A Pelican Book
Electricity

Rupert Taylor was born in 1946. He is a noise
consultant, running his own practice, and designs
methods of noise reduction for machinery and buildings
as well as providing expert evidence in court cases. He
is the author of the Pelican book *Noise* and many
articles and papers on the subject. In addition to
lecturing and broadcasting he has been a member of the
U.K. Noise Advisory Council since 1971, and of the
council of the Institute of Acoustics since its formation.
His involvement with electronics is as an outsider who
has to make use of it, as it overlaps the world of
acoustics in several ways. This led him, after finishing
Noise, to want to get to the bottom of electricity and
electronics and to write this book for other people in a
similar position. His pastimes lately have tended to
involve a soldering iron, which he occasionally puts
down in favour of a paint brush.

D1471283

Rupert Taylor

Electricity

Penguin Books

Penguin Books Ltd, Harmondsworth,
Middlesex, England
Penguin Books Inc., 7110 Ambassador Road,
Baltimore, Maryland 21207, U.S.A.
Penguin Books Australia Ltd, Ringwood,
Victoria, Australia
Penguin Books Canada Ltd,
41 Steelcase Road West, Markham, Ontario, Canada
Penguin Books (N.Z.) Ltd,
182–190 Wairau Road, Auckland 10, New Zealand

First published 1975
Copyright © Rupert Taylor, 1975
Made and printed in Great Britain by
Richard Clay (The Chaucer Press) Ltd,
Bungay, Suffolk
Set in Monotype Times

This book is sold subject to the condition that
it shall not, by way of trade or otherwise, be lent,
re-sold, hired out, or otherwise circulated without
the publisher's prior consent in any form of
binding or cover other than that in which it is
published and without a similar condition
including this condition being imposed on the
subsequent purchaser

To Alison

Contents

Introduction

Many of us know something about electricity, but deep down are in a fair state of confusion about what really goes on inside all those wires and circuits. The problem is not helped by the way most books on electricity tackle the subject, by ignoring the nature of the phenomenon itself and plunging headlong into all its complex properties.

Chapter 1 starts from the first rung of the ladder, with the task of finding out what electricity really *is*; it then becomes easier to understand why it behaves as it does. This means starting with atoms and electrons and the structure of matter. If you are itching to get on with the volts and the amps, rather than hear of particles, shells and valences, you can by all means skip straight to Chapter 2. On the other hand, if you are not content with being told to think of electricity as being 'like water in a pipe' and if you want to know *why* conductors conduct and insulators insulate, start with Chapter 1; it will certainly be helpful when you come to semi-conductors and transistors.

Electricity is usually looked upon as a separate business from electronics, but in many ways such a split is artificial. You certainly cannot tackle electronics without first mastering the basis of electricity, and though electricity as a power source is an important subject in its own right, its impact on twentieth-century life has probably been overshadowed by that of electronics.

Electricity, in the form of electrical engineering, is put to work so that power inherent in it can be extracted to work machines of many kinds, often of vast size: electronics is the manipulation of electricity, usually in tiny quantities, to provide communications and control systems. A modern portable television uses little power (some can in fact be run from torch batteries), but the job it does of extracting and filtering a clear colour picture, together with sound, out of a space saturated with all kinds of radio waves, is infinitely more subtle than the work done by an electric motor.

Introduction

This book covers a lot of ground, starting with electricity and graduating to electronics. If your electronic curiosity will be satisfied merely by understanding how a transistor works and by fathoming the mysteries of simple circuits, you may wish to go straight from Chapter 6 to Chapter 11 and gain a similar understanding of computers, leaving out such things as the way colour-television transmissions work, or the pros and cons of the British, American and French colour systems.

If you simply want an explanation of the workings of an amplifier, go straight to Chapter 7; if, on the other hand, you already understand everything but the nature of radio waves, go right away to Chapter 9. If, like most of us, you find the whole subject strangely opaque, read on.

1 An Irresistible Attraction

What is electricity?

Electricity is a remarkable phenomenon. Think of it: neat energy piped straight to where you want it. At the touch of a switch, pure, unadulterated power streams out of a socket in the wall. The dirty work has all been done for you; the fuel obtained, burned and converted into energy. All you have to do is to turn it on.

Electricity is almost taken for granted – but what actually is it? Some sort of invisible liquid? A strange ethereal gas? A lot of little bits of something rushing through a wire? It is none of these, but like them all. Electricity does, at times, behave like a fluid, but it is also made up of a myriad of basic units. These units, as well as being the 'corpuscles' of electricity, are also fundamental components of all atoms. One of these units is called an electric charge, and because it is the key to understanding all electricity, we must first find out more about it, and therefore about atoms.

If you could chop up a piece of an element, such as lead or carbon, into ever decreasing lumps, you would reach a point when you were left with the smallest piece which could exist and still have all the properties of the element. That piece would be an atom, one of the fundamental 'building blocks' of matter. Democritus probably coined the word *atom*, which comes from the Greek verb *temnein*, to cut, and means 'uncuttable'. Shakespeare's Queen Mab,

> 'In shape no bigger than an agate stone
> On the forefinger of an alderman,
> Drawn with a team of little atomies'*

shows Elizabethan knowledge of some sort of tiny, basic particles, but neither Democritus nor Shakespeare's contemporary scientists had really done more than logically conclude that if you go on cutting a substance into smaller and smaller pieces, you

*Romeo and Juliet, I, iv, 53–5.

11

probably reach a stage where you cannot go any further. They presumed you would then be left with elementary specks of matter which go together to make up the original material.

The atom has long since been debunked as an indivisible particle, and although the consequences of its division have shifted the course of mankind's development we are not concerned here with the results of splitting the atom, but with the particles that make it up. Modern science in the form of 'wave mechanics' has shown that even recent concepts of atomic structure are over-simplified. Nevertheless, it is still best to start by thinking of an atom as a minute solar system, with a sun, and at least one planet.

The sun is the nucleus and is made up of particles known as protons and neutrons; the planets are electrons. These particles are the same, no matter what kind of atom they are in. A hydrogen atom with only one proton and one electron is the most basic form but it is possible for an atom to have over 100 electrons in orbit round the nucleus, which normally contains the same number of protons as there are electrons in orbit. The number of protons in the nucleus of an atom is its atomic number (Table 1).

What are these mysterious particles that constitute an atom? Here comes a most fundamental problem, which lies at the root of the point about the electrical charge. In order to start to describe an atomic particle, let us think how we describe any object at all. We can give its shape, its size and its weight. An atomic particle certainly has weight; weight is only the effect of gravity on an object of a given mass and in most scientific contexts it is better to talk about mass rather than weight, because even weightless objects in space still have mass. The mass of an electron is 0·00000000000000000000000000009107 grams; that of a proton or neutron almost 2,000 times as great. Unfortunately a particle does not have size. Its length, breadth and height are all 0 in whatever units you choose! It consequently has no shape, but it is not deprived of having a very precise position in space at any particular moment.

These extraordinary non-objects, endowed with incongruous properties, are called 'particles' purely as a matter of convenience. The mathematician arrives at a point where he can only produce a semblance of a logical conclusion if he invents the particles as a means of accounting for the mechanical properties which he has found to exist.

Although they have no geometrical dimensions, some of these particles have other properties besides mass. An electron has wave characteristics (a feature which will turn up again later in the book); above all it possesses what is known as a negative charge, while a proton has a positive charge and a neutron has neither. A charge is a quantity of electricity, and the charge on an electron is the smallest 'piece' of electricity you can have. Once again, this charge is a figment of the mathematician's mind which is invented as the only means of explaining the things which electrons do. Nevertheless, without these figments, only the Einsteins of this world could cope.

Our rule of thumb for dealing with these irrational concepts is to state their properties. The principal property of a negatively charged particle is that it is attracted to a positively charged particle, and repelled by another negatively charged particle. In the same way, a positively charged particle is repelled by another of like charge, and attracted to one of opposite charge. Comparatively, neutrons are cold and frigid.

Now let us have another look at a complete atom. The nucleus, because it has protons in it, has a positive charge, which simply means it will attract a negatively charged particle. To maintain equilibrium in the atom, an equal number of electrons is required in orbit round the nucleus, and complicated forces caused by their orbits prevent the electrons from being sucked into the middle by the attraction of the protons. Most nuclei have neutrons in them as well, the effect of which is to raise the mass of the atom without changing any of its chemical properties.

The factor which distinguishes an atom of one element from an atom of another is simply the number of protons in its nucleus, and thus the number of electrons normally in orbit around it. Any two atoms which normally have the same atomic number have the same chemical properties. Any atom with only one proton in its nucleus, and one electron normally in orbit, is a hydrogen atom; any atom which normally has ninety-two protons is a uranium atom.

However, the nuclei of two atoms of the same element can be

rather different. For instance, a hydrogen atom can have a nucleus consisting of just one proton, or one proton and one neutron, or one proton and two neutrons. It is the neutron complement that can vary, and when it does, the different types of atom are called isotopes, with differing atomic weights or mass numbers depending on the number of neutrons. A hydrogen iso-

Element	*Atomic Number*
Hydrogen	1
Carbon	6
Nitrogen	7
Aluminium	13
Calcium	20
Iron	26
Copper	29
Zinc	30
Silver	47
Iodine	53
Gold	79
Lead	82
Uranium	92

Table 1. The atomic numbers of some common elements

tope with one neutron is called 'deuterium', with two, 'tritium'. 'Heavy water' is water in which the hydrogen atoms are deuterium atoms.

Electrons revolve round nuclei in a very special way. In simple Newtonian physics, we know that two identical objects, such as two billiard balls, can be endowed with different quantities of energy. If you put one ball on the top step of a staircase, and another on the bottom, although both billiard balls will still be exactly the same size, shape and mass, and still be electrically neutral, they will not have the same energy. Because work has been done on the ball at the top of the stairs in overcoming gravity to get it there, it is possessed of greater potential energy than the one on the bottom step. Similarly, if you shoot both balls from a gun, and one travels faster than the other, that ball will

14

have greater kinetic energy than the other by virtue of its greater momentum. The same applies if you whirl it in a circle on the end of a piece of string; the faster it revolves, the greater its energy.

All electrons are as alike as two peas, or billiard balls, but they can also be possessed of different energy-levels. This is because they orbit in different ways, at different distances from the nucleus, at different speeds, and in different-shaped orbits; and in addition they also spin. In any atom, there is always a limited number of electron states that have very nearly the same energy, and electrons in one of these groups of states are said to be in a single shell of the atom. An electron in a hydrogen atom in a certain shell will always have the same energy, but in multielectron atoms, because of interaction between electrons as well as between electrons and the nucleus, there is something of a spread in energy within a shell.

We have so far ignored a subtle piece of deception: only in very rare cases is it in fact true to say that an atom is the smallest particle of any substance which can exist freely and still exhibit all the chemical properties of the substance. It is true in the cases of neon, argon, krypton, xenon and radon, but with most other elements, including hydrogen, the smallest free particle possessed of the required chemical properties, known as a molecule, consists of more than one atom. By looking at the reasons for this we will gain an insight into the very nature of electricity.

All the atoms of the obscure elements just mentioned have in their outer and weakest 'shell' eight electrons. You might describe this as a full house; these atoms are at peace with the world, and constitute chemically inert substances. An atom with less than or more than eight electrons in its outer shell is a troubled soul, either hungry or dyspeptic.

Hydrogen is an exception, with an 'appetite' in its outer shell for only two electrons. But a hydrogen atom, we know, has only one electron orbiting round its single proton, and therefore, in order to satisfy its need for two electrons, it will club together with another hydrogen atom and, by mutual agreement, they share each other's electron and are thus contented. A hydrogen atom is said to have a valence of one.

A similar type of electron sharing goes on among atoms with

15

the normal appetite for eight electrons in their outer shells. Oxygen atoms are normally short of two electrons to make up the satisfactory octet, and thus are described as having a negative valence of two.

It is now possible to see how a molecule of water can exist. An oxygen atom, needing two electrons to make up its eight, joins forces with two hydrogen atoms and their electrons. The three atoms share out their electrons so that, for at least some of the time, the oxygen atom has eight to call its own, and each hydrogen atom has moments when it can lay claim to two passing electrons, and so satisfy its need. This is called a covalent bond.

Now there is another type of molecular bond called electrovalence or polar valence. Take a sodium atom, overburdened with nine electrons in its outer shell, and imagine that by some means it can be relieved of its ninth electron. It will be delighted to achieve its ideal state of having only eight electrons in its outer shell, but wait a minute; in its original state it has the same number of electrons in orbit as it had protons in its nucleus, and thus was electrically neutral. Take away an electron, and the atom will have a positive electrical charge. An atom in this condition is called an ion, and this sodium atom has become a positive ion.

Now a chlorine atom has only seven electrons in its outer shell. Let us give it the extra electron to make up an octet. It will now have an electron too many compared with the number of protons in its nucleus, and although happy because it has an outer shell of eight electrons, it has acquired a negative charge, and turned into a negative ion.

Remember that we said earlier in the chapter that the principal property of a positive charge was that it was attracted to a negative charge. So if a sodium ion and a chloride ion (an ionized chlorine atom) come together they will be attracted to one another, form an electrovalent bond and become a molecule of sodium chloride. All that fiddling with test tubes is simply in order to organize the atoms of acids and alkalis so that they can be ionized and form the schoolboy's hard learnt 'salt plus water'.

(As a point of interest, alkali atoms always have 'one over the eight' electrons and halogen atoms, e.g. iodine, or bromine, lack one electron. In interactions between alkali and halogen

16

atoms, an alkali atom will lose an electron, becoming a positively charged ion, and a halogen atom will gain this electron, becoming a negatively charged ion; both thus acquire the 'outer eight' electronic stability, and they are joined to form a molecule by the electrostatic attraction between them. Elements like magnesium and calcium, which have ten outer electrons, tend to become doubly charged positive ions and are then attracted to doubly charged negative ions formed when atoms of elements like oxygen and sulphur acquired two more electrons to augment their normal outer six.)

So let us dissolve some of the salt, sodium chloride, in water. Unfortunately for the salt, the attractions between the sodium and the chloride ions are affected by the water, which itself absorbs the attraction between the ions, and they drift apart. Salt water contains not molecules of sodium chloride, but sodium ions and chloride ions drifting about on their own.

The same phenomenon occurs with other compounds in liquids, for example when hydrochloric acid is diluted with water. A molecule of hydrochloric acid has one chlorine atom with an extra electron attached, thus becoming a (negative) chloride ion, and a hydrogen atom which has been robbed of its electron and become a (positive) hydrogen ion: in fact, a single proton (because, of course, a hydrogen ion is a positive one).

Let us take a tank of this liquid (see Figure 1), which is water with chloride and hydrogen ions drifting about in it, and put a zinc rod into it. Zinc has ten outer electrons, and is therefore keen to get shot of two of them. It goes about it in a novel way; when the rod is inserted into the liquid, zinc atoms float off it, leaving two electrons behind. Because they have lost two negatively charged electrons, the zinc atoms are in fact doubly charged positive ions. The rod, however, is left with a number of abandoned, negatively charged electrons and so, after a few zinc ions have floated off, there begins to exist some back-attraction between the rod and the ions and the process stops. In just the same way as two negatively charged particles repel each other, so will two positive ions do likewise. This will mean that the positive zinc ions coming off the zinc rod will repel the positive hydrogen ions towards the other end of the tank.

17

Electricity

Now let us put a copper rod in the other end of the same tank. The atoms in copper and zinc molecules are not subjected to either covalent or electrovalent bonds, but to what is called a metallic bond. A copper atom has nine outer electrons, but when a number of atoms exist together in a lump of copper, they get over their 'one over the eight' problem by divesting themselves of electrons and indulging in an extreme case of electron sharing. There then exists a crystal lattice of copper (positive) ions and a sort of electron gas swimming around the lattice, the ions borrowing stray electrons here and there to balance their positive electric charges. The atoms are kept together because they have got their electrons so mixed up with one another.

Now, suppose we let the tops of the two rods touch or, better still, connect a copper wire from the copper rod to the zinc rod. What will happen? Let us summarize the state of affairs that exists in the tank: positive zinc ions have floated off the zinc rod (leaving an excess of free electrons on the rod) and are swimming among negative chloride ions and positive hydrogen ions. If the two rods are connected, the excess of electrons on the zinc rod will tend to push over the electrons in the copper so that the excess is evenly distributed over the zinc and copper. The result will be that where the copper rod is immersed in liquid, there will be a few superfluous electrons. In the liquid there are a whole lot of hydrogen ions in search of an electron, and so if they come close enough to the copper rod, they will pick up the free electrons that have become available as a result of connecting the zinc and copper rods. Having gained their missing electrons, the hydrogen ions become atoms again, linking together into molecules which are then capable of existing on their own as hydrogen gas. They then bubble to the top and disappear off into the atmosphere. The zinc ions each pick up the extra electrons from two chloride ions to form zinc chloride. The excess of electrons on the zinc rod is now reduced, as is the back-attraction that they caused, and so more zinc ions can float off, leaving more electrons behind to wander on to the copper rod and start the whole process over again. The tank will go on bubbling until the zinc rod is completely eaten away. Something of fundamental interest is happening. Electrons are flowing from the zinc rod to the copper rod. This is none other than an electric current.

Break the connection between the two rods, and very soon an excess of electrons will build up again on the zinc rod until stopped by back-attraction between electrons and zinc ions in the liquid, and the hydrogen forming on the copper rod will leave it slightly deficient in electrons. What does this mean?

Electrons have, as we have said, a negative charge, and as there is an excess of them on the zinc rod, then the rod itself has a negative charge. The copper atoms, on the other hand, have been made abnormally short of a few electrons by the hydrogen formation, and so their protons are more in number than their

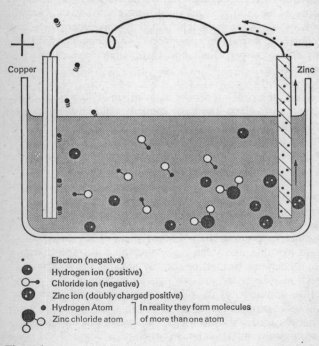

Figure 1

electrons, giving the copper rod a positive charge. Positive charges attract negative charges; so, as soon as the copper touches the zinc, the negatively charged electrons flow from the zinc rod to the copper rod and away we go.

We have, in fact, just described a battery. It is a rather impractical type of battery called a voltaic cell, but it has served very well indeed to lead us to a fundamental understanding of electricity. We have learnt some very important facts, one of which came right at the end: the nature of the bonds between atoms of metals. Copper is not the only material that has a metallic bond; many other metals are made up in the same way. They all have this unique system of ions sharing a common 'gas' of electrons to make up their tally of eight in their outer shell at any moment. Because of the relative freedom of these electrons, they are able to move about in the metal if attracted by some external electrical phenomenon. Metals are therefore good conductors of electricity. Silver, copper, aluminium, platinum and mercury are good examples.

Let us now leave metals for the moment, and take a piece of very different stuff: glass. The basic element which makes up glass, silicon, has a tendency towards positive ionization. In other words, a silicon atom is not averse to discarding an electron. If you take a piece of glass and rub it with a material that likes to collect electrons, ionization of the atoms of both materials will occur. This is what happens when you rub a glass rod with a piece of silk. The silk picks up electrons from the glass, leaving the glass positively ionized. It will then attract light objects like little bits of paper in order to share some electrons and try to neutralize its positive charge. Many pairs of substances in fact behave like this, and some types of comb will cause charges to build up between themselves and the hair they are combing. The attraction caused by the positive ionization of one and the negative ionization of the other is the reason why the hair will stand up towards the comb.

This is called static electricity, because it will stay put rather than flow anywhere, although when the hair and the comb actually touch, the ionization will be eliminated as the electrons jump the short distance back to their rightful owners. The crackling which some people experience when pulling a woollen pullover over their hair is caused when static electricity builds up on ionized hair and ionized wool and then discharges between them. The electrons sometimes continue to jump across if a small gap is made between the two materials, causing sparks and a crackling sound.

It is the static qualities which are important to us, and lead us to another vital property of a group of substances; the glass which we have talked about is what is called a dielectric, and its most important electrical feature is that if you used it to connect the zinc and copper rods in a voltaic cell, nothing much would happen. All the atoms in the substances which constitute glass have very personal relationships with their electrons, and although they can be ionized, they will not indulge in the kind of free love which goes on in metals with their maelstrom of free electrons. Although there are plenty of electrons on the zinc rod which are eager to flow to the copper rod, they cannot do so

Silver	1·6
Copper	1·7
Aluminium	2·8
Platinum	10
Iron	12
Lead	22
Carbon	5,000
Silicon	300,000
Glass	10,000,000,000
Sulphur	200,000,000,000,000,000,000,000

Table 2. Relative electrical resistance of some common materials (e.g. platinum is one thousand million times better than glass as a conductor of electricity).

through a rod of glass. Glass, and many substances like it, is in this respect the opposite of copper, and whereas the latter is a good conductor of electricity, the former is very poor indeed. Conversely, you can say that glass is a very good insulator, and copper a very poor insulator indeed.

However, there is no such thing as a perfect insulator any more than there is a perfect conductor (although modern science enables us to come very close to this). Any material can be classed in terms of its conductivity; Table 2 gives a list of better known substances in ascending order of resistance. Static electricity is not confined to rods of glass and combs: it crops up in the most unusual places. Motor cars acquire a static charge when the tyres are ionized through friction with the road. When the car comes to a halt and passengers get out, the misplaced electrons dislodged by the ionization will sometimes try to return to their rightful owners by flowing through the body of a passenger who touches the metal body of the car while standing on the ground. The effect is a small spark, a click and a slight electric shock. Some think that the static charge in a car body causes travel sickness, and owners try to offset this by providing a permanent electrical connection with the ground. Metal chains are the most commonly used, but become useless after a few miles when the ends get worn off.

Much more spectacular in the world of static electricity is, of course, lightning. The earth as a whole has a slight excess of electrons all the time, thus having a slight negative charge, while the upper atmosphere has a mild positive charge, increasing with altitude. The air between is a dielectric (like the glass rod) across which there is a constant small leakage of electrons, or current. The means by which the charge is maintained against this leakage is not really understood, but in fine weather the charge is evenly distributed over the earth's surface.

In a rapidly developing rainstorm, the clouds also become charged. There comes a point when the charges can be held apart no longer, and there is a sudden discharge of electrons between the surfaces of the cloud, or between two clouds, or between the cloud and the earth beneath. There is in fact always a thunder storm going on somewhere in the world and it is estimated that there is an average of 100 lightning flashes every second, causing sufficient electric current to run 4,000 million electric fires!

Lightning flashes can be very long, even up to several kilometres, and be over 100 millimetres in diameter. 'Forked' lightning is not really forked at all. It is the result of several flashes in quick succession, each of very short duration and taking a different path. There is nothing different about 'sheet' lightning. It is simply ordinary lightning at a distance, the light from which is reflected or scattered by clouds. 'Ball' lightning, though, is a very different phenomenon. It occurs as a small, incandescent, hissing globe, moving slowly along in the air, sometimes even indoors, scorching obstacles it touches, sometimes exploding. It has even been known to gouge great furrows out of the ground. Nobody really knows what causes it. A recent theory sounded like an extract from a science fiction story; it talked about nuclear reactions between particles called positrons (not normally existing in our world, being the exact opposite of electrons) and electrons which they annihilate with the consequent powerful radiation of energy. The positrons were said to be caused by cosmic rays.

Lightning is most dangerous when the discharge is from a cloud to the ground. In these cases, the ground beneath the cloud acquires a charge as well, normally negative, and when the electrical 'stress' between the cloud and the ground becomes great enough, there will be a discharge between the cloud and the nearest object connected with the ground, such as a tree or a tall building. Trees and buildings, of course, are not normally made of materials that are particularly good conductors of electricity, but we have already seen that there is no clear distinction between conductors and insulators, and in fact any substance will conduct to a certain extent.

Benjamin Franklin is credited with first identifying lightning as an electrical discharge, when he conducted his famous kite experiment. There is none better to describe it than Franklin himself:

'Make a small cross of two light strips of cedar, the arms so long as to reach the four corners of a large silk handkerchief when extended; tie the corners of the handkerchief to the extremities of the cross, so you have the body of a kite; which being properly accommodated with a tail, loop and string, will rise in the air like those made of paper; but this being of silk, is fitter to bear the wet and wind of a thunder-gust without tearing. To the top of the upright stick of the cross is to be fixed a very sharp pointed wire, rising a foot or more above the wood. To the end of the twine next the hand, is to be tied a silk ribbon, and

23

where the silk and twine join, a key may be fastened. This kite is to be raised when a thunder-gust appears to be coming on, and the person who holds the string must stand within a door or window or under some cover, so that the silk ribbon may not be wet; and care must be taken that the twine does not touch the frame of the door or window. As soon as any of the thunder clouds come over the kite, the pointed wire will draw the electric fire from them, and the kite, with all the twine, will be electrified, and the loose filaments of the twine will stand out every way, and be attracted by an approaching finger. When the rain has wet the kite and twine, so that it can conduct the electric fire freely, you will find it stream out plentifully on the approach of your knuckle; and from the electric fire thus obtained, spirits may be kindled, and all the other electrical experiments can be performed, which are usually done by the help of a rubbed glass globe or tube, and thereby the sameness of the electrical matter with that of lightning completely demonstrated.'

It should be added that the chances of Franklin killing himself by this experiment were very high indeed, and readers conduct it at their own risk!

Franklin, like all his contemporaries, got one thing wrong. He talks about the electric fire being drawn from the thunder clouds, and streaming out plentifully from the twine to the approaching knuckle. In fact it is the other way round: the earth has the negative charge, due to an excess of electrons, and the cloud has a deficiency of electrons, giving it a positive charge. The wet twine can be regarded as an extension of the cloud (dry, it would be too poor a conductor), and when there is a spark from your knuckle to the end of the twine, which is insulated from your hand by the dry silk, you are in fact supplying electrons from the earth to flow up the wet twine and make up the deficiency in the cloud. What a good thing rubber-soled shoes were not in existence in Franklin's day: think how the march of progress in electrical engineering might have been delayed!

The names 'positive' and 'negative' as applied to charges are in fact totally arbitrary. As a result of the early researchers getting their ideas back to front, electricity has always been regarded as flowing from positive to negative, and for engineering purposes it is still customary to do so. In this book we generally follow this practice and talk of 'conventional current flow' unless we say otherwise. However, we shall see later that it becomes necessary eventually to take note of the fact that the electrons are actually flowing in the reverse direction. Had it been worth the trouble, the terms might have been transposed when the error was discovered, but the resulting confusion would outweigh the advantages.

One of the most important points in Franklin's description of his experiment is the fact that the wire on top of the kite must be very sharply pointed. If a charge is put on a pointed conductor, most of the charge piles up at the point. Only if the point is quite sharp may the charge actually leak off to the surroundings. The sharpness of the kite wire therefore made it easier for the electrons from the earth to leak off into the cloud.

Franklin put his discovery to very good use; he realized that if a sharp-pointed conductor were permanently erected at a height, and earthed by means of a conducting wire, such as lead, thunderclouds could be steadily neutralized of electric charge as they pass over the conductor, and no electrical potential would accumulate between the cloud and the earth. You will, of course, find one of these on pretty well any church steeple in the land, because that is what a lightning conductor is. Lightning conductors do not, as some believe, attract flashes of lightning; they allow the electrical discharge to occur peacefully over a period of minutes or more instead of violently in a few microseconds.

Interesting though the phenomenon of lightning undoubtedly is, man has not yet found much of a use for the electricity which it involves. As we are not going to power any electric motors by rubbing hair with woolly jumpers, we had better discover some more practical means of producing electricity. We have already met a simple sort of battery, the zinc and copper rods immersed in dilute hydrochloric acid, but in that form it does not really come under the heading of 'practical'. Nevertheless, zinc, copper and hydrochloric acid are by no means the only three substances which when used together in this way produce an electric current. The zinc and copper rods which are correctly called electrodes are only two of the several pairs of dissimilar materials such as those in the following list:

1	Aluminium	6	Copper
2	Zinc	7	Silver
3	Iron	8	Gold
4	Nickel	9	Carbon
5	Lead		

The list of possible electrode materials is arranged in a special way: if any two of the materials are used to form a battery or cell, the one that is higher on the list will be the one consumed in the same way as the zinc rod; it will be the supplier of electrons, making it negative. The lower material will be the positive terminal. The other important thing about the list is that the further apart the two electrode materials are on the list, the greater will be the difference in charge on the two terminals. The hydrochloric acid, known as the electrolyte, may be replaced by one of a selection of many acids, salts and bases which, when in solution, contain positive and negative ions. It is now much easier to make a practical voltaic cell, with all these different materials available to us.

The most common cell of all, the dry cell, is none other than a voltaic cell of the sort we have been looking at. If you cut one open, you will find that it has a case made of zinc and a core made of carbon. These are in fact the electrodes, the counterparts of the zinc and copper rods, but from now on we shall call the zinc electrode which is the emitter of electrons the cathode, and the carbon electrode the anode.*

The electrolyte in this case is ammonium chloride, a compound which contains hydrogen, nitrogen and chlorine, as opposed to just the hydrogen and chloride in hydrochloric acid. The ammonium chloride in the dry cell is dissolved in a damp paste, and consists of ions of nitrogen, hydrogen and chloride. When the cell supplies current, doubly polarized positive zinc ions leave the cathode, giving it a negative charge. Connection of the cathode to the anode makes spare electrons available on the anode, which in turn are picked up by some of the hydrogen ions. Meanwhile, the

---

* An electrode which emits electrons is always called a cathode and one that absorbs them an anode (from the Greek words meaning 'way down' and 'way up').

remainder of the hydrogen ions join up with the nitrogen and form ammonia (ammon*ia* is a compound with one less hydrogen atom than ammon*ium*).

However, in practice, the anode becomes covered with hydrogen bubbles, and loses contact with the electrolyte, stopping the reaction. This effect is known as polarization and to overcome it in the dry cell the anode or carbon core is surrounded by another damp paste, this time of manganese dioxide. This parts with some of its oxygen to react with the hydrogen and form water, thus preventing the formation of a layer of bubbles. A metal cap is now fitted atop the protruding carbon rod which is surrounded by an insulating washer (Figure 2) and forms the positive terminal of the cell; the bottom of the zinc case becomes the negative terminal. At last we have a practical battery!

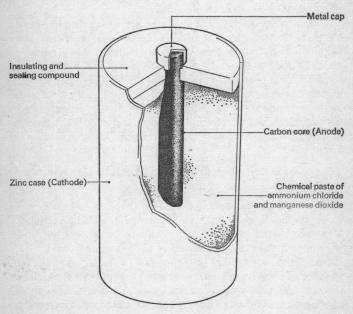

Metal cap

Insulating and sealing compound

Carbon core (Anode)

Zinc case (Cathode)

Chemical paste of ammonium chloride and manganese dioxide

Figure 2

A dry cell will go on delivering electricity until the ammonium chloride is used up. There is then not a hope of recharging it. Although many people have found that if you put a cell on a radiator and heat it up it will give it a new lease of life, all you are doing is accelerating the final death-throes of the battery and squeezing the last drops of energy out of it in a shorter time. Is it not possible to produce a cell where the chemical reaction which generates electricity is reversible? The answer is of course, yes, because that is what a car battery is.

A car battery is a rechargeable set of cells known as a lead–acid accumulator. Each cell consists of a pair of lead plates, one of which is coated in lead peroxide (PbO_2 in chemical notation) and is the cathode. The anode is plain lead, and both are immersed in dilute sulphuric acid (H_2SO_4). The lead reacts with the sulphuric acid by combining with the sulphate (SO_4) to produce lead sulphate ($PbSO_4$) which coats the anode.

This complex reaction can only take place with the aid of extra electrons, and this gives the anode a positive charge. It also leaves behind two hydrogen ions which are repelled away from the anode by the positive charge. Meanwhile over at the cathode, the sulphuric acid is attacking the lead of the lead peroxide to make more lead sulphate. This will produce an excess of electrons, some more water and some free oxygen ions which, too, are repelled by the negative charge created. They meet the stray hydrogen ions and join them to make even more water. In chemical notation the reaction is

$$PbO_2 + Pb + 2H_2SO_4 = 2PbSO_4 + 2H_2O$$

As current is discharged, the sulphuric acid becomes more watery. This is the reason why, since the acid is heavier than water, the best way of checking the charge in a lead accumulator is to measure the specific gravity with a hydrometer, from which you can calculate the concentration of the sulphuric acid.

Now let us look at what happens when the battery is recharged; an external negative charge is connected to the cathode which will become crammed with electrons, and a positive charge to the anode which will then be hungry for them. Hydrogen ions will be attracted to the now negatively charged lead peroxide cathode and, on arrival, recombine with the sulphate in the lead sulphate molecules formed during discharge to create sulphuric acid and lead again. At the anode, sulphate ions are attracted and, to balance their ionization, take the two hydrogen atoms out of a water molecule to form more sulphuric acid. Finally, lead sulphate molecules at the cathode also split up, the sulphate ions breaking up more water molecules; the oxygen ions from the broken-down water molecules now join with the remaining lead ions from the lead sulphate, and form lead peroxide again. This completes the circle and restores the battery to the same state as it was in before it discharged.

Even car batteries, as any motorist will know to his cost, will not go on for ever. There are a number of reasons for this: active material is lost from the plates during the hundreds of two-way reactions which take place; plates get buckled, the non-conducting members which separate the plates deteriorate.

Dry cells and lead accumulators are by no means the only, or best, batteries available to us. They have nevertheless adequately provided us with some electric current to play around with in the next chapter.

2 Current Affairs

Volts, amps and ohms

How does one measure electricity? We have found one or two ways of creating it, talked about some charges being greater than others, and seen electrons flowing from one terminal of a battery to another. We have nowhere mentioned any units at all.

The first thing that is needed is a measure of quantity. What is the quantity of charge on a glass rod rubbed with silk? This can be measured in terms of the number of electrons transferred by the rubbing process. Electrons are rather small, and so to obtain a workable unit they must be measured in large doses. The unit of quantity or charge is the 'coulomb' and is equivalent to about 6,300,000,000,000,000,000 electrons.

Now that we have a unit of quantity, it is possible to measure current, since there is already a unit of time, the second, and current is 'quantity per second'. If 6.3×10^{18} electrons or 1 coulomb of electricity flow along a conducting wire in a period of one second, then that is a current of 1 coulomb per second, or of 1 ampere (amp, for short).

Unfortunately, electrons do not flow along conductors completely unimpeded; the very definition of a conductor is that it passes current more easily than an insulator, and another way of saying this is that insulators offer a very high resistance to current, conductors a low resistance. The atoms in insulators are reluctant to part with electrons and considerable energy is required to get them to do so. On the other hand the electrons in good conductors are fairly free to move, but these electrons still have to get past the lattice of nuclei which exert forces on them, and energy is used up in the process.

The unit of resistance is the ohm, and it is really a measure of force that will b needed to get a given current to flow along a conductor, and overcome the energy lost because of the resistance. A copper wire about 1 square millimetre in cross-section and 60 metres long has a resistance of about 1 ohm. The resistance across the thickness of the insulation round the wire will probably be over 1 megohm (1,000,000 ohms).

There are some important points about resistance to take note of. Remember that the object of the exercise is to get as many electrons as possible along the wire or conductor in one second. Suppose the wire is cut through and the surface area of the bare end is 1 square millimetre. If we double the size of the wire, so that it has a cross-section of 2 square millimetres, there will then be twice as many electrons on an end section, and so twice as much current will get through without any extra force. This means that the resistance is halved; the resistance is therefore inversely proportional to the cross-sectional area of the conductor. In addition, the resistance is directly proportional to the length of the conductor. A copper wire with a cross-sectional area of 1 square millimetre, 1 metre long, will have the same resistance, all other things being equal, as a copper wire with an area of 2 square millimetres, 2 metres long.

If we want to get a current of 1 ampere through both a wire of 1 ohm resistance, and another of 2 ohms, we shall have to push the electrons twice as hard in the second case as in the first. Volts measure the strength of the push.

To get a current of 1 ampere through a conductor having a resistance of 1 ohm, a push, or in more conventional terms, an electromotive force (e.m.f.) of 1 volt is required.* To maintain the same current through a conductor with a resistance of 2 ohms, 2 volts would be required. Voltage is equal to current multiplied by resistance, and this relationship is called 'Ohm's Law', after Georg Simon Ohm, the German scientist.

The volt as a unit serves a double purpose. As well as measuring e.m.f., it measures the amount of potential electrical force which exists between two points, usually the difference between the force at two ends of a resistance. This is known as potential difference and to all intents it is the same thing as e.m.f., both of which are crudely referred to as 'voltage'. Consider a conductor 2 metres long, of constant diameter, with a resistance of 2 ohms. The potential difference (p.d.) between the two ends, if a current

*This is no longer the precise definition of a volt, but is true enough for our purposes.

31

of 1 amp is passing through it, will be 2 volts whereas the p.d. between one end and a point half-way along will be only 1 volt. Voltage is proportional to resistance, and resistance is proportional to length.

Before we go any further, let us have a look at Ohm's Law in all its forms:

$$\text{current} = \frac{\text{voltage}}{\text{resistance}}, \text{ or amperes} = \frac{\text{volts}}{\text{ohms}}, \text{ or } I = \frac{V}{R}$$

so

$$\text{voltage} = \text{current} \times \text{resistance, or } V = I \times R,$$

and

$$\text{resistance} = \frac{\text{voltage}}{\text{current}}, \text{ or } R = \frac{V}{I}.$$

Many people who are far from being novices in electricity have to stop and think sometimes to get these laws right, and the only easy way to remember them is to understand their meaning. Voltage is a pressure-like unit; current is really volume flow. Resistance is what it says it is, and amounts to back-pressure. It really is fairly logical: the more back-pressure there is, the more pressure you need to apply if the flow is to be maintained. If the back-pressure alone rises, the flow drops and if the pressure alone rises, the flow increases. That is all there is to it.

We still need another unit, the unit of power. If on the one hand, a current of 1 ampere is being pushed through a resistance of 1 ohm (by an e.m.f. of 1 volt) and, on the other hand, another current of 2 amperes is being pushed through a similar 1-ohm resistance (by an e.m.f. of 2 volts), it is easy to see that more work is being done in the same length of time in the latter case than the first. In fact exactly twice as much work is being done in the second case than the first. It is being done in the same time in both cases, and therefore twice as much power is being used in the latter case, since power is the rate of doing work. Power is therefore current times voltage, and is the amount of energy supplied each second, since current is the amount of electricity supplied each second and voltage is the force behind it.

The unit of power is the watt,* and it is the product of voltage and current, so that:

$$\text{watts} = \text{volts} \times \text{amps}.$$

One watt is the energy expended per second by a current of 1 ampere flowing through a conductor, the ends of which are maintained at a potential difference of 1 volt. Suppose you are supplied with electricity at 240 volts, and you plug in a heater rated at, let us say $8\frac{1}{3}$ amps, you will use $240 \times 8\frac{1}{3}$ watts of power, which equals 2,000 watts, or 2 kilowatts.

This brings us to the last of the units we need: the unit of energy. The basic electrical unit of energy is the joule, which equals volts $\times$ coulombs. Energy is the capacity for doing work, and power is the rate at which the work is actually done, so if energy is supplied at the rate of 1 joule per second, what have you got? A watt! Taking this the other way round, if a current 'works' at a rate (power) of 1 watt, in a second it will supply a watt-second of energy – or 1 joule. You may have scarcely heard of the joule, because since it is such a small unit one usually measures electricity in bulk terms of a thousand watts and an hour: hence the kilowatt hour or kWh, the 'unit' measured on an electricity meter by which the consumer pays for electricity. One kWh is equal to $1000 \times 60 \times 60 = 3\cdot6$ million joules.

Let us now put together the elements of a simple circuit. In order to do this, we shall need a method of representing the elements of a circuit on paper. We could, at a stretch, draw little pictures of them: Figure 3 shows one of the voltaic cells described in the last chapter, connected by two lengths of straight wire to a resistance, which in this case is just a considerable length of thin copper wire wound in a coil. Figure 4 shows a simplified diagram of the same circuit, using idealized standard symbols for the elements instead of complete pictures.

A voltaic cell can seldom produce an electromotive force or voltage greater than 1·5 volts. Let us say that the resistance to

*The watt as a unit of power is not confined to electrical power, and can be used to measure any sort of power, including horse-power. One horsepower in fact is 746 watts.

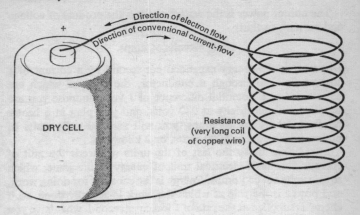

Figure 3

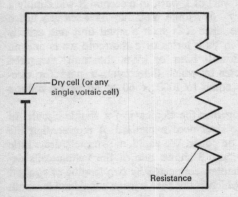

Figure 4

which the cell in the diagram is connected has a resistance of 10 ohms.* What will be the current that will flow round the circuit?

* It would in fact require over 50 metres of copper wire less than a tenth of a square millimetre in cross-section to have a resistance of 10 ohms.

34

If we use the formula:

$$\text{current} = \frac{\text{voltage}}{\text{resistance}},$$

we will have the sum:

$$\text{current} = \frac{1 \cdot 5}{10} = 0 \cdot 15 \text{ amps.}$$

Now let us connect another identical pair of wires in parallel with those already there (Figure 5). Since resistance is inversely pro-

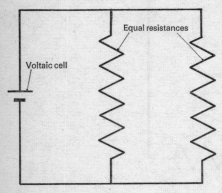

Equal resistances

Voltaic cell

Figure 5

portional to cross-sectional area, we can conclude that the joint value of two equal resistances in parallel is half that of one of them (and similarly for other numbers). The sum thus becomes:

$$\text{current} = \frac{1 \cdot 5}{5} = 0 \cdot 3 \text{ amps.}$$

This means that more current is flowing through the circuit because the resistance has been lowered. Had the two resistances been connected in series (Figure 6), then the total resistance would have doubled and the current would have *dropped* by half.

There is no way of hotting up a cell to give more voltage; all we can do is bring in another one. In just the same way as the total

35

resistance of two resistances in series is twice their individual values, so the voltage of two batteries connected in series is twice their individual voltages. To connect two batteries in series means to connect the positive terminal of one straight to the negative terminal of the other, and use the remaining free terminals to connect to the circuit. If, therefore, two cells are connected in series as in Figure 7, then we shall effectively have a battery with

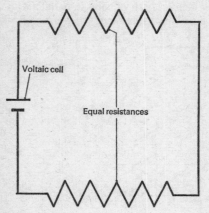

Figure 6

an e.m.f. of 3 volts. Why stop there? How about taking another pair of similarly wired cells and connecting the free positive terminal of one pair to the free negative terminal of the other; the answer – a 6-volt battery. It is even possible to have combinations of cells giving several hundred volts. Figure 8 shows the configuration of a typical 9-volt, multi-cell dry battery, and the symbol which would represent it on a circuit diagram.

We have seen that for resistances connected in series one simply adds up their individual values, and this presents no problems even if the values are all different. However, if resistors of different values are connected in parallel, the matter is not so straightforward. The easiest thing to do is to convert the resistances into the complementary values of 'conductances'. The

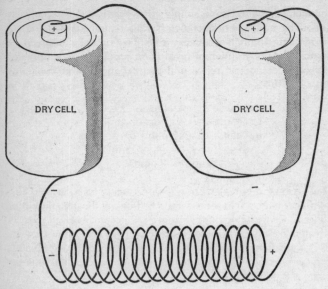

Figure 7

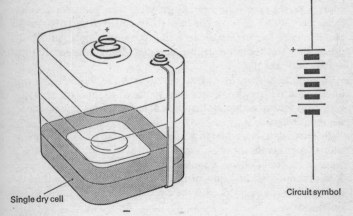

Single dry cell

Circuit symbol

Figure 8

conductance of a resistor is simply $1/R$ where R is the resistance in ohms. The unit of conductance is rather amusingly called the 'mho' being 'ohm' spelt backwards. To find the combined resistance of a set of different resistors in parallel, you simply add their conductances in mhos and convert the answer back into ohms, like this:

$$\text{resistance a} = 4 \text{ ohms or } \tfrac{1}{4} \text{ mho}$$
$$\text{resistance b} = 6 \text{ ohms or } \tfrac{1}{6} \text{ mho}$$
$$\text{resistance c} = 12 \text{ ohms or } \tfrac{1}{12} \text{ mho}$$
$$\tfrac{1}{4} + \tfrac{1}{6} + \tfrac{1}{12} = \tfrac{6}{12}, = \tfrac{1}{2} \text{ mho}$$
$$\tfrac{1}{2} \text{ mho} = 2 \text{ ohms.}$$

Let us take a circuit with a 2 ohm resistance connected to a 12-volt car battery. Six amps would be flowing through the circuit and so, since watts = volts × amps, the power involved must be 72 watts. We also know that if power is used at a rate of 1 watt, this is equivalent to 1 joule of energy per second. If we leave our circuit connected for 60 seconds, then 72 × 60, or 4,320 joules of energy will be used up.

Energy cannot just be 'used up'. Because of the law of conservation of energy, it must in fact turn into another form of energy. In the case of our circuit, it turns into heat. As the electrons flow along thin copper wire, they continually come under the influence of the forces around atoms of copper, and in so doing they get the atoms quite agitated. Heat in a solid is just agitation of atoms.

A joule as a quantity of heat energy is equal to 0·239 calories, and a calorie is the amount of heat required to raise the temperature of 1 gram of water through a temperature increase of 1 degree centigrade.

Because watts are equal to amps × volts, and volts are amps × ohms, then watts must be amps × amps × ohms. A watt is a joule per second, and as a joule is a measure of energy and therefore potentially a measure of heat, it is possible to say that the quantity of heat produced by a circuit in terms of current and resistance is:

$$\text{heat} = (\text{amps}^2 \times \text{ohms} \times \text{seconds}) \text{ joules.}$$

Obviously if the heat generated in a circuit is too great, the metal which forms the conductor is liable to melt, and then the circuit will be broken. If you connected a short copper wire across the two terminals of a car battery, the wire would quickly burn out. Because heat increases in proportion to the square of the current and is only directly proportional to the resistance, high current is more responsible for heat than high resistance, particularly since high resistance causes less current anyway.

If there were a fault, for instance, in a lighting circuit where the wires connecting to the lamp both touched, a 'short-circuit' would be created, because the current would no longer have to flow through the high resistance lamp, but can go straight round the wire. There would clearly be a danger of the wire burning out, and not only would this be extremely inconvenient and expensive, but it could also be very dangerous and start a serious fire. If the wire were long and thick, it might not actually burn out, but instead the insulation would start to smoulder.

The heating effect of current can be turned to advantage to prevent this dangerous situation happening. A very short section of wire is introduced into the circuit made of a metal with a low melting-point, and of thin cross-section. Let us say that if the circuit is working normally, 10 amps of current flow through it. The short section of different wire is selected so that if a current of more than 15 amps flows through it, so much heat is generated that the wire melts; if there is a short-circuit and a massive current tries to flow, the wire will instantly burn out and break the circuit.

This device is of course a fuse, and it serves two functions. It burns out the moment the current tries to exceed a safe level, and it also means that when a short-circuit does occur, one knows exactly where it will have burned out and can go straight to the fuse box to repair it. (Providing you have labelled all your fuses to show which circuit they apply to.)

Needless to say, or so it should be, it is most important to rectify the cause of the fuse 'blowing' before mending the fuse, and if a cause cannot be found great care should be taken and an expert consulted.

Let us look again at the heat formula: heat equals current

squared times resistance multiplied by the time in seconds. In a circuit carrying 10 amps, a fuse with a resistance of 0·02 ohms would, in 1 second, produce $10^2 \times 0·02 \times 1 = 2$ joules of heat. Suppose that the resistance of the fuse were raised to 0·1 ohms, by making it thinner. Because the fuse is in series with the (much greater) resistance of the rest of the circuit, the drop in current through the fuse will be negligible, since the total circuit resistance is insignificantly increased. The heat produced would be $10^2 \times 0·1 \times 1 = 10$ joules, and one can see that a thinner fuse will burn out at a lower current. Fuse wire is classified according to the current required to burn it out. It is made of an alloy of tin and lead, for its low melting-point, and the normal values are 2 amp, 5 amp, 10 amp, 13 amp, 30 amp and, in motor vehicles, 35 amp. In industrial applications, the values go much higher. Care must always be taken to select the correct fuse for an electrical appliance: its value must be sufficiently high to permit the rated current to flow, but must fail when this is exceeded.

This is by no means the only benefit available from the heating effect of electric current. Perhaps more important is our ability to make use of the heat which is generated. By using a resistor which has a high melting-point, using special alloys, any temperature up to red heat may be maintained. In order to obtain a high enough resistance, it is usually necessary to employ a considerable length of resistance wire in the form of a spiral around a heat-resisting core, and this is what the bar of an electric fire is.

There is however, one problem when it comes to calculating heating effects, and that is that the resistance of a conductor is dependent on its temperature. This can make the sum rather complicated, but it also leads to a fascinating corollary.

If you cool a conductor down, its resistance falls progressively; if you could reach absolute zero, the resistance would fall to nothing. However, there is a strange group of materials, of which lead and aluminium are two common ones, which suddenly offer virtually no resistance at all to electric current when their temperature gets down to a few degrees above absolute zero. The temperatures at which these materials become 'superconducting' can fairly easily be maintained by immersing the conductors in liquid helium, which liquefies at just above 4°C. The astonishing result is that something approaching perpetual motion is achieved when a superconducting material is made into a ring: a current in the ring will go on flowing round and round for months on end as a result of the insignificant resistance offered to it.

The potential applications of superconductors are innumerable. One of the most attractive is the transmission of electric power over long distances without any overheating problems and with negligible losses of energy. Because of the problems of keeping them at such low temperatures, superconductors are obviously very expensive, but it is possible to construct cables in which a central aluminium core is surrounded by liquid helium contained in a tube, around which is another layer of liquid nitrogen, which in turn has insulating layers around it.

Let us now have a further look at some of the implications of the set of units which have just been described. Let us go back to the coulomb for a moment, which was the measure of the quantity of electrons and thus the quantity of electricity. Is it not possible to measure the quantity of charge in a battery? It certainly is, and this is one of the important differences between a 12-volt car battery and a 12-volt torch battery. A car battery, or lead accumulator, can store current in proportion to the size of the cells, and therefore the energy which can be converted by the reversible chemical reaction. A battery's capacity is normally quoted in amp hours. A battery with a capacity of 35 amp hours will deliver electricity at a rate of 35 amps for 1 hour, or 1 amp for 35 hours, or any intermediate permutation. However,

$$\text{amps} = \frac{\text{coulombs}}{\text{seconds}} \text{ or } I = \frac{C}{S},$$

so amps multiplied by seconds equal coulombs;

$$I \times S = C,$$

so 1 amp hour equals 3,600 coulombs.

A 35-amp-hour battery has a capacity of 126,000 coulombs. Since a coulomb is about $6 \cdot 3 \times 10^{18}$ electrons, a car battery like this will push round 800,000,000,000,000,000,000,000 or 8×10^{23} electrons, give or take a few billion, before it gets completely flat. If you put a spanner across the terminals, those electrons will all

41

whiz through the spanner in such a short time that the terminals will melt, the spanner will get red hot, the plates of the battery will get completely buckled and the whole thing will be wrecked. Put a 120-ohm resistance across the terminals, and the current will happily trickle round at a rate of one tenth of an amp for 250 hours, before the battery finally becomes flat. It can then of course be recharged; it is better for the battery to be recharged at a modest rate of a few amps, although it could in theory be done in a very short time with a high enough current, but with a serious danger of damage to the battery.

Now a 12-volt dry battery will not have anything like the quantity of charge in it that a car battery would; even the most sophisticated set of cells would provide little over a fifth of an amp hour, or no more than 20 coulombs. The other important difference between these types of battery is the current they can maintain. Even if a circuit of a fractional resistance is put across the terminals of a car battery, there is a limit to the current which will flow, caused by the fact that it takes time for the chemical reaction to take place. To compensate for this, the voltage will drop and, in the case of a car battery, 500 amps is about the limit. A dry battery can only deliver a tiny fraction of this, and that is the reason why you can happily short circuit a dry cell without burning the wire, or even heating it. The current will reach its maximum and then the voltage drops.

Perhaps the role that voltage plays in electricity is now becoming plainer. It is not necessary to have a high voltage to extract a large amount of power, but if you have less voltage you must have proportionately more current in amps (by having lower resistances) to get the same amount of power. The wires in a car are thick because they carry heavy currents sometimes; if a 24-volt battery were used instead, less current would be needed. In the same way, it is just as possible to power a 35-watt headlamp with a 6-volt battery as with one of 12 volts, but the lamps must have half the resistance so as to pass twice the current.

This brings us to another vital effect of electric current: the production of light. If you were to take a heating coil, as described earlier in the chapter, and start increasing the voltage across it, it would get hotter and hotter as more current flowed. It would eventually get white hot and finally burn out because of oxidation or simply by melting. Before burning out, it would emit a fair amount of light. Now if a small coil of metal with a very high melting-point is enclosed in a vacuum, or in a space filled only with an inert gas, it will not burn out. Provided it does not reach its melting-point temperature, it will continuously emit light. This is of course what a filament lamp is.

A common light bulb, more correctly called a lamp, consists of a fine coil of tungsten wire mounted inside a glass bulb which has been evacuated or filled with nitrogen or other inert gas. The coil has a high resistance, and is thin enough so that the heat produced by the passage of current is all concentrated on a small length and size of wire with the result that it reaches about 2,500°C and becomes white hot. As you find out to your distress, when you touch an electric lamp, only a small proportion of the energy used in a lamp actually comes out as light, the rest is lost as heat.

Another type of light source is the carbon arc, which is perhaps most commonly found in the form of the light source in a cinema projector. It consists of two pointed carbon electrodes which have a potential difference between them and are momentarily touched together to allow current to flow and then drawn a small distance apart. Electric current continues to flow through the gas of burning carbon which forms between the electrodes and the points of the carbon electrodes become white hot, reaching around 3,500°C. A brilliant white light is emitted, and both electrodes are gradually consumed, the positive one acquiring a characteristic pit or crater.

There are several other ways of producing light by means of electric current, but in order to understand them, it will be necessary to get to know something about the type of current provided by mains electricity, as these methods of lighting will not work from batteries.

3 Fields, Flux and Force

Magnetism and electromagnetism

In Chapter 1 a statement was slipped in that seemed irrelevant at the time: that electrons in addition to pulsating in orbits round the nucleus also spin on their axes. This has a very important effect; it creates what is known as a magnetic moment.

A moment, apart from being something you wait for, is a quantity such as mass, inertia or force, multiplied by the distance at which the force is acting upon a point, such as the length of a lever from a fulcrum. This particular kind of moment is called torque: if you pull a lever you are creating a torque or moment of force which is the product of the force on the handle and the distance from the handle to the pivot of the lever. Torque in the drive of a car is the rearward force on the road at the tread of the tyre multiplied by the radius of the tyre.

A magnetic moment consists of two opposite attractions separated out by a certain distance, although of course when associated with electrons the distance is unimaginably small. What it boils down to is that in order to have a pair of attractions, such as positive and negative, there has to be a distance between them otherwise they will cancel each other out. If an electron and a proton have no distance between them they would both be in the same place and their individual attractions would cancel each other out.

A magnetic moment is a separating out of attractions: the attraction in this case is due to the spinning of electrons. It is not quite the same as the attraction between, for instance, a rubbed fountain pen and a little piece of paper, called electrostatic attraction; the type of attraction we are now talking about is magnetic attraction.

A very few substances have atomic structures of such a kind that the magnetic moments caused by electron-spin can be aligned so that they all point in the same direction. These substances are the ferromagnetic materials, and consist of iron (and steel), nickel and cobalt. The only one of much interest to us is iron in various forms.

The Earth has a magnetic moment: there are two types of attraction, the north and south magnetic poles, which are separated by a distance rather less than the diameter of the Earth. This magnetism is thought to be due to the fact that the core of the Earth is molten iron which is slowly spinning round. Over the ages, ferromagnetic minerals which have lain in the Earth's crust have had the magnetic moments of their electrons more or less permanently aligned in the direction of the forces exerted by the north and south magnetic poles. They are said to be magnetized. (Some of the moon rocks brought back by the Apollo astronauts are magnetized in this way, showing that the Moon once had a magnetic field as the Earth does, but it has long since disappeared.)

Centuries ago magnetized minerals on the Earth were discovered to exhibit strong attraction for iron, and were known as lodestones. Magnetite, which is the name for the mineral of which lodestones are constituted, is an iron ore which can become permanently magnetized. It is purportedly named after a puzzled Greek shepherd who got into difficulties one day when he found that he was rooted to the spot. It turned out that he was wearing hob-nailed boots and was standing on ground containing lodestone.

A lodestone, or any magnetized piece of iron or steel, possesses poles in the same way that the Earth does, and will attract another lump of ferromagnetic material whether magnetized or not. If the other lump happens to be magnetized, then 'opposite poles attract; like poles repel'. On the other hand, if the other lump of iron or steel is not magnetized, the lodestone or magnet will cause the magnetic moments of the lump to all face the same way, and the lump itself will then be found temporarily to have poles also. It is then said to be polarized. When the magnet is taken away, the lump of iron will normally go back to being an ordinary lump of metal again.

However, as originally happened to the lodestone, if the lump of iron, or better a bar of iron, is affected by a strong enough magnet for long enough, it will itself retain some permanent mag-

45

netism. In the old days magnets were made by stroking bars of iron with lodestones, as the stroking process speeds things up.

Most schoolboys have done the trick of sprinkling iron filings over a sheet of paper and placing a magnet underneath; the iron filings are polarized, becoming temporary magnets. The poles of a magnet tend to be at its furthest ends and the filings line themselves up in a special way. The position these lines of filings take

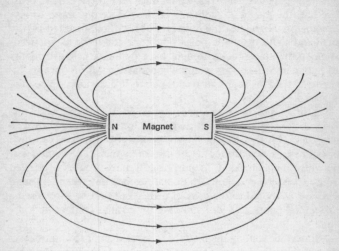

Figure 9

up and the direction in which they point will be determined by the relative strength of attraction felt by each filing from the different poles of the magnet. For this reason the iron filings form a pattern which looks like a squashed figure of eight, and the pattern clearly shows the direction in which the force from the magnet acts at any particular point. If you were to join up all the individual filings you would have drawn a series of lines curling round from one end of the magnet to the other, again like squashed figures of eight (Figure 9).

These lines are called lines of force. They show three things: they show the angle a little magnet like a polarized iron filing would adopt if dropped into the vicinity of the magnet, and they also show the strength of the magnetic 'field'. A field is just an area under the influence of something, such as magnetism, and the strength of it is shown diagrammatically by the number of lines of force that are drawn (Figure 10).

The third thing shown by lines of force is the direction a tiny

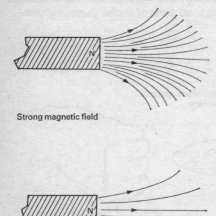

Strong magnetic field

Weak magnetic field

Figure 10

magnet would point if dropped on to a line, in addition to the angle it would adopt. The poles of magnets are named after the effect terrestrial magnetism (the Earth's magnetism) has on them. The end of the magnet which is attracted towards the north magnetic pole is called the north-seeking or just north pole, the other one the south-seeking or south pole. Remember that if the north pole of a magnet is attracted towards the north magnetic pole of the Earth, it does in fact possess the type of attraction that the Earth's south pole does, because only opposite poles attract.

In order to show the direction of the force in a magnetic field,

47

arrows are drawn on the lines of force, pointed so that the head of the arrow is where the north-seeking pole of a little magnet would be after it has taken up its position in the field of the large magnet.

What have magnets got to do with electricity? The answer is that the Earth is not the only source of magnetism. Magnetism can also be created electrically, and when electromagnetic fields and magnetic fields interact, all sorts of useful things happen.

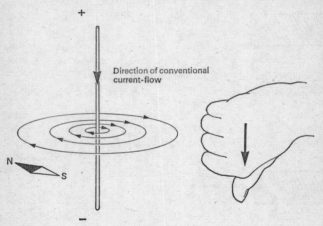

Figure 11

We already know that the behaviour of electrons can have very odd effects, and that electron-spin causes magnetism. Electrons can also cause another associated effect, and this happens whenever a stream of electrons travels from A to B. It may be in space, as happens with a spark (a process we shall look at in more detail later), or while electrons are flowing along a conductor, such as a copper wire. A stream of electrons is surrounded by a magnetic field. We shall call it an electromagnetic field to distinguish it from fields around permanent magnets, but it is a similar phenomenon.

The special thing about the electromagnetic field around a stream of electrons, which for most purposes means a current-carrying wire, is the direction of the lines of force. A little magnet, like the pointer of a compass, will always try to line itself up with the circumference of an imaginary circle round a current-carrying wire. In other words the lines of force round the wire are circular (Figure 11).

If you imagine a wire passing through a hole in this page, and that the electrons are travelling up towards you (i.e. that the conventional direction of current was down into the page), then a compass needle will always try to turn so that it lies on a tangent* to an imaginary circle drawn round the wire with a radius equal to the distance from the pivot of the compass needle to the centre of the wire. This imaginary circle is a line of force, and its direction will be *clockwise*. This means that the north-seeking pole of the compass needle will be pointing in a clockwise direction. If the direction of the current flow is reversed, so will be the direction of the lines of force. There is a convenient rule to help remember the direction of the lines of force known as the right-hand wire rule. Clench your right fist and stick out the thumb, and if the conventional direction of the current is the way your thumb is pointing, then the lines of force will follow the direction of your fingers.

The nearer you get to the wire, the smaller the imaginary circle gets, so the force is therefore distributed over a smaller area and becomes stronger. In fact if you halve the distance between the point of interest and the centre of the wire, the force is doubled. As you near the centre of the wire itself, the force increases steeply, and the electrons themselves, inside the wire, are all probably spinning in a clockwise or anti-clockwise direction themselves, as they whiz along the wire.

On its own like this, the electromagnetic field round a current-carrying wire is not much use, but if you wind the wire into a coil and pass a current through it, what will happen? Each loop of the coil is certainly surrounded by its cylindrical force-pattern, but the coils being in proximity to one another their forces have a mutual effect on one another. Between the coils the directions of force are always opposite, cancelling each other out; outside the

*To the non-geometrical reader, a tangent is an infinite straight line which only cuts a circle in one place, i.e. just touches it.

coils the forces are all tending to one direction so they all act together in that direction; inside the coil they all act even more strongly in the other direction because the curvature of the coils concentrates the force into a smaller space (Figure 12). A compass needle in the vicinity of the top end of the coil in Figure 12

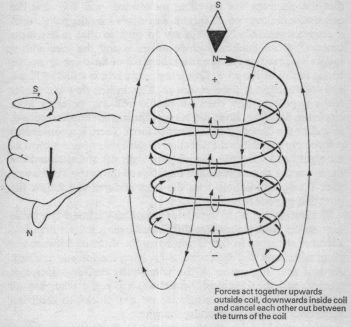

Forces act together upwards outside coil, downwards inside coil and cancel each other out between the turns of the coil

Figure 12

would whip round so that its north-seeking pole pointed down the centre of the coil. It is important to realize that all these phenomena are caused purely by the electric current, not by any effect the current is having on the conductor itself. Copper alone cannot be magnetized.

There is another rule of thumb to help work out the direction of force produced by a coil called the right-hand coil rule. If you

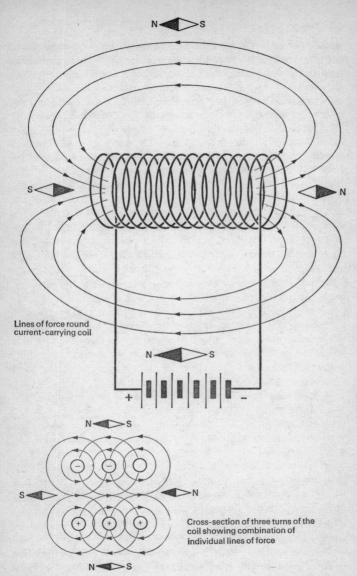

Lines of force round
current-carrying coil

Cross-section of three turns of the
coil showing combination of
individual lines of force

Figure 13

wrap your fingers round the coil in the direction the current is conventionally flowing round the coils and stick out your thumb, then the thumb end of the coil will have a north-seeking type of attraction.

Now place an iron bar down the centre of the core, and the result will be a massive increase in the force created by the coil. Why does this happen? A bar of copper or lead would make no difference to the force at all. The answer is that iron is ferromagnetic and is capable of being polarized. The electromagnetic field of the coil polarizes an iron bar stuck down the middle, and the bar is then a temporary magnet. In this condition it adds its own magnetic field to that of the coil, with the result that there is a marked increase in the overall strength of the field. If the iron core is subjected to a strong enough electromagnetic field, it will retain some of the polarization and become a permanent magnet, although this can be done much better with steel.

Iron is what is known as a soft magnetic material, because it is easily demagnetized; those which are not are called hard magnetic materials, of which silicon steel and steel alloyed with chromium and tungsten are among the best. However, for the purposes of our coil, it is to our advantage to have a core which when the current is switched off ceases to be polarized. Permanent magnets have their uses, but electromagnets which can be switched on and off at will are even more useful.

'Lifting magnets' capable of holding on to several tons of iron and steel are used as cranes to move metal about, and can exert a force big enough to lift cars with ease. They are also useful for sorting ferrous metal from scrap or refuse, and some refuse disposal depots use electromagnets to separate all the cans and other ferrous metal objects which are then baled and sold. ('Tin' cans are only tin-plated steel.)

At the other end of the scale, small electromagnets sometimes called solenoids can be most useful. A relay is a device which can be activated by one electrical circuit to make or break another circuit. For instance, a weak current in one circuit can be just enough to power a solenoid which attracts a mechanism and closes the contacts of another circuit carrying a heavier current.

Figure 14 shows a typical relay. A relay can in fact have an extensive combination of contacts, some opening when others close, operated by the energizing circuit.

As well as being used for remote switching, relays are valuable safety devices operating like reversible fuses. In these cases they can be designed to protect against excess current (like a fuse), too little current, over-voltage, under-voltage, reverse current and many other abnormalities. Many householders may in fact have a trip mechanism in their fuse cupboard which breaks the mains

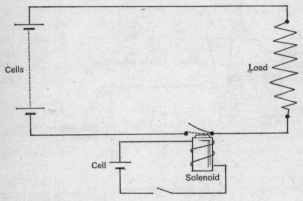

Figure 14

circuit if overloaded by switching too many appliances on at once, and can be reset when some of the appliances have been switched off without the labour of mending a fuse. These mechanisms are usually found where the supply is limited in terms of current, and we shall see more of them in Chapter 5.

An electric bell is another device which relies on an electro-magnet or solenoid. In the simplest design the clapper is spring loaded, and in the relaxed position closes a pair of contacts. When the button is pressed, current at first flows through the circuit, activating the solenoid. This immediately pulls the spring-loaded clapper towards the core of the solenoid (striking the bell), and breaks the circuit which relied for contact on the clapper being

53

relaxed. Immediately the circuit is broken like this, the solenoid's magnetic field collapses, and the clapper springs back to its rest position, closing the contacts again and restarting the whole cycle. By adjusting the stiffness of the spring on the clapper, the clapper can be made to fly back and forth at a suitable rate to keep up a continuous ringing of the bell (Figure 15).

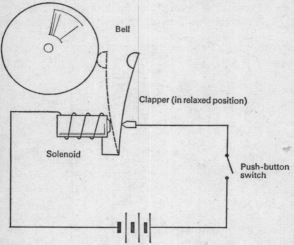

Figure 15

However, electromagnets or electromagnetic fields have many more tricks to reveal to us than these. What do you suppose happens if you mix an electromagnetic field with a magnetic one? What is the effect of current in a wire which runs between the poles of a permanent magnet?

To help in answering this question, consider what happens when one magnet is brought into the field of another. Figure 16 shows a magnet and its lines of force, the north pole at the top, south at the bottom. A secondary magnet is placed close to it at an angle, also with its north pole at the top. Because unlike poles repel, the magnets will tend to twist round and push one another apart.

54

Now any point on a line of force is really a tiny invisible magnet. Drop an iron filing on to that point and it will play the role of the tiny invisible magnet. Therefore in just the same way as the two magnets in Figure 16 try to straighten up and push themselves apart, so do the lines of force always tend to push

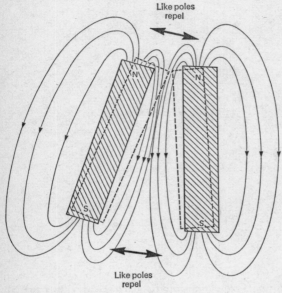

Like poles
repel

Like poles
repel

Figure 16

themselves apart. This effect has most interesting results. We have already seen that the number of lines represents the strength of the field – that is, the strength of the pull it can exert – and if on a drawing of force-pattern the lines seem bunched together, it is not because they want to be close together, because their natural tendency is to separate; they would only be there under the influence of some other force, such as the proximity of another magnet.

Now let us see what happens when a current-carrying wire

passes through a magnetic field. For our magnetic field let us take either a curved magnet whose poles face one another across a gap or, for greater simplicity, two magnets, opposite poles of which are separated by a gap. The lines of force across the gap will be as shown in Figure 17. (Notice how they bulge as a result of their

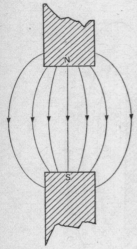

Figure 17

mutual repulsion.) Now introduce the current-carrying wire with its circular lines of force.

The first thing one notices is that to the left of the wire, the electromagnetic lines of force run in the opposite direction to the magnetic ones, and so cancel each other out. To the right they all tend to go the same way and the force is increased. The combined force-diagram looks like Figure 18.

The result is going to be that the lines of force to the right of the wire will object to being bunched up and, as before, tend to repel each other. This will push the wire over to the left. If the directon of current-flow is reversed, the wire will be pushed to the right.

This is one of the most important phenomena in electrical engineering; the implications are immeasurable. Let us take it a step further, and instead of a current-carrying wire, use a coil of wire. Let this be mounted on a swivelling axis as in Figure 19, and placed between the poles of a specially shaped magnet.

On one side of the coil, there will be a lot of wires going one way, and on the other side of the coil they will be going the other

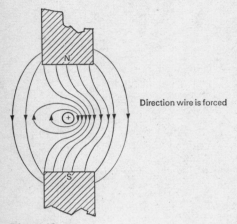

Direction wire is forced

Figure 18

way. When the current is switched on, the effect of the magnetic field will be to push the wires outwards and, since the wires are part of a pivoted coil, this means that the bottom of the coil is pushed to the left, and the top to the right. The coil will swivel on its axis.

For the moment, let the coil be spring-loaded, so that there soon comes a point where the torque exerted by the interaction of fields equals the strain on the spring and it swivels no further. We now have a most useful instrument.

The strength of the electromagnetic field round the wires of the coil is determined by the amount of electricity flowing through them or, in other words, the amount of current. The stronger the electromagnetic field, the greater the force resulting from the

57

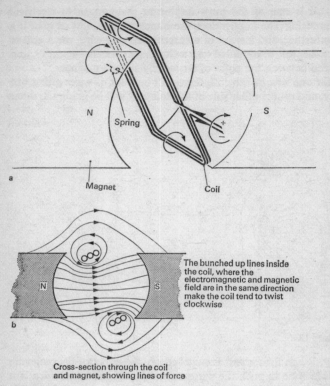

a

Spring

N

S

Magnet

Coil

b

N

S

The bunched up lines inside
the coil, where the
electromagnetic and magnetic
field are in the same direction
make the coil tend to twist
clockwise

Cross-section through the coil
and magnet, showing lines of force

Figure 19

interaction of the electromagnetic and magnetic fields. Consequently, the greater the current, the stronger the torque exerted on the coil, and the further it will swivel against the spring. Fit a pointer to the axis of the coil and put a scale behind the pointer, and here is a means of measuring currents: an ammeter, no less.

This type of ammeter will be somewhat limited in the size of current it will measure and it is normally called a galvanometer. There are several variations to the design, one of which is to place a fixed iron core in the centre of the coil to concentrate the field.

here, by building up the resistance of the ammeter to a value many times greater than that of the resistor across whose terminals we are measuring the voltage. This will mean that the proportion of current that flows through the ammeter will only be a fraction of the proportion in the main circuit so that the meter will have a negligible effect on the circuit.

Inside the meter, although it has a high resistance and therefore carries little current, that current will still be proportional to voltage, and so if the scale on the meter is calibrated directly in volts instead of amps, here is our voltmeter.

Let us summarize the difference between these types of meter. A galvanometer has a relatively low resistance and is wired in series with the main circuit. The more current which flows in the circuit, the greater will be the needle deflection. If the needle goes off the top of the scale, then the galvanometer can be partially by-passed by connecting a shunt (a resistor) having a lower resistance than the galvanometer, across the terminals. Less current will flow through the meter, and the reduced reading is then multiplied by the multiplying power of the shunt and the result is an ammeter. A voltmeter is a similar device to an ammeter but is not wired into the main circuit. It is wired in parallel with and across the section of the circuit where the potential difference or electromotive force is required to be measured in volts. In order that the voltmeter does not short-circuit the section it is connected across, it has a high resistance and so takes only a negligible fraction of current. Although fractional, this current is still proportional to voltage, and so the scale on the meter can be calibrated directly in volts. The higher the voltage across the terminals, the higher the current that flows through the meter (although it is a small proportion of the current in the main circuit) and so the greater deflection of the needle.

So far, all we have done is generate light to watch meters measuring current that is keeping us warm. Now let us get the electricity to move us about as well.

We must, for a moment, return to the galvanometer and start taking it to bits. Remember that there is a coil pivoted inside the field of a permanent magnet. Current in the pivoted coil creates an electromagnetic field around the coil, and the mutual influence of the magnetic and electromagnetic fields forces the coil to swivel. We prevented it from rotating far by spring-loading the coil. Let us remove the spring and see just what sort of a muddle the thing would get into.

Figure 22 shows again the fact that if current flows from terminal A of the coil to terminal B, then the direction of the electromagnetic field is such that the coil will turn clockwise. If

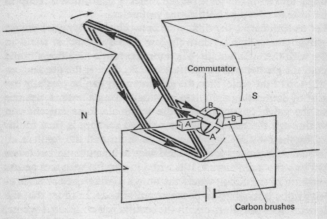

Figure 22

the current flows in the reverse direction, from B to A, then the direction of the lines of force of the electromagnetic field will be reversed and the coil will turn the other way. Now if, instead of reversing the current flow, the coil is turned upside-down as would happen if it went on swivelling, the same result is achieved and the coil will want to turn the other way, anti-clockwise. It would therefore, in practice, just settle down in a middle position and not move at all.

To make a motor, we want the coil to go on turning in a clockwise direction, so let us kill two birds with one stone, and both ensure that this happens and at the same time stop the wires getting tangled. This can be done by connecting the terminals of the coil to a copper ring mounted on the shaft of the coil. The ring has a break at the top and the bottom and is in fact made up of two semicircles insulated from one another. This split ring is called a commutator. To get the current through the coil, spring-loaded carbon 'brushes' are pressed against the commutator. Carbon is used because it is a convenient conducting material which reduces wear on the commutator.

The introduction of the commutator and brushes greatly alters the situation. Now when the coil starts to turn upside-down under the influence of the interacting fields, instead of reaching a point where it wants to turn back in the other direction, the brushes which are stationary find that they come in contact with opposite halves of the commutator, reversing the direction of current flow. However, the coil is now upside-down, and reversing the direction of flow has repeated the original state of the electromagnetic field with relation to the magnetic field, causing the coil to go on turning clockwise. There are no wires to get tangled because the commutator and brushes supply current and yet permit rotation.

This is a pretty basic sort of motor: it would not run very smoothly or be very efficient because, as each half-turn of the coil neared its end, the turning force would diminish, causing jerky movement. A typical battery-operated motor. such as the self-starter of a car engine, has several sets of separate coils wound into notches in a soft iron core, and for each separate coil there is a corresponding pair of opposite segments on the commutator. This is why the commutator has a whole series of separate copper 'pads' all the way round, and the effect is to make for much smoother operation.

The magnetic field in the simple motor was provided by a permanent magnet, but often this is replaced by an electromagnet, being an iron core with windings through which all or part of the current supplied to the motor is passed. We shall have a great deal more to say about motors later on, but for the moment we shall leave them there and have a look at some more electromagnetic effects of current.

Although we have spent a fair amount of time measuring attributes of electricity, nothing much has been said about quantities in magnetism and electromagnetism. How do you express an amount of magnetism? The simple answer is to give arbitrary values to the lines of force and to express the quantity of force in terms of the total number of lines; indeed a *line* is a unit of magnetic quantity. 100,000,000 lines are equal to one *weber*. What in fact does a weber measure? The thing that we have rather vaguely described as magnetic quantity is correctly called magnetic flux density, the degree of closeness together of the lines of force. This is measured in webers per square metre. We are not in fact very interested in the actual units here; the thing we want to look at closely is the quantity itself, magnetic flux.

It is reasonable to think that electrons being particles of attraction, they could perhaps be induced to move along a conductor by magnetism. This is in fact not far from the truth. Although you would not get very far by holding a magnet to one end of a wire and hoping electrons would come running towards it, if you were to play around with a magnet and a coil, you would indeed be extremely successful in inducing electrons to move.

What you do is to connect the coil to a galvanometer and sharply jerk the pole of a bar magnet into the mouth of one end of the coil. This will cause electrons to spiral round the coil, inducing current in the circuit and deflecting the needle of the galvanometer. There is no battery in the circuit and the current is entirely caused by the magnet. The moment the magnet comes to rest, the current stops. Notice that stationary magnetism does not induce electrons to go anywhere, it is only when the magnet is moved that anything happens. What, then, is different between the electromagnetic state of affairs when the magnet is still and when it is moving? The answer is that lines of force, in the second case, are cutting across the wires. In other words the wires are experiencing a change of flux. Whenever there is a change in the number of lines of magnetic force near a conductor, an electric current will be induced in the conductor. The direction of current-flow is dependent on the direction of the lines of force and the direction in which they change. In Figure 23(a) the conventional current-flow is anti-clockwise. Reverse the polarity of the magnet or jerk it in the opposite direction and the direction of current-flow will be reversed to clockwise – Figure 23(b).

Now of course current in a coil turns the coil into an electro-magnet, and if you apply the right-hand coil rule (page 50) to Figure 23, you will see that the coil becomes an electromagnet with its north pole at the left. This is going to repel the north pole of the magnet which was jerked into the coil to induce the current.

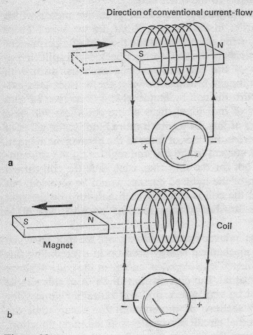

Direction of conventional current-flow

N

S

a

S   N

Coil

Magnet

b

Figure 23

Since you never get anything for nothing in this life, the energy in the current induced by the magnet came from the energy supplied by your arm in overcoming the repulsion between the magnet and the coil the moment there was any current in it.

Now for some units; an electromotive force of 1 volt would be generated in the coil in Figure 23 for every weber (100,000,000 lines) of flux which cuts a conductor in 1 second.

There is yet another rule to help work out the direction of current flow, as follows: 'If the thu*M*b (of the right hand) points in the direction of *M*otion, and the *F*irst finger in the direction of *F*lux, the se*C*ond finger will point in the direction of *C*urrent-flow.' When doing this, the fingers should be extended so that each is at right angles to the other two.

Suppose we now resurrect the rather primitive motor which was described earlier in the chapter. What did we have? There was a coiled conductor pivoted to rotate the field of a permanent magnet. The terminals of the coil were connected to a split ring so that the polarity of the coil was reversed each half-turn with respect to the stationary brushes. Connect the brushes to a galvanometer, and turn the coil by hand: what will happen? From the point of view of individual turns of the coil there will be a continuing change of flux, or to put it more bluntly, the wires of the coil will cut across the lines of force of the permanent magnet. This will induce a current in the coil and register on the galvanometer. If it were not for the split ring, each time the coil turned over the direction of the induced current would be reversed, but as the polarity of the coil is reversed each half-turn by the split ring, one of the brushes always remains positive, the other always negative.

The effect of the induced current is to oppose the motion which produces it. The mechanical energy used up in overcoming this opposition is converted into electrical energy in the coil. We have an electrical generator! The current that flows from this simple generator will not be very much, and will be rather lumpy, for although the two sections of the commutator ensure that the current in the external circuit always flows in the same direction, during each half-turn the current grows from near nothing to its maximum and then back to near nothing.

By replacing the simple coil with a large set of coils each with their own pair of segments on the commutator, the current can be smoothed out in the same way as the operation of the motor was improved. The set of coils is known as the armature, and large ones incorporate cooling slots to remove heat generated by the resistance of the coils.

The coils, of course, are not the only part of the armature

which cut the lines of force of the field magnet; the iron core of
the armature also does. The core is not connected to a circuit, so
the currents that are generated in it as it rotates just go round in
small circles and are called eddy currents. In so doing, they tend
to heat up the iron and this is clearly a waste of energy. There are
two principal ways of reducing this effect. One is to make the
armature out of metal having a high resistance, but the other,
more common method, is to use a built-up armature consisting of
a multiple sandwich of relatively thin metal stampings. The

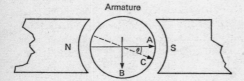

Armature

A – Direction of field due to field magnet
B – Direction of field due to armature
C – The combined effect of the two
θ° – Angle of lead

Figure 24

stampings are insulated from one another so that eddy currents
are confined to individual 'leaves' and this prevents the build-up
of any considerable voltage in the armature as a whole.

The field magnet for our generator has so far been a permanent magnet, but in practice field magnets tend to be electromagnets. Often there are more than just two poles, so that each
conductor passes north and south poles more than once during
one half-turn. This tends to make for extremely complex connections between the coils and the commutator to ensure that one
brush always picks up only positive or negative as the case may be.

In the same way as the coils are not the only part of the armature which cut the lines of force, so is the field magnet not the only
source of magnetic field. The armature has a field of its own while
current is induced in its coils, and going back to the simple
generator, Figure 24 shows that the field due to the armature is
always at right angles to that of the field magnet. The net result of
the interaction of the two fields is to skew the overall field round

a bit. This is called armature reaction, and what it means is that the armature (and the current induced in it) behaves all the time as though it were a few degrees further round than it actually is. The extent of this is known as the angle of lead, and the effect is that the changes of polarity at the brushes are out of step causing frightful sparks. In order to prevent this, the brushes must be positioned further round.

Generators, as we have said, usually have electromagnets as field magnets, and they usually supply their own current to energize the field magnets. There is always a little magnetism left

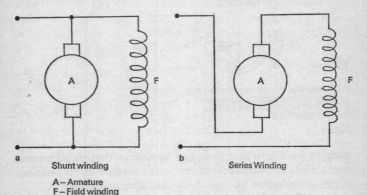

a   Shunt winding   b   Series Winding

A – Armature
F – Field winding

Figure 25

in the iron to start things off. When the generator is first rotated, a small voltage is generated in the weak field due to the residual magnetism of the iron, and this provides a little current to start a small electromagnetic field which in turn causes more induced current, and so on until everything builds up to the full.

There are two ways of connecting the field magnet – shunt and series (as shown in Figure 25). With a shunt winding, if a heavy load is connected to the generator terminals, the voltage tends to fall, but in a series-wound generator, if extra current is taken by the circuit, more current flows through the field-magnet windings, increasing the flux and causing the voltage to rise. Neither of these effects is particularly desirable, and a crafty way out of the problem is to incorporate both types of winding in one generator. The field magnet then has two windings, one in series with the armature and one in parallel. This is called a compound winding, and with increase in load, the voltage drop due to one winding is offset by the voltage rise due to the other.

All these side effects have their counterparts in motors. Armature reaction occurs in the opposite way, requiring the brushes to be turned so that they lag slightly behind. Eddy currents are taken care of in the same way as in generators. However, the effects of shunt and series windings are rather different. A heavy load on a shunt-wound motor does not decrease its speed very much, but series winding causes the speed to drop. This means that starting under load is easier, but if the load is removed, the motor is liable to run too fast. Here again, compound winding is a useful way out of the problem.

There is another, perhaps unexpected, side effect which occurs with electric motors. We have seen that basically the same device will serve as either motor or generator. How does it know which it is to be? The answer is that it doesn't and that while a motor is running, its coils are also cutting lines of force and generating what is called back-voltage. If the coils of the armature had no resistance the back-voltage would be equal to the applied voltage (but we would then be in the land of perpetual motion machines). As it is, the back-voltage is always less than the applied voltage, and the difference is the voltage required to overcome the armature resistance. The back-voltage and the current in the armature are the way in which the mechanical load on the motor manifests itself electrically. The product of the back-voltage and the armature current gives us the power in watts developed by the machine (746 watts are equal to one horsepower).

Problems arise when it comes to starting a big motor under load. When it is not rotating, there is no back-voltage to oppose the applied voltage. This means that there is only the resistance of the copper windings (not much) to oppose current-flow, and a dangerously excessive current is likely. Large motors therefore have to have a starter, consisting of a bank of resistances which are switched into the armature circuit for start-up of the motor. As the motor speed rises, the resistances are switched out one by one until normal running speed is reached and the starter is cut out altogether. To prevent inadvertent attempts to start the motor without the starter switched in, its control lever is usually spring loaded towards the 'off' position, and held in the 'on' position by an electromagnet wired into the field magnet circuit. The moment the current is switched off, the starter control lever returns automatically to the 'off' or start-up position, with all the resistances switched in. A similar safety device is often found which trips the starter when current-flow to the motor increases too greatly.

4 The Power Game

Alternating current

Electricity is consumed in vast quantities all over the world, but far and away the greatest proportion of it is used in a form which is fundamentally different from that so far talked about in this book. We have been talking exclusively about direct current, where one terminal of the generator or battery is always negative, and the other always positive; where there is a flow of electrons from the former to the latter, or a conventional flow of current in the reverse direction. Mains electricity, as most of us well know, is not direct current; it is alternating current and it has surprisingly little in common with direct current. What is alternating current, and why is it so different?

In the last chapter, we took to using a simple motor as a current generator by applying a rotational force to it, and cutting the lines of force between the poles of the permanent magnet with the coils of the armature, thus inducing a current to flow. Remember that both with the motor and the generator, it was necessary to fit a split ring or commutator and brushes, to make sure that the polarity of the machine stayed the same while the armature rotated.

It would obviously be simpler to be able to leave out the complication of the split ring. What sort of current would we get if we did? Figure 26 again shows a simple loop of wire in the field of a permanent magnet. In Figure 26 the loop begins to be turned clockwise, cutting the lines of force of the magnet, and inducing a (conventional) current flow from the terminal A to terminal B of the loop. As the loop nears the end of the first quarter-turn, it almost ceases to cut any lines of force, and a momentary point is reached where no current flows at all as the loop is in a vertical position.

As it enters the second quarter-turn, the two strands of wire start to cut lines of force again, but the direction of flux is reversed. The loop completes its first half-turn, and the current flow builds up to its maximum as the loop cuts the greatest number of lines of force. It then falls off and, as the loop nears the end of its third quarter, almost no lines are cut, the current momentarily drops to nil, and in the final quarter the direction of current-flow again changes and builds up to its maximum at the end of the first complete run.

Although a commutator can be dispensed with, it is still neces-

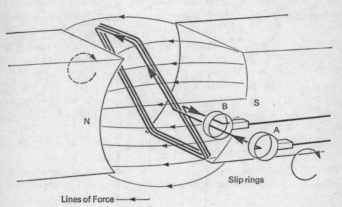

Lines of Force ◀

Figure 26

sary to get the current away from the loop, and so a pair of slip rings can be used, as in Figure 26, to connect the rotating wires with the stationary ones. What will the current be like at the two terminals? It has been established that the direction of flow changes once every half-turn and, in between, points are reached of no flow in either direction, but that is all. To look at the problem more closely, a graph has to be drawn.

The loop rotates at constant speed, and the strength of the current generated is proportional to the number of lines of force which are cut in a given time. The graph in Figure 27 shows the numbers of lines which one side of the loop is cutting as it passes through sixteen positions spaced around the circle through which it rotates. The poles of a magnet are placed either side of the circle of rotation, so that the lines of force between the poles cross the

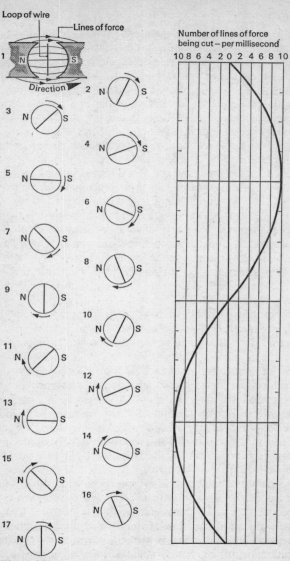

Figure 27

circle. At position number 1, the wire is, at that instant, moving in the same direction as the lines; it is therefore cutting none, so no current is induced to flow. The graph is marked to show 0 lines of force being cut at position 1.

By the time it reaches position 2, the wire has started to move across the lines, and let us say that at position 2 it is cutting 4 lines per millisecond. The figure increases until position 5 is reached and a maximum of 10 lines per millisecond are being cut, because the conductor is now moving at right angles across them. The current then falls in an identical pattern until at position 9, at the end of the first half-turn, the wire is back to cutting no lines at all. The pattern for the last half-turn is then identical to that of the first, but the current-flow is reversed. So let us plot the number of lines being cut as a negative quantity on the graph.

Repeat this routine for several rotations, and the graph takes on a beautifully uniform serpentine shape, smoothly oscillating above and below the centre line as the direction of current-flow alternates. 'Alternates' is the operative word, because this type of electric current is called alternating current, or A.C., as opposed to direct current or D.C.

The beautifully smooth shape of the graph is no accident, and in fact it should be familiar to anyone who remembers their trigonometry. It is a graph of the trigonometrical function, the sine. To be more precise, in this case we have got a cosine, and the number of lines being cut at each position is equal to ten times the cosine of the angle between the loop and the vertical position 1.

Sine waves are rather fundamental things in many walks of life. The sound waves of pure musical tones are sine waves; the purest types of light waves are sine waves, and in fact they crop up all through physics. In simple language, a sine wave is circular motion converted into oscillatory motion. The connection between sine waves and circles is evident if you take a small spring, like the one in a ball-point pen, and stretch it out slightly. If you look down it the coils are circular, but if you look at it from the side you will see a sine wave. If you are still puzzled, think of a water wheel half-submerged so that its axle is on the surface of the water. One of the spokes is painted red, and a tape measure hung from the outer end of the spoke. As the wheel turns, the distance from the end of the spoke to the surface of the water will change as the angle between the red spoke and the water changes. If, when the spoke is vertical, the tape measure has ten divisions showing out of the water, then when the wheel starts to turn, the number of divisions still showing is equal to ten times the sine of the angle formed between the red spoke and the surface of the water. When the spoke goes beneath the surface, the sine has a minus value, and the tape gets very soggy.

Looked at another way, the conductor which is busily rotating in the magnetic field is only doing useful work in so much as it cuts lines of force. The sine curve is in fact a representation of the amount of 'sideways motion' that the conductor is doing at points around its circle of rotation.

Looking at the graph in Figure 27, it is evident that the sine wave can be given two quantities; height and width. The width, or the amount of paper taken up for the line to swoop from one high point to another, is more important than you might think. If we know, for example, that the idealized conductor is rotating 50 times per second, so that the paper width can be calibrated in terms of time, the curve will plunge from peak to peak in a distance representing 1/50th of a second. Another way of stating this is to say that the alternating current which we are dealing with here has a frequency of 50 cycles per second, because it completes a full cycle 50 times each second. 'Cycles per second' are called hertz, and it is now common practice to talk about frequency as 50 hertz rather than 50 cycles per second; they both mean exactly the same.

What does the height of the sine wave represent? Voltage? Current (amps)? Power (watts)? The infuriating answer is: 'It depends.' Odd things happen to alternating current which do not happen to direct current, and volts, amps, watts, ohms, mhos and their colleagues reveal new ramifications. We will also soon have to get to grips with farads and henrys. However, before pressing on, we had better pause and consider just how one can possibly measure the voltage, current or any quantity which will not stay still for long enough to clap a meter on it.

We have mentioned that the height of the wave is the dimension which signifies quantity, such as number of volts or amps, but the height is always changing. Do we measure the peak that the wave reaches? That will give us a rather over-optimistic result, because for almost all the time the curve is not at its peak, only for an instant twice every cycle, once positive and once negative. Then perhaps we need an average. What do we average? One way of doing it would be to draw a whole series of vertical lines as shown in Figure 28, and to take an arithmetic average of the height of the lines. The trouble is that the answer will be 0 because the lines

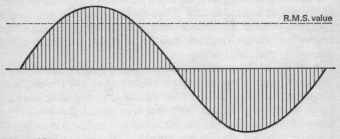

R.M.S. value

Figure 28

below zero have a minus quantity and will cancel out the lines above zero. The answer to the problem is to square the lengths of all the lines, and as a minus quantity multiplied by itself gives a positive answer, if we average the squared values we will again have a positive answer. Now take the square root of the answer, and this brings us back down to what is called the root-mean-square (R.M.S.) value of the sine wave. This gives us the effective voltage or current or whatever else the curve represents.

For mathematical reasons which it is not worth going into here, the root-mean-square value of a sine wave is equal to the maximum or peak value divided by 1·414 (the square root of 2) which is the same as the peak value multiplied by 0·707. This problem solved, though, we still have to discover whether the curve represents voltage, or current, or what.

The first complication arises when you make the very simplest circuit through which alternating current flows. The simplest circuit is just a resistance connected across the terminals of the source of electricity, so let us connect a carbon rod as an idealized resistor across the terminals of our alternator, and see what happens.

Ohm and his law told us that you divide the voltage by the resistance to arrive at the current, and as in this case the resistance does not alter in value, the current is directly proportional to voltage, and with alternating current both the voltage and the current oscillate as sine waves. Figure 29 shows the waves for volts and amps in our simple circuit; there is no significance in the

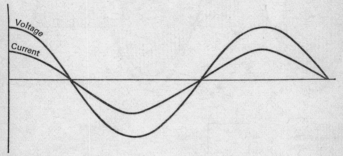

Figure 29

fact that one is higher than the other, they are measured in different units so there is no comparison of amplitudes. The important thing is that both the curves oscillate at the same frequency because they both reach their highest and lowest points together and both pass through zero at the same time. The technical words used to describe this state of affairs are 'in phase', which really just means 'in step'.

Now volts multiplied by amps give power in watts, so take a series of points along the curves in Figure 29, read off the values of volts and amps in each case, multiply them together and plot the answer on the graph. What you will get is another sine wave, but this time it is all above zero, that is, it has no negative values (Figure 30).

To obtain the average power, you simply halve the peak value. The total energy involved (power × time) is equal to the area

77

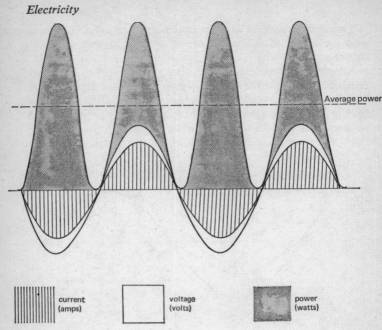

Figure 30

under the power curve (shaded with dots). The power curve is still in phase with the voltage and the current curves, but its value is always positive, and its frequency is double that of the voltage and current.

The next complication to be dealt with is a great deal more complex and takes very much more understanding: inductance.

Remember that whenever a coil cuts lines of force (and vice versa) an electromotive force (e.m.f.) is induced. Until now though, the lines of force have been provided only by the poles of a magnet. We have also come across electromagnets and know that they produce magnetic fields similar to permanent magnets. The basic component of an electromagnet is a current-carrying coil of wire, and the complications set in when you apply to a coil an alternating current instead of a direct one.

The electromagnetic field around a coil with direct current going through it looks like Figure 31a. If you reduce the strength of current, the field will weaken and become like Figure 31b. Notice that in Figure 31b, the lines of force have shifted as the current weakened. Now you can imagine that with the constantly changing strength of an alternating current applied to the coil, the lines of force of the electromagnetic field will also oscillate and in so doing will cut the loops of the coil itself. This causes none

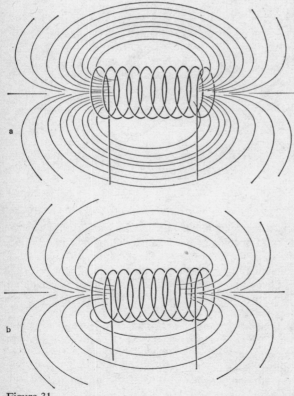

Figure 31

other than an induced e.m.f. (voltage) and if you puzzle over it long enough you will discover that the direction of the induced e.m.f. is such that it will oppose the change of current that caused it.

Figure 32 shows the graph of the oscillating current, together with the oscillating e.m.f. that is producing the current. The induced e.m.f. opposes the change in current and appears in Figure 32 as the exact opposite of the applied e.m.f.

There is another important point. The effect of an induction

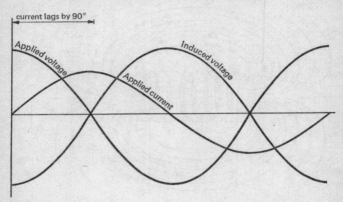

Figure 32

coil is to cause the current to lag behind the voltage. Previously in the circuit with nothing but resistance the current and voltage were in phase; now with nothing but inductance in the circuit, the current is found to be proportional to the rate of change of the voltage, not the voltage itself. The rate of change of an oscillating quantity is shown by the steepness of the curve on the graph representing its progress, and the steepest part of the voltage curve is as it passes through zero. So when the voltage is passing through zero, the current reaches its peak. It is in fact lagging by a quarter of a cycle. Remember that the frequency of the current is measured in cycles per second or hertz and that one cycle is equal to the interval between the positive peaks of the curve; if you treat one cycle as having gone a full circle, it makes sense to measure parts of a cycle as fractions of 360°. We can now say that the current in the inductive circuit lags behind the voltage by 90°.

What happens to the power in this case? Let us follow the same procedure as with the resistive circuit (Figure 30), and multiply a succession of values of the voltage and current curves together, since volts × amps = watts. This time a very odd result appears: the power curve still oscillates, but instead of being conveniently always above the zero line, it neatly alternates from a positive value to a negative one (Figure 36b, p.85). The average power is therefore zero, and the total energy involved is equal to the shaded area above the centre line minus the shaded area below the centre line: both areas are the same, again giving an answer of zero.

Does this mean that there is no net transmission of power? In theory, yes. Here is a paradox: in a circuit with pure inductance, you have both voltage and current, but no power. This sort of current is sometimes said to be wattless, and one of the side effects is that it will not turn an electricity meter! The unit of induction is called the henry, and having introduced it, we must leave it for a while and come to the other new unit, the farad, the unit of capacitance.

Of all the ways in which alternating current is different from direct current, perhaps the most radical is that whereas with a flow of direct current there is also a flow of electrons, with alternating current there is no net transfer of any electrons at all. If you could earmark one of these mites somewhere along a wire in an A.C. circuit, switch the circuit on and run it for hours, when you switched it off again, you would in theory find the earmarked electron still in its original position. As the voltage builds up it is pushed forward a bit, and as the voltage falls again it slips back; when the voltage falls through zero, the electron passes through its rest position, and when the voltage reaches its greatest negative value, the electron is displaced by an equal amount in the reverse direction. If it is situated in the business part of the circuit, the electron does its bit of work and transmits its bit of power by its action of moving to and fro. The actual amount of power involved is governed by the number of other electrons it has got oscillating with it (because the total number of electrons is proportional to the current), and also by the distance they are displaced fore and aft (the effect of voltage). The product of the two values gives power in watts.

Because there is no net flow of electrons in an A.C. current, you do not actually need a continuous loop of wire to complete a

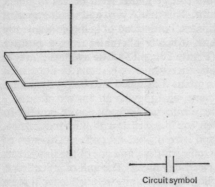

Circuit symbol

Figure 33

circuit. In fact, a common component in electronic circuits, a capacitor, incorporates an insulating layer. A capacitor in its simplest form is a device consisting of two metal plates separated by a layer of air (Figure 33) which acts as an insulating layer

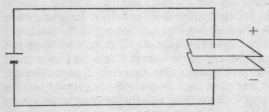

Figure 34

known as a dielectric. Let us first of all apply a direct current to the two terminals of this capacitor. The e.m.f. of the cell in Figure 34 causes a whole lot of electrons to pile up on the negative plate and there to be a scarcity of them on the positive plate. Does this sound familiar? The negative plate is going to exert an attraction towards the positive plate. The excess of electrons on the negative plate gives it a slight electrostatic attraction of a negative kind, and a correspondingly opposite attraction is formed on the other plate.

Remove the cell, and the state of affairs will not immediately alter. The attraction which exists across the airspace will cause the electrons to want to stay where they are, and the disconnected capacitor will retain a charge. If you then make a circuit across

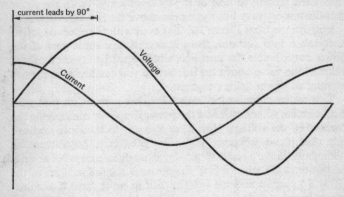

Figure 35

the terminals again, the capacitor will discharge and will show a deflection on a galvanometer.

Your mind will perhaps boggle at the thought of what will happen when a capacitor is introduced into an A.C. circuit. Let there be yet another graph (Figure 35). As the voltage increases electrons pour into and out of the respective plates of the capacitor, so current is at its maximum. The voltage starts to reach its peak, the capacitor is nearly full, it cannot accept many electrons and the current nears zero. Then the voltage starts to fall, the capacitor starts to discharge, and current starts building up in the reverse direction. Then, when voltage reaches zero, the current reaches its maximum negative value and so on. The effect of a purely capacitive A.C. circuit is therefore very similar to that

83

of a purely inductive circuit, but instead of the current lagging by 90°, this time it is leading by the same amount.

You can appreciate that almost all A.C. circuits cannot in fact be purely capacitive or inductive; they are bound to have resistance as well, even if it is only in the wires leading to and from the capacitor or induction coil. What effect does this have? One more graph will show the answer: whereas with either pure capacitance or pure inductance the power curve has an equal area above the zero line as it does below, the introduction of resistance causes the current to lead or lag by less than 90° with the result that the power curve has more area above the line than below.

You can see from Figure 36c that even with the effect of resistance taken into account, there is nevertheless some part of the power curve below the zero line, which must be knocked off the value of the curve above the line before you can arrive at the net amount of power being transmitted.

This rather complicated business makes you realize that with A.C. circuits you cannot find the power simply by multiplying the current by the voltage. You have also got to take into account this vital phase difference which is the effect of capacitance or inductance in the circuit. When the phase difference is 90° there is no power at all; when it is 0° the power is the full product of the (R.M.S.) current and the voltage. But in most cases it is somewhere between the two: the circuit is neither purely resistive nor purely capacitive or inductive. The relative amount of these ingredients is termed the power factor.

In a circuit which is purely inductive or capacitive, the power factor is zero. You multiply the current by the voltage, and then multiply the answer by the power factor; when the power factor is zero, then there is no power. In a purely resistive circuit, the power factor is one, and the power is the same as it would be with an equivalent D.C. circuit. In the vast majority of A.C. circuits which are resistive with some inductance or capacitance, the power factor turns out to be a figure rather less than one, such as 0·85.

How do you work out the power factor? You simply measure the phase angle between the current and the voltage, and the power factor is the cosine of the angle. The cosine of 90° is 0, of

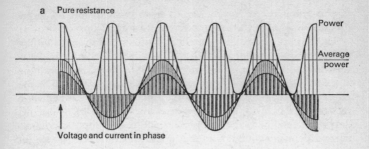

a Pure resistance

Power

Average power

Voltage and current in phase

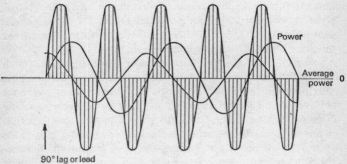

b Pure capicitance or inductance

Power

Average power

0

90° lag or lead

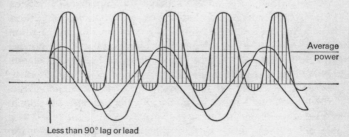

c Capicitance or inductance AND resistance

Average power

Less than 90° lag or lead

Figure 36

0° it is 1. 0·85 is the cosine of 32°, so in this example the phase difference between the current and voltage is 32°.

The power factor can cause some confusion in the calculations of electrical engineers; to avoid this, with large loads, the straightforward product of volts and amps, known as the apparent power, is measured in kilovolt-amperes (1 kilovolt equals 1,000 volts), abbreviated kVA. When this is multiplied by the power factor, one gets the true power, measured in kilowatts (kW).

It must now be becoming plainer and plainer that alternating current is a very different animal indeed from direct current. To start with there is no net flow of electrons, and on top of this you can have current without power. Here is another problem: you know the voltage, and you need to find out the current. What do you do, besides reach for an ammeter? Divide the voltage by the resistance as in D.C. circuits? Yes, if it is a purely resistive circuit, but what effect do these wretched inductances and capacitances have on current? Do they offer any sort of resistance?

In a D.C. circuit, inductances just act as any old conductor, offering a mild resistance by virtue of the material of which the coil is made, and the thickness of the coils. A capacitor in a D.C. circuit allows no current at all to pass. The insulating layer between the plates may permit electrostatic fields, but only if the voltage builds up to a high enough level to cause a spark across the plates will any electron have a hope of getting through, and in D.C. electrons have to travel for any current to flow.

Now let us turn the D.C. into A.C. by starting it oscillating very, very slowly, say once a second – a frequency of 1 hertz (1 Hz). At the induction coil, this slow oscillation will cause slow changing of lines of force around the coil, but the lines will not cut the turns of the coil at much of a rate, and very little induced e.m.f. will result. At low frequencies, then, an induction coil will pass A.C. almost as well as D.C.

What will happen to the capacitor when the current starts slowly oscillating? Because of the low frequency, a very large number of electrons are going to move forward in the time available, before the polarity starts to change, allowing them to move back again past their rest positions and out in the reverse direction. With a 1 Hz frequency, there is a quarter of a second during which electrons surge forward before the sine wave reaches its crest and the voltage starts to fall again. Our capacitor only has room for a limited number of electrons, so for the very low-frequency A.C. a mere trickle of current will get through, whereas the D.C. would not.

If the frequency of the A.C. current starts to rise, there is less time for electrons to move, and so less of them are involved in the same sized current. Because there are less of them, the capacitor will take a better proportion of current. In other words, the higher the frequency, the higher the current in a capacitive circuit.

The opposite happens with an induction coil; the higher the frequency, the higher the rate at which lines of force cut the turns of the coil, and therefore the higher the induced e.m.f. Induced e.m.f. opposes the applied current, and so the rule is that the higher the frequency, the lower the current in an inductive circuit.

We have to have a new word to describe the capability of a capacitor or an induction coil to allow current in an A.C. circuit. We cannot use the word resistance, because there is no heating effect or anything like that, and resistances do not alter with frequency. The new word is reactance.

Reactance has resistance-like properties, in that if the circuit is purely capacitive or inductive, current will equal voltage divided by reactance, just as in a resistive D.C. circuit current equals voltage divided by resistance. The big difference is that reactance varies with frequency. The reactance of an inductance increases with frequency, that of a capacitance decreases.

Reactance is in fact measured in ohms as resistance is, but before we come to the means of calculating reactance, we must become familiar with another way of expressing frequency. We have already taken to describing the interval between two crests in the sine wave by dividing it up into fractions of 360° (a full circle). Frequency is measured as the number of times the wave swoops from crest to crest in 1 second. Now for reasons which become clearer later, it is sometimes better to express this 360° between crests in terms of the other units for measuring angles: radians.

The circumference of a circle is about 6·28 times as long as the radius, and this ratio is more commonly expressed as 2π. 360° is equivalent to 2π radians, $180°$ to π radians, $90°$ to $\pi/2$ radians, and so on. This other sort of frequency scale we need is in fact angular frequency, and it is simply the frequency multiplied by 2π. The units are radians per second, and the usual symbol is the lower-case version of the Greek letter omega, ω. For an inductance, the reactance in ohms is simply the product of the inductance in henrys and the angular frequency in radians per second. For a capacitance, it is

$$\frac{1}{\omega C}$$

where C is the capacitance in farads and ω is again the angular frequency.

Most circuits incorporate a fair amount of resistance as well, and the effects of reactance and of resistance must be combined into one universal quantity: impedance.

Unfortunately impedance is not just the straightforward sum of the reactance and resistance. You have to square each of them, add the squares, and then extract the square root of the total, so that:

$$\text{impedance} = \sqrt{\text{reactance}^2 + \text{resistance}^2}.$$

Now at last we have arrived! The current in the A.C. circuit is equal to the voltage divided by the impedance, and full marks if you have tumbled to the fact that the ratio of the resistance to the impedance is none other than our old friend the power factor. If the impedance is no greater than the resistance, the power factor is 1, which is what you would expect because there is no inductance or capacitance to give reactance; the circuit is purely resistive, and the power is the straightforward product of the voltage and the current.

Here is a summary of the differences between D.C. and A.C. circuits.

1. In a D.C. circuit you have only resistance to worry about; inductors behave like simple resistors, capacitors allow no current to pass at all and behave like insulators.

2. In an A.C. circuit, in addition to resistance you have also reactance, which is the effect of capacitance and inductance opposing current flow. With capacitance, the reactance falls as the frequency is increased; the opposite happens with inductances.

3. The overall impedance of a circuit takes into account resistance and reactance, which each have to be squared, added and the square root extracted from the total to give the impedance in ohms.

4. The ratio of resistance to impedance gives the power factor. Capacitance and inductance put current out of phase with the voltage, so that when the two are multiplied together to give power, there will be negative power as well as positive power, reducing the true power available. In a purely capacitive or inductive circuit, the negative power completely offsets the positive power, causing wattless current. The ratio of the true power to the apparent power (volts × amps) is again given by the power factor.

What we have learned about alternating current so far is that, among other things, it is considerably more complicated than direct current. Yet all but a small proportion of the electricity generated and consumed the world over is in the form of alternating current. What sort of masochistic technicians are electrical engineers to have burdened themselves with all these complexities, when it could all be brought within the understanding of a plumber or gas man by supplying electricity as a steady flow of electrons in the form of direct current?

There are some surprisingly cogent reasons for generating and using electricity in the form of A.C. and we shall soon see that far from making life difficult for themselves, engineers would find it nearly impossible to do without A.C.

One of the most important factors in the argument is the enormous magnitude of the generating and supply problem. The Central Electricity Generating Board, which operates the largest power system in the world, controls power stations capable of generating 60 million kilowatts (more conveniently known as 60,000 megawatts) of power. By contrast, in the 1920s there were over 500 electrical supply companies with a consequently chaotic range of supply systems and voltages. Some provided a D.C. supply while others supplied a range of A.C. voltages, usually between 200 and 250 volts. (It was not until the early 30s that the National Grid came into being, and in 1948 the whole system was nationalized so that today, for England and Wales, the C.E.G.B. looks after the generating, while the area boards sell the electricity to the consumer.)

The heart of a power station is, not surprisingly, an alternator, and when we come to consider the problems associated with alternators the size of those in power stations, we begin to find advantages in generating A.C. Before going into the question of their design, though, it is interesting to digress a little into a non-electrical problem, that of providing enough power to drive these giant generators.

The majority of power stations still burn coal, and they burn over 70 million tons per year. Many of the early power stations were built on the coal fields to reduce the cost of transporting the fuel, since the cost of transporting the end product, electricity, was a good deal cheaper. However, at the newest power stations, coal is transported to them in specially designed trains with hopper wagons which pass directly from the main line on to a loop of track. Their cargoes are unloaded directly into bunkers beneath the rails and the trains return to the main lines without stopping. This way costs are reduced enough to make it economical to build power stations some way from the coal fields.

A small number of oil-fired power stations exist near to oil refineries, burning the equivalent of about 20 million tons of coal. An even smaller number burn natural gas, but ironically the fuel for these stations is supplied by the rival Gas Council. Much to the Electricity Council's chagrin, the gas is provided on a 'seller's option' basis, meaning that it is used when available but is liable to interruption at short notice. The equivalent of half a million tons of coal is burnt in gas-fired power stations.

Still in its infancy is the nuclear power station, although the proportion of Britain's power supply generated in nuclear stations will soon be over 10 per cent in spite of the engineering difficulties that have been met with. For every 25 tons of coal, about the same amount of electricity is generated that can be made from one pound of enriched uranium. This makes the transport of fuel a rather easier matter, until the uranium has been used. After that it becomes radioactive and has to be loaded into thick steel flasks weighing 45 tons and taken by rail to Windscale, near the Lake District, for reprocessing.

In all but nuclear power stations, the first stage in generating electricity is to burn fuel in a boiler to heat water, circulating at high pressure in the boiler tubes, thus generating high-pressure steam. In the case of present-day British nuclear stations, carbon dioxide gas is used in the first stage of the heat exchanging process. The steam is piped to the turbines, which consist of several series of highly sophisticated 'windmills'. The pressure of the steam turns the turbine shafts at high speed. From the turbine, the steam enters a condenser and passes over cooling water tubes to turn it back into water. This creates a partial vacuum which helps to draw the steam through the turbine. The water is then returned to the boiler.

The turbines are coupled to the alternators, and these may be capable of generating over 600 megawatts of power. That is enough to keep almost 100,000 houses going on an average day, from one alternator alone. In designing an alternator to produce this much power, one must clearly look very closely indeed at the question of efficiency, and the first question to answer is: how best to supply the power? Remember that all electrical power takes the form of a certain amount of current at a certain voltage, and that for the same power you can either have a large current at a small voltage, or a small current at a large voltage. To help in answering the question, consider that there are over 10,000 miles of cable in the National Grid in order to get the electricity to all the distribution points. You can by now appreciate that the total resistance of all that cable dissipates an astonishing amount of energy, and our electricity supply system will have to be designed to minimize the loss in the distribution network. It is no good overcoming it by lowering the resistance of the cables through increasing their size, because with the price of copper as high as it is the cables would cost more than the power stations.

The problem can best be solved by generating the power at as high a voltage as possible, involving as little current as possible so as to enable moderately slim cables to be used and still keep the resistance of the distribution system within acceptable limits. This sounds an excellent idea, until you work out the figures; to have the best practical system you must supply the electricity at well over 100,000 volts, even as high as 400,000 volts if the power station is capable of it. To do this is no mean feat, and even if the generators work at only, say, 25,000 volts, there are many problems that have to be overcome. The thought of producing 25,000 volts with a D.C. generator is daunting. We have already seen how complex even a small D.C. generator can be in order to produce a reasonably steady current, involving a large number of separate windings on the armature with separate pads on the commutator. Imagine the brushes for a commutator of this size; brushes would in fact present a nearly insuperable problem. In any case, even with a large number of windings, no generated direct current is absolutely smooth and free of ripples.

Fortunately, as we shall shortly discover, D.C. is not particularly convenient as a power supply anyway, so the fact that an alternator on the scale required is a much more practical proposition is no bad thing. An unexpected advantage, though, is that it is easier to achieve high voltages with alternating current, by using it in a slightly different way from that we have discussed so far.

This type of A.C. is called three-phase supply. To achieve it, the windings of the alternator are in three parts. There are no permanent magnets: the windings are stationary and are incorporated in the outer, fixed part of the machine known as the stator. The rotating part, the rotor, is wound as an electromagnet which is energized by a small D.C. current from an exciter generator coupled to the end of the rotor shaft. Electricity is generated by the rotating electromagnetic field of the rotor whose lines of force cut the coils of the windings in the stator. The power output of the alternator is thus taken from the windings of the stator, and there is no question of having to design gargantuan slip rings.

The stator is wound on three separate systems spaced around it so that the current in each set of windings reaches its peak 120° before the current in the next winding. The effect is like that of three alternators delivering A.C. whose waves are each lagging behind the other by a third of a cycle. The windings are usually connected in a star arrangement as shown in Figure 37, but instead of having two wires for each circuit, the 'return' wires can all be connected together in a single wire to carry the return current. As a result there is a four wire system in which the fourth wire is known as the neutral wire.

If you look at Figure 37b, you will see that at any instant, if you add the currents in each of the circuits together, the answer is

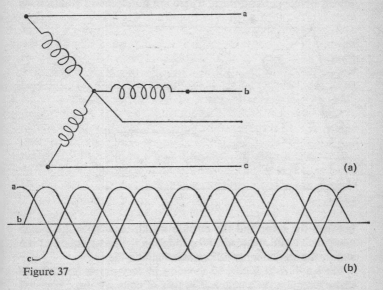

Figure 37

zero. Therefore, provided that the loads on the three circuits are equal, the current in the neutral wire will be zero and it can be omitted to form 'delta' winding (Figure 38).

What is the point in complicating an otherwise simple alternator in this way? Part of the answer is that for a given physical size a three-phase alternator gives a larger power output than a single-phase machine, and that from the industrial consumer's point of view, three-phase electrical machines give a smoother output with less vibration.

Let us have another look at the working of some electrical machines, notably motors. A large proportion of big electric motors run on three-phase supply, the most common type being the induction motor. Motors of this type are rather different from those we looked at in Chapter 3, which worked by having an armature and field magnet.

In an induction motor there is no armature fitted, but merely a rotor consisting of heavy copper conductors fitted in slots and joined by copper end-rings. There are no electrical connections

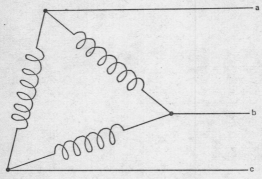

Figure 38

between the rotor and the outside world. How does the motor work then? The answer is to be found in the construction of the stator, the stationary windings surrounding the rotor.

Have a look at Figure 39 showing, in very simple form, three-phase windings on a stator. The pair of coils a–a are connected to one phase, the pair b–b to another phase and the pair c–c to the third phase. Let us pick an instant when the current flowing through coils a–a is at its maximum: there will be an electro-magnetic field at an angle of 0° across the circle in the centre. One sixth of a cycle later, the current in the second phase, wired across b–b, will have reached its maximum, and there will be an electro-magnetic field at an angle of 60°. Another sixth of a cycle later, the current across c–c will have reached its maximum and there will be an electromagnetic field at an angle of 120°. We shall then be back to a–a again another sixth of a cycle later, when the current in the first phase will reach its maximum in the opposite direction, the sine wave having plunged to its lowest negative point. There will then be an electromagnetic field at 180°.

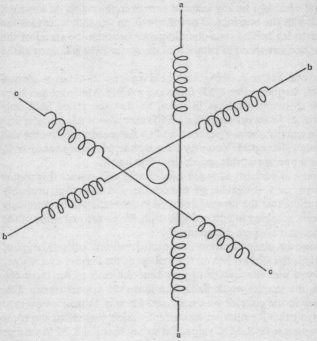

Figure 39

This process will go on, getting back to a field at 0° every whole cycle, and you can see that what it amounts to is a rotating electromagnetic field in the windings of the stator. Now as the electromagnetic field rotates, it cuts the conductors of the rotor and induces currents in the conductors and the end-rings. These currents of course produce their own electromagnetic field, and this reacts with the rotating field of the stator. The effect is to

95

produce motion of the rotor in the direction which will tend to prevent what is technically known as 'change of flux linkage' and in effect means that the rotor follows the stator field round.

Thus the rotor is induced to turn, but never up to the speed at which the field rotates. For one thing, if this came about, there would no longer be any induced current in the rotor. At any rate, friction in the bearings, if not the load on the motor, causes the rotor to lag behind, and the difference between the speed of the rotor and the speed of rotation of the stator field is known as the slip.

In our example, the stator field rotates 50 times a second (mains frequency) or 3,000 times per minute. Many motors have twice as many windings in them, so that the stator field only rotates 25 times per second, or 1,500 revolutions per minute. The slip is usually about 4 per cent, and so the speed of the motor will be only 1,440 r.p.m. You may have wondered why so many A.C. motors operate at this speed; now you know.

You can perhaps now see how simple and robust this motor (known as a squirrel-cage motor) is; you can also probably appreciate that the torque produced in the rotor will be extremely smooth, resulting in reduced vibration. These are just some of the advantages of three-phase supply.

However, one of the more unexpected results of using this type of supply is the effect it has on the voltage of the current as a whole.

If you plot the voltage against time for each of the three circuits, the graphs would look like those we saw in Figure 37b. Earlier in the chapter we discovered the way to take an average voltage value for alternating current, which was called the root-mean-square or R.M.S. value. Let us say that the R.M.S. voltage of each of the circuits connected to a three-phase alternator with respect to earth is 10,000 volts. This means that if you took any one of the three circuits and used it and the neutral wire as an ordinary single-phase power supply, you would have 10,000 volts. Now we know that when all three phases are used, for instance to drive the squirrel-cage motor we have already looked at, the individual phases are not connected across an impedance to earth, but to the next phase round in the circle (Figure 38). This means that the voltage involved is the voltage between two phases.

Suppose, for the sake of argument, the two phases were 180° out of phase; they would be in direct opposition, one at its positive peak when the other was at its negative peak. The result would be an R.M.S. voltage between them of double that of a single phase with respect to earth. This is not the case, as we know, because the circuits are only 120° out of phase with one another. The R.M.S. voltage between a pair of circuits is therefore a bit less than double: it is 1·732 (which is $\sqrt{3}$) times the voltage between one circuit and earth. This means that the effective voltage of the alternator in our example is 17,320 merely by virtue of its being three-phase.

All this leads us to two serious problems. One is that we have already decided that the most economical way to supply electricity from a power station is to have it at a potential of 400,000 volts, and yet we have talked of alternators capable of little more than 25,000 volts. The second problem is that if you were supplied with electricity at 400,000 volts, life would be exciting, to say the least. Both these problems amount to the same thing: how do you achieve large changes in voltage without using a significant amount of power? You could in theory get down from 400,000 volts to 250 with a gigantic resistor, but you would use up almost all the power at the same time.

One thing is certain – this problem could not be solved if the power supply were D.C. One of the many advantages of using alternating current is that, for a given power, you can quite easily and efficiently transform it into any permutation of current and voltage. This means that if you have a 1 megawatt power supply which happens to consist of 1,000 amps at 1,000 volts, you can transform it into, say, 10,000 amps at 100 volts or for that matter into 40 amps at 25,000 volts, or any other combination.

The trick is achieved by using a transformer. A transformer is a device which takes advantage of one of the side effects of A.C. which we have already discussed: the behaviour of induction coils. We found that alternating current through a coil caused the lines of electromagnetic force which surround any current-carrying coil to swish back and forth as the current swooped from positive to negative and back again. We found that the swishing of the lines made them cut across the turns of the coil itself, thus inducing a voltage in opposition to the applied voltage. All we deduced from this was that coils offer impedance to alternating current, which increased with increasing frequency.

However, what we did not stop to consider was what would happen in another, separate, coil if it were laid beside the one carrying the current. Surely the lines of force of the original coil in waving back and forth will also cut the turns of the second coil as well. This is true, and as you would expect the result is that a current is induced in the second coil in accordance with the right-hand coil rule. This news may not surprise you, but the interesting part of it is that when the secondary coil has a large number of turns, a large number of electrons, in series along the turns, are given an inducement to move. Because the electrons are one behind the other along the turns, their individual electromotive forces (voltages) combine like a number of cells in series so that their voltages are additive. If the secondary coil has a smaller number of turns, the electrons which are induced to move are more side by side than strung out along the coil, and since cells connected in parallel give a higher current but no increase in voltage, the electrons in parallel give increased current at the expense of voltage.

If you ignore resistive and other losses in the coils, you can simply state that the voltage induced in the secondary coil is proportional to the number of turns it has compared with the number of turns in the primary coil. It then follows that, since you cannot gain something for nothing, the current in the secondary coil is inversely proportional to the number of its turns. A high voltage and a low current is achieved by having a large proportion of turns in the secondary coil; a low voltage but high current is achieved by having a small proportion of turns in the secondary coil, both compared with the primary coil. This is exactly what we need for a transformer.

For a transformer to be efficient, we have to design it to ensure that as many of the lines of force as possible cut turns of the secondary coil. This can be done by using an iron core which, as a ferromagnetic material, will channel the lines of force along it. The two windings can then be placed around the core in one of two ways, shown diagrammatically in Figure 40. Three-phase

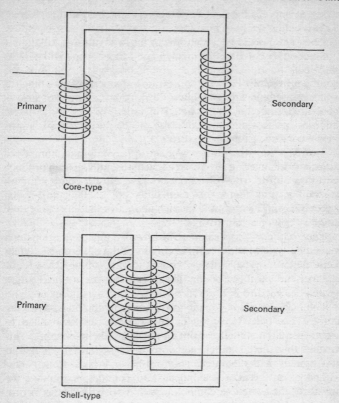

Figure 40

currents may have a separate transformer for each phase, or in a single transformer there may be a separate limb of the core carrying a primary and secondary winding for each phase. The core will usually be made of a number of plates laminated together to reduce the problem of eddy-current losses that we came across when looking at motors; there are, however, other losses, one of which is caused by the fact that the core tends to hang on to some magnetism each time the current alternates and for a

99

Electricity

moment opposes the new, reversed magnetic field that is created. This is called the hysteresis loss.

Losses also occur because some of the lines of force still do not cut secondary coils, but all in all, a good transformer will pass 95 per cent or so of the power in the primary circuit into the secondary circuit. Power station transformers can be as big as a small house, and are usually oil-filled. A fair amount of heat is generated, and the oil is cooled in radiators to remove it. In addition, quite a high level of noise can be created by vibrations in the core due to magnetic forces.

Now you can see how a power station containing a number of alternators delivering current at a few thousand volts can produce an output of up to 400,000 volts. In fact, not all power supplies start off quite as high as this, and voltages of 132,000 and 275,000 are common. The output from each alternator is connected to the primary coil of a transformer.

The secondary coils of the transformers are connected to a switching system, with the three circuits of the three-phase system kept separate. The switches consist of an isolator, a circuit-breaker and another isolator. The circuit-breaker is a heavy-duty switch designed to operate in a fraction of a second in order to switch off the current flowing to the transmission lines. After the current has been interrupted, the isolators can be opened to isolate the circuit-breaker from all outside electrical sources. This ensures that there is no chance of high voltages being applied to its terminals when maintenance work is being carried out.

The circuit-breaker is connected to conductors running the length of the switching compound called busbars. These in turn are connected to another circuit-breaker and from there the current is fed into the National Grid.

You may by now be getting the first understanding of what those extraordinary fields of triffid-like excrescences outside power stations are actually for. Much of the weird appearance is due to the fact that with voltages like the ones we have been talking about, it is no easy job to insulate a conductor from the ground. Not only are long ceramic insulators called for, but they must also have the best shape for preventing sparks jumping down their sides and short-circuiting the insulation.

Talking of sparks, if you have seen a domestic light switch, with the cover off, operate in the dark, you will know that when you break a circuit the current will continue to jump a small gap between the conductors in the switch until they have separated to a great enough distance to prevent this. You can imagine that the circuit breakers in a power station would create terrific sparks when opened. Why don't they?

The answer is that the spark, or arc as it is correctly known, does occur, but the switch is designed to ensure that it lasts only a very short time so that no damage is done. One way of doing this is to immerse the contacts of the circuit breaker in oil, itself an insulator. When the switch is opened by springs or electro-magnets the arc is quickly extinguished by the oil. In another design air-blast switches are used in which compressed air 'blows out' the arc as soon as it is struck.

The brain-centre of the power station is the control room, where the output of electricity is monitored, the operation of the generating plant is controlled and supervised, and the high-voltage switch gear directing the power to the Grid system is operated. Faults in the system, caused by things like abnormal voltages or excessive current, are quickly isolated by protective fuses, and similar devices prevent disturbance to the operation of the rest of the equipment or the overstressing of insulation. Over-heating can also occur, with consequent danger of fire or other serious damage. The protection mechanism is designed to operate quickly and without disturbing the remainder of the system.

All the power systems are connected via transformer sub-stations to the National Grid, which is basically about 10,000 route miles of cable. Energy distribution on a countrywide basis, even with international links, has become an important factor because it is a great deal cheaper to generate power in very large quantities in a large power station, and then transmit it in bulk to where it is needed, than to site a whole lot of smaller generating stations around the country.

In addition, it pays to remember that it is almost impossible to store electricity in the quantities we are now talking about, and it has to be used the instant it is generated. In hydro-electric schemes where natural water pressure is used to drive turbines and power the alternators, it is possible to pump water back up to a higher level during off-peak periods and convert electricity from the Grid back into potential energy, ready for re-use at periods of peak demand. However, in all other cases, if electricity is only being consumed on a nationwide basis at a low rate, then you cannot possibly keep the excess for a rainy day.

Britain and France do not always have the same pattern of demand for electricity, and so the National Grid is connected with the control centres of Electricité de France in Paris and Lille. At times, electricity is exported in either direction to help smooth out the demand. You can see from Figure 42 that the demand on the National Grid can be as much as over 40,000 megawatts at the end of a popular television programme in winter, or less than 8,000 megawatts in the early hours of a summer morning. The effect of television is not that the sets themselves take power; in fact while the sets are on, very little power is being consumed elsewhere in the house. It is when such stimulating entertainment as the Eurovision Song Contest or Miss World comes to an end, everyone tends to rise from their stupor and turn on lights, ovens, kettles, hot baths and so on. In fact this phenomenon is now so well established that the audiences of major attractions can be gauged by watching the needles of the meters in the C.E.G.B. control centre soar as the programme ends.

Since it is pretty plain that you do not have an electricity supply in your home at 400,000 volts, there is obviously quite a lot between the National Grid and the consumer. At Grid supply points, transformers step the voltage down to 33,000 volts in each of the circuits of the three-phase system, and bulk supplies of electricity at this voltage are taken for primary distribution in the towns and to industrial areas, groups of villages and similar concentrations of consumers (see Figure 41).

Heavy industry actually uses electricity at 33,000 volts, and the factories have their own transformer substations to give them the lower voltages they also need. Otherwise, the voltage is further stepped down to 11,000 volts at a large number of intermediate substations. Some light industries and hospitals take power at this voltage. Secondary distribution carries the power into the area to be supplied and the lines terminate at distribution sub-

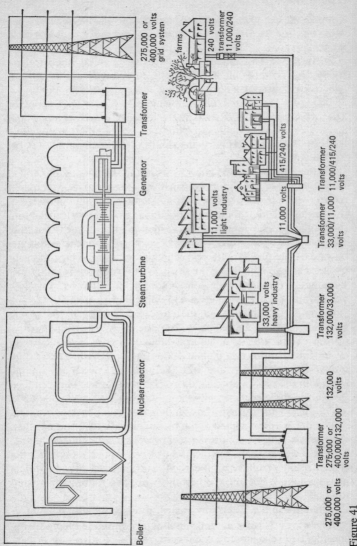

Boiler Nuclear reactor Steam turbine Generator Transformer 275,000 or 400,000 volts grid system

275,000 or 400,000 volts

Transformer 275,000 or 400,000/132,000 volts

132,000 volts

Transformer 132,000/33,000 volts

33,000 volts heavy industry

Transformer 33,000/11,000 volts

11,000 volts

11,000 volts light industry

Transformer 11,000/415/240 volts

415/240 volts

240 volts transformer 11,000/240 volts

farms

Figure 41

stations. At last the voltage is stepped down to its final level of 240 volts for use in shops, commercial premises, schools and homes.

There are one or two exceptions to the general rule of electricity distribution. One is that the electrified railways have their own substations, usually supplying the railway with power at 25,000 volts. (London Transport generates its own D.C. supply.) The other exception is that where existing power stations are already close to consumers, for instance in London, the power is fed into the local primary distribution network at 66,000 or 33,000 volts.

We seem to have gone straight from 11,000 volts to 240 volts. What about 415-volt supply, such as is used to power many motors in factories and industrial installations? The answer to this question is that industrial consumers take their electricity in three-phase form, and we saw earlier in the chapter that the effective voltage of a three-phase system is 1·732 times the voltage on one of the phases with respect to earth. The voltage in each phase, which in isolation from the other two phases is exactly the same as an ordinary single-phase supply, is 240 volts, and 240 volts multiplied by 1·732 gives 415 volts.

Power is distributed and sold to the consumer by the Area Electricity Boards. Distribution from the transformer is by means of four cables: one is the neutral cable taking the return current of all three phases, and is black. The three phases are carried in red, yellow and blue cables, and the voltage between any one of them and the black cable is 240 volts;* the voltage between any two of the three is, as we have seen, 415 volts.

The supply to a private house, or any single-phase consumer, will be one wire connected to the black neutral cable, and another wire which may be connected to any of the three-phase cables. Since the neutral wire is just a sort of drain pipe and carries no supply itself, you have no means of knowing at your end which phase you have got in the other, live wire, and it does not matter to you.

It matters to the Electricity Board, though, because they must

*There are still some electrical backwaters where the supply is at a non-standard voltage, such as 210 volts.

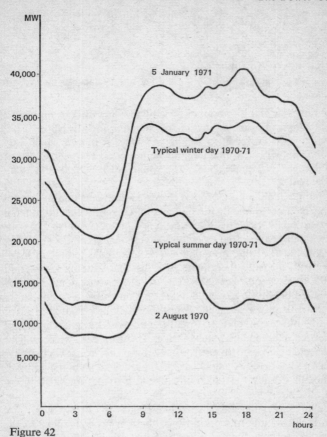

MW

40,000 —

5 January 1971

35,000 —

30,000 —

Typical winter day 1970-71

25,000 —

20,000 —

Typical summer day 1970-71

15,000 —

10,000 —

2 August 1970

5,000 —

0   3   6   9   12   15   18   21   24
                                        hours

Figure 42

try to get a fairly even distribution of load on the three different phases. An approximately equal number of houses will, therefore, be connected to each phase. Any consumer who wants to impose a large load on the supply can be connected to all three phases and receive in consequence 415 volts, three-phase supply.

5 Juice on Tap

*Electricity in the
home and car*

We have learnt a bit about electricity now, about volts and watts
and things, and about how it is generated and distributed, but
what does it all mean in the home? Does it matter which way
round you wire an appliance, and what is polarity anyway? When
do you get an electric shock, and when will it be fatal? Why do
fuses blow?

In the last chapter, we found that in an ordinary house, you are
connected up to one of three phases of current transmitted from
the National Grid. This gives you single-phase supply at 240 volts
and an alternating frequency of 50 cycles per second, or 50 Hz.

Whichever of the three phases you are connected to, in isolation from the two other phases, it is just plain alternating current
without any complications. The wire in your house will be
coloured brown (in the old days, red). You will also be connected
to the neutral wire, and the connection will be coloured blue (or
in the old days, black). Finally, you will have a third wire
coloured in green and yellow stripes, or just green, which will be
connected to your own earth connection. This is just what it says
and is sometimes a metal bar or pipe driven into the ground,
although usually the Electricity Board provides an earth along
with the supply.

In principle, the only live connection is the brown wire and,
contrary to some misconceptions, there is no equivalent to the
positive and negative connection of a battery. This can sometimes
be difficult to understand. With a battery, when a circuit is made,
there is a continuous flow of electrons from the negative terminal,
round the circuit and back to the positive terminal. While, indeed,
the Earth is an almost limitless supply of electrons, you will not
get a circuit by connecting the positive terminal to earth because
in order for the battery to work you have got to remove electrons
from the negative terminal as well.

Now with alternating current, when a circuit is made, there is no net flow of electrons; they just oscillate to and fro in the wire. The alternator in the power station is just a pump sucking and blowing on the electrons. Although there is no net flow of electrons, this is not to say that they do not move. In fact, it is their movement backwards and forwards that provides the power, and does the work. If they cannot move backwards and forwards, there is no power to be had. In an open-ended live wire carrying A.C., electrons cannot move much, in spite of sucking and blowing from the power station, because, if they move forwards, there is nowhere, at the end of the wire, for them to go, nor if they move backwards, is there any temporary replacement supply of electrons to fill the space left. If, however, you connect an open-ended live wire to earth, the Earth is such a vast receptacle of electrons that the electrons in the wire can flow into it and out of it with ease. A circuit is made.

The neutral wire in a power supply is not only connected to the other ends of the stator windings, but also to earth. Consequently the normal way of making a circuit with the mains is to connect across the live wire and the neutral wire. Don't do it, except for testing purposes, but you can get a perfectly good circuit across the live wire and your own earth wire. It is even more inadvisable, and sometimes downright dangerous, but you can get a circuit if you connect the live wire to the cold water pipes.* Finally (literally so!) you yourself, if connected well with the ground, can make a ciruit with the live wire.

You can probably see now why those two wires, the live and neutral, although connected to similar looking terminals in a power point, are very different. In some cases, you could touch the neutral wire and nothing whatever would happen, because by being earthed at the power station, no current from the alternators comes through it. However, you will appreciate that, once a circuit is made somewhere, if you are touching the neutral wire you will get the brunt of the current from the live wire as it is then connected through the neutral wire to earth. You can, therefore,

---

*In some circumstances, the cold water supply is actually used as an earth, but for obvious reasons the earth must be arranged so that the pipes in the house never become live.

get an electric shock by touching either the neutral wire or the live wire, but you can only be sure of a beauty from the live wire.

Sometimes an electric shock is worse than at other times. If you touch the neutral wire and it is carrying current, the shock will not be too bad because you will generally offer a much higher resistance to earth than the rest of the neutral wire would. Remember Ohm's law; the higher the resistance, the less the current. If you are wearing rubber soles you will be fairly well insulated from the ground, and you would probably get away even with touching the live wire. If you are in the bath and touch a live wire you have had it, because the water* will offer a lowish resistance and connect you well to the pipes, and these are splendidly well earthed. A very high current will flow through you, and stop the brain and nervous system from functioning. Of course, if you touch both the live wire and the earth wire or the neutral wire, no matter how well insulated you are from the ground, your skin will get burnt where the wires touched.

In the U.S.A. the mains supply is at half the voltage it is in the U.K. Consequently it is a good deal safer, because your body will offer the same resistance in both countries, but for reasons of Ohm again, only half the current will flow through you in the U.S.A. The disadvantage is that to get the same amount of power, you have got to have twice the current, and, therefore, American cables have to be much fatter to carry it.

Let us now have a look in more detail at the electricity supply to your home. First of all there is a main cable which comes either from underground or from an overhead line. This is connected to a sealed box containing the Electricity Board's main fuses, and in turn to the electricity meter. If you have off-peak supplies, there will be two meters and a time-switch to turn you from one tariff rate to the other as the off-peak periods start and finish.

How does an electricity meter work? Basically it consists of a small electric motor, a magnetic brake and a set of dials with pointers driven by the motor. The motor is in fact an induction motor of the sort we discussed in the last chapter, but in a rather unusual form. The equivalent of the squirrel-cage rotor is a light

---

*Pure water is not a good conductor, it is the impurities in tap water that make it conduct well enough to give fatal electric shocks.

aluminium disc on a spindle. There are two electromagnets near
to the disc, one designed to produce more force when the voltage
increases, and the other when the current increases. The magnetic brake is provided by permanent magnets.

What happens is that the more current that is consumed the
faster the disc will be made to rotate by one electromagnet, and
if, for any reason, the supply voltage fluctuates, the other electromagnet will compensate for it. The revolving disc drives round a
train of gear wheels, each of which has a pointer attached to it, so
that the number of rotations is recorded.

The scale of the dials is such that if you put a load of exactly
1 kilowatt on the supply for a period of exactly one hour, one
unit will register on the dial. This unit is called a kilowatt-hour or
1 kWh, and it is for these units that you are charged by the Electricity Board.

Next, after the meter, comes the main switch, which in turn
connects to the distribution boards and fuse boards. There may
be separate fuseboards for lighting and power circuits, the fuses
in the latter being sized to burn out if the current exceeds 30 amps,
the others if it exceeds 15 amps, or 5 amps. Only the live wire of
the circuit is connected through the fuse board, the neutral wires
are just connected straight to a terminal block, as are the earth
wires to a separate terminal block of their own.

Although appliances which consume more than 3 kW of power
will normally be wired separately back to a fuse on the fuse
board, all the power points in a modern installation will be connected to what is called a ring-main circuit. This is shown in
Figure 43 and you can see that it consists of a long loop of wire
for each of the live, neutral and earth connections. The fact that
there is a loop does not mean that there is any sort of short-
circuit, because the loop only connects live to live, neutral to
neutral and earth to earth. This arrangement makes it easy to tap
the circuit at any point and connect sockets in parallel. You do
not have to run a cable from every single power point back to the
fuse boxes. In awkward cases it is an easy matter to run a 'spur'
out from the ring-main to a more remote point.

At a suitable point on the ring there will be a spur box with
switch and fuse from which the lighting circuit is taken and, in

modern lighting circuits, a similar principle to that of the ring-main is employed. Recently regulations have been introduced requiring the provision of an earth in lighting circuits so that the metal parts of light fittings can be earthed.

Each power plug will also have a fuse built into it, and it is important to realize that they are nearly always supplied with

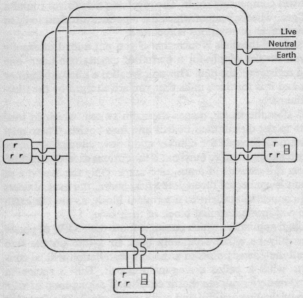

Figure 43

13-amp fuses. Very often one connects things to them which do not require anything like as large a fuse as this and consequently much of the value of having a fuse is lost. It is extremely important when connecting a plug to an appliance to check on the value of the fuse. It is not difficult to calculate the right value when you remember that amps = watts/volts.* If you have a 100

*Except with large rotating machines when the power factor comes into it (see p. 84).

110

watt lamp, the current it will use will be $100/240 = 0.42$ amps, approximately. The available ratings of fuses are 2-amp (blue), 5-amp (grey), 10-amp (yellow), and 13-amp (brown); clearly, in the case in question, only a 2-amp fuse is needed.

One of the most important points about circuits concerns switches. We have learnt about the difference between the live wire and the neutral wire, and consequently it is essential that the switch, which is normally only capable of disconnecting one wire, should break the circuit by disconnecting the live wire, not the neutral wire. Disconnecting the neutral wire certainly switches the appliance off all right, as the circuit is broken. However, after the switch has been turned off, the live terminal will still be as live as ever and itching to give someone a shock. It is difficult enough to persuade some people to turn a switch off before pulling out or putting in a plug, but if after turning off the switch the live pin is still live, you have not achieved anything. We have already found that you do not need the neutral wire to get a perfectly good shock.

Unfortunately, if you were to go round many houses with a testing device you would find a lot of cases where power points have been wired up with the wrong polarity (meaning that the live wire is on the wrong side). In many cases it is also important for you to connect up the plug correctly as well. It does not matter with things like lamps because they are symmetrical in all respects, but many machines incorporating electric motors or electronic devices are extremely touchy about which way round they are wired. Consequently, it always pays to get the polarity right, whether it matters in an individual case or not. Most modern plugs have the letters L, N and E marked near the terminals, and so long as you remember what the colours of the wires mean you are all right. Blue is a cold colour, so think of that as neutral, brown is a warm colour, so logically it is live, and the earth wire is green and yellow stripes and stands out from all the rest because it is absolutely imperative that you do not connect it to anything other than the earth. If the plug has no markings, when you are looking down on it with the cover off and the terminals exposed, the live terminal is on the right. As an *aide-mémoire*, remember that brown has an 'r' in it, blue does not. In any case, the plug will usually have a fuse in it, and the live wire must be connected to the fused terminal.

What makes a fuse blow? Obviously a direct short-circuit, formed for instance by letting the live wire touch an earthed metal part of an appliance, will cause such a heavy current that even the largest fuse would blow. Sometimes then, the cause of a fuse blowing is that the insulation of the wiring or of the components of a machine is inadequate or has become ineffective, or it has just been wrongly connected.

Another cause can be overloading of the circuit. If you plugged an electric fire into every single socket on a ring-main system, you could get something like a 24 kW load. To work out the current this would take, you divide the watts by the volts, and the answer is 100 amps. Needless to say, this would blow a 30-amp fuse! Many modern installations with a ring-main system have circuit-breakers instead of fuses in this case. These consist of automatic switches which cut out or 'trip' if the current exceeds the set value, and thereby isolate the supply. Because overloading is easier with a ring-main system than with a system using a separate supply for each power point, it is a considerable advantage not to have to mend a fuse each time it goes, merely to reset the trip switch, after having switched off enough appliances to prevent overloading again.

The golden rule is never to mend a fuse without finding out what caused it to blow in the first place, and never use fuse wire other than of the correct value. A good way of setting your house on fire is to get sick of a fuse repeatedly blowing and put thicker wire in to stop it. This will then allow excessive current to flow and cause overheating somewhere along the line.

*

The home is not the only place where our lives are dominated by electricity. One tends to forget how essential to the functioning of a motor car are all the electrical parts of the engine. In fact the electrics of a car are in some ways much more complicated than those of a house. Most people know that electricity is needed in a car to power the lights and things like that, but if you start talking about high-tension leads you lose them immediately. As for the workings of coils and contact-breakers, voltage regulators and condensers, they are in another world altogether.

We are fairly familiar with the battery in a car; in fact it was described in Chapter 2 at some length. It provides direct current at a voltage of, in most cases, 12 volts. The only new thing we really need to know about the battery is the way in which it is connected up. One way would be to run a positive wire and a negative wire to every point in the car where electricity is needed. This would require rather a lot of wire, and since most cars are made from steel, a fairly good conductor of electricity, it is much easier to connect one terminal of the battery to the body of the car, so that you then only have to run wires of either positive or negative to the point of use. The other terminal of the item to be powered is then just connected to the car body, or 'earthed'. As a result, the entire car body has a voltage potential with respect to the un-earthed terminal of the battery. The term 'earth' is borrowed from its equivalent in mains electricity, but of course it is not quite accurate as the car is insulated from the ground. In cars with a fibreglass body, there has to be much more wiring to cope with the earth, which is usually connected to the engine itself.

Cars for many years had the positive terminal earthed, and all the wires carried negative current. However, in recent years it has become standard practice to earth the negative terminal instead, and it is most important not to get confused. Many electrical components will work only when connected with the correct polarity, and you would create havoc by earthing the wrong battery-terminal or by fitting an accessory like a radio with the wrong polarity.

If your car has a negative earth, it will probably have a prominent label under the bonnet saying so. If there is no label you can examine the battery to see whether it is the terminal marked with a '+' or a '−' that is connected to the heavy braided earth wire. If you buy a new accessory, such as a radio, it will be labelled 'negative earth' or 'positive earth' and if you buy the wrong kind you will damage it if you connect it.

The battery is capable of delivering a very large current and so, in contrast with dry batteries of the same voltage, it stores a fair

113

amount of power. The resistance of the human body is too high for you to get an electric shock direct from the battery, but that does not mean you cannot get a shock from any part of the system, as we shall soon see.

One's first encounter with the battery is usually when one asks it to turn the starter; and, if in good condition, the battery will turn the engine at a fair speed. Those of us who have owned cars with starting handles and had need to use them will appreciate the amount of power delivered by the self-starter, which turns the engine much faster than it can be turned by hand.

The main electrical feature of a starter motor is that it is a series-wound D.C. motor. In Chapter 3 we found that D.C. motors can either be shunt- or series-wound. The effect of a shunt winding was that under heavy load, although it can maintain its speed quite well, it is not very good at starting. A series-wound motor delivers much more torque and is ideal for turning an engine from rest.

Turning the engine with the starter will get the mechanical parts going, fuel and air aspirated and so on, but the engine cannot possibly start without the most vital electrical part of all, the ignition. The ignition is of course there to provide a spark in the cylinders in order to ignite the fuel. There are basically five parts to the system: the battery, the coil, the points, the distributor and the sparking plug.

The battery we know about, and although you may not appreciate the fact, we already know a good deal about the coil. It is really a sort of transformer, and it contains a primary winding with a small number of turns and a secondary winding with a very large number of turns. One end of the primary winding is connected to the ignition switch and thereby to the positive battery terminal (assuming a negative earth system). It is useful to know that this connection on the coil is marked SW, for switch, so there should be little difficulty in connecting it up correctly.

The other end of the primary winding leads to the terminal marked CB, for contact-breaker. This is connected to the low-tension terminal of the distributor. The term 'low-tension' just means that the voltage is at 12 volts. However, before we leave the coil, we should take a look at the connections of the secondary winding. One end is connected between the primary winding and the CB terminal; the other end emerges at the top of the coil right in the centre, and the fat high-tension distributor lead is plugged in there.

Inside the distributor are housed both the contact-breaker and the distribution mechanism, which we shall come to later. The contact-breaker consists of a pair of metal points, one of which is connected to the low-tension lead, the other to earth. Most of the time the two points are touching, and current can flow across them. All the time the ignition is switched on, even without the engine running, current is flowing from the battery through the primary winding of the coil, through the points to earth (the car body), and thus completing a circuit and using power. Consequently, don't leave a car with the ignition on unless you mean to, or you will run the battery down.

When the starter turns the engine, a cam in the distributor, connected to the main engine camshaft, rotates. Each time it rotates it opens and closes the contact-breaker points four times (with a four-cylinder engine). While current is flowing through the primary windings of the coil, there is an electromagnetic field around the winding. However, each time the points open, there is a sudden interruption in the flow of current, and this causes an abrupt collapse of the electromagnetic field in the coil. The collapsing of the field causes the lines of force around the winding to sweep back, cutting the turns of wire of the secondary winding. This has so many turns that a very high voltage is induced in it, building up to 25 kV at the high-tension terminal of the coil. It is from here on that you can get a nasty, if not dangerous, electric shock.

Fitted to the end of the cam in the distributor is the rotor arm, which is synchronized so that, as the points open, its electrode is nearly touching one of the electrodes ranged around the inside of the distributor cap. The high voltage induced in the coil is, therefore, distributed to whichever sparking plug needs a spark at the time. A four-stroke engine fires twice each revolution, and since the distributor cam rotates at half the engine speed, it will deliver two sparks per revolution.

There is a high tension lead from each electrode in the cap of

115

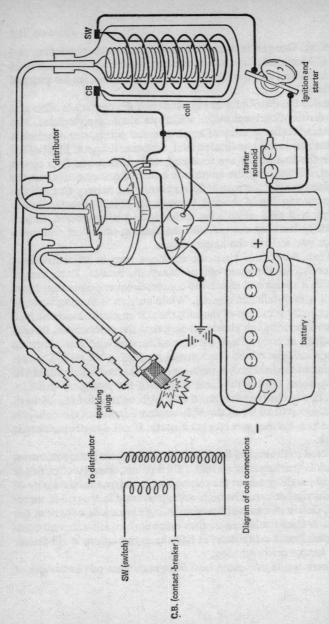

SW

CB

coil

distributor

sparking
plugs

ignition and
starter

starter
solenoid

+

battery

−

To distributor

Diagram of coil connections

SW (switch)

C.B. (contact-breaker)

Figure 44

the distributor to the top of each sparking plug. The plug consists of two electrodes, a central one fitted in the ceramic insulating body of the plug, and a bent one fitted to the metal base of the plug, which is screwed into the cylinder head. The engine itself is earthed by a flexible lead to the car body.

As soon as the very high-voltage impulse is transmitted from the distributor, it jumps the gap between the two sparking plug electrodes, and the spark caused by its jump across ignites the fuel in the combustion chamber. At least you would think it would, in theory. In practice, this arrangement would not work very well because each time the points opened there would be a smaller spark across them also, preventing the sudden interruption of current that is required. To avoid this happening, a capacitor is connected across the points. The effect of this is to provide a spring-like buffer to 'absorb the impact' of the sudden break in the path for the current and relieve the electrons in the points of enough energy to prevent them jumping across.

If the capacitor, sometimes called the condenser, fails to work, the engine will not start. This is because, at the speed at which the contact-breaker points operate, there would be a constant flow of current across the points due to the sparks, and the coil will not produce high-tension current unless the low-tension circuit is abruptly interrupted.

The fat size of the high tension leads is not because they carry more current than the others. In fact they carry less current, because, for a given amount of power, if you push up the voltage, you do so at the expense of the current. On the other hand, because of the very high voltage extremely good insulation is necessary.

The next most important electrical component is some means of replacing power used from the battery while the car is running. This is still done in most cars with a dynamo run from the engine.

The dynamo is a shunt-wound D.C. generator of fairly simple design. The complicated part is the means of regulating the output voltage to limit it over the wide range of running speeds of the engine. Basically, the output from the commutator is shunted by an electromagnet which controls the opening and closing of a pair of contacts. When closed, the contacts short-circuit a resistance in

117

the circuit of the field windings of the dynamo. When the voltage reaches a certain value, the attraction of the electromagnet is enough to overcome the retaining spring of the contacts and pull them open. This brings the field-circuit resistance into play and reduces the strength of the field. This in turn drops the output voltage, and the contacts close again, by-passing the resistance.

The contacts, therefore, oscillate between being open and closed and keep the voltage at the correct value. However, in practice the device has to be a bit more sophisticated than this, and incorporates a current regulator as well as a voltage regulator, together with a cut-out to prevent reverse flow of current from the battery when the dynamo's voltage falls below that of the battery. The ammeter, if there is one, is fitted between the voltage control box and the battery.

You may have wondered how the ignition warning light works. It is connected between the dynamo output (marked D, as opposed to the field winding input, marked F) and the ignition switch. When the ignition switch is on, a positive voltage from the battery is connected to the warning light. If the dynamo is not charging for any reason, the current from the battery will flow to earth through the warning light and the commutator of the dynamo, lighting the light. When the dynamo is charging, the 'D' terminal has a positive potential, as does the battery terminal, and so no current flows through the light.

A good car nowadays will have an alternator instead of a dynamo, because alternators are much more efficient, having no commutator and much simpler control equipment. The alternator design will be similar to those we have already met, in most cases single-phase. Some now are three-phase, but all are fitted with rectifiers to turn the alternating current into D.C. The voltage regulating device is a transistorized, solid-state equivalent of the mechanical dynamo regulator. Alternators are lighter and smaller than dynamos, and give a high rate of charge at quite low speeds, even when the engine is only idling.

6 Controlling Electrons

Transistors and valves

'Electronics' is a word which slips off countless twentieth-century tongues as readily as words like 'plastic', but plastic is stuff which most of us can describe reasonably well; electronics, to most, is just a word to cover that awe-inspiring latticework of coloured, shining, space-age jungle which reveals itself when the television man takes the back off the set.

Radio valves are fairly familiar looking things and so they should be; they have been around for half a century. Valves are things which 'blow', rather like electric lamps, but what do they actually do? As for transistors, well, how could that gaggle of coloured blobs possibly bring you the nine o'clock news?

Most of us appreciate that radio and television are only two of the scores of applications of this fantastic science. We have all heard of computers, even if we sometimes confuse them with the people who travel to towns to work, but we probably do not quite appreciate that electronic computers have had almost as far reaching an effect on our lives as radio and television put together. Although one of the biggest agents of the transformation of society in the last couple of decades has been the communications explosion (thanks to electronics), it would have been more of a feeble bang than an explosion had it not been for computers. Far from being there simply to confuse your gas bills, computers design, control the manufacture of, and in many cases operate, machines of all kinds. From setting type to landing aircraft, and from launching satellites to teaching children, electronic computers will be to the next half-century what motor cars were to the last.

So back to the fundamental question; what is electronics? It is obvious that it has to do with electricity, but what is special about it? The key is in the name '*electron*ics'. Electronics is the science of manipulating electrons, whereas electricity is the putting of electrons to work to get heat, light and power. Electronics is using electrons to control things; using electrons for communication. Very little power is ever involved, and if a direct end-product is required of an electronic system, electric power is brought in from outside. A radio tuner and amplifier will extract a symphony from space, but it calls for a power amplifier to bring in enough watts to work a big loudspeaker.

Perhaps the most fundamental application of electronics is in the storing, transmission and reproduction of sound. A high proportion of the science of electronics has to do with the processing of waveforms, and sound and waveforms are inseparable. Before going any further then, it will be worth making sure of what sound actually is.

Air is elastic. Although it will not hold your socks up, it will always spring back when squeezed. You realize this when you try to work a bicycle pump that is blocked at the outlet; in fact air is such a good spring that some vehicles use it in their suspension systems. Air is made up of millions of molecules all jostling around, and the springiness of air is due to the fact that the molecules are kept apart from one another by spring-like forces. If you could squash a pair of air molecules together they would spring back when you released them.

If a surface vibrates, like the body of a violin, it pushes and pulls on the layer of air molecules next to it. The springiness of air means that the push or pull is not instantaneously transmitted, but takes time rather like the effect of a shunt on a train of railway wagons. In fact it takes about a second for a wave to travel 344 metres.

When the layer of air molecules next to a vibrating surface is pushed forward, it is squashed against the next layer, until this squashing of the spring-like forces between molecules overcomes the inertia of the next layer of molecules and sets them going. The squashing amounts to an increase in pressure, and a sound wave is really a pressure wave which is passed along by the air molecules at 344 metres per second.

Take a very pure sort of sound, a whistle; if you can measure the relatively tiny pressure fluctuations it causes at one point, and draw a graph of the pressure over and above (or below) atmospheric pressure, your graph ought to be rather familiar to you. It is our recent acquaintance, the sine wave. A single pure tone has a sinusoidal waveform; more complex musical tones have over-tones or harmonics which are sine waves of frequency once, twice, three times etc., the frequency of the fundamental tone. On the graph, these are added arithmetically to give the more complex waveforms shown on Figure 45. Non-musical sounds may be a mixture of sine-waves, either related in frequency or in dis-cordant combinations, or mixed with waves which rise and fall above and below atmosphere in a random manner. Some noises are just random pressure fluctuations without any repetitive pat-tern to them.

Electronics was perhaps born of the need to transmit sound

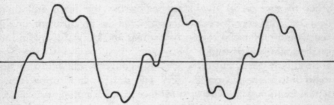

Figure 45

over distances, and it could be said that Alexander Graham Bell not only invented the telephone, but also sowed the seeds of the gargantuan electronics industry of today. The very first thing, though, which has to be done, before progress can be made in transmitting sound electrically, is to convert acoustic pressure fluctuations into electrical fluctuations. We had better take a look at some microphones.

A microphone is just a pressure transducer, meaning that its only job is to sense variations in air pressure and convert them into variations in voltage which fluctuate in magnitude in an identical way. What sort of an instrument do we need to achieve this? The first thing to be done is to sense the pressure fluctua-tions in the air. As in many things, nature did it first, by stretching a very light diaphragm across a circular orifice. This is what the tympanic membrane or eardrum is in the human and many animal ears.

121

When a pressure wave arrives at the eardrum, any small and momentary rise in air pressure has the effect of pushing the eardrum inwards. A small drop in air pressure sucks the eardrum out a little. If one of the ubiquitous sine waves arrives down the ear canal, the eardrum will be pushed in and pulled out in a smoothly alternating manner, and if its relative position at any one moment is plotted as a graph, there is the familiar wavy line.

Beyond the eardrum, the ear is vastly more sophisticated than any electronic device, and until we learn to copy it further, our microphone must make use of rather more primitive means of turning sound into an electrical signal. Although some microphones use slightly different means of picking up air-pressure fluctuations, the best example for our purposes employs a fine sheet of say, metal foil, stretched across the open end of a cylinder. This acts in exactly the same way as an eardrum, and it too would be pushed regularly inwards and outwards by an impinging sinusoidal sound.

So far so good, but how does one convert mechanical movement into electrical oscillation? The most logical thing to do would be to find a device or substance which is pressure-sensitive, and which has an electrical resistance or impedance which varies with pressure. Take a simple example, and one that has been used in telephone microphones. Figure 46 shows a little pot of carbon granules packed not too tightly into a small drum, with a membrane stretched across the top.

Carbon is an electrical conductor, we know, and it is not difficult to see that a collection of granules is not going to be quite such a good conductor as a solid lump would be, because the granules only touch each other over a relatively small area. On the other hand, if you press the granules closer together, they will conduct slightly better, and more like a solid lump: here is our microphone.

If the pot containing the carbon granules in Figure 46 is made of non-conducting material, and an electrode is introduced into the carbon on each side, the wires from the electrodes may be wired into a circuit with a battery and voltmeter. Let us connect up this circuit, with the voltmeter connected across the terminals of the pot, and see what happens. Current will flow round the circuit in a quantity depending upon the resistance across the carbon granules.

Remember that there is always a potential difference between the two terminals of a resistor, which will be large if the value of the resistor is high. Potential difference is measured in volts, and so the voltmeter connected across the pot of carbon granules will register. Now apply pressure to the diaphragm across the top of

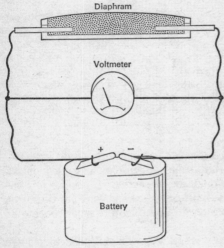

Figure 46

the pot, thus pressing the granules closer together. There will be an easier path for current to flow through the carbon, and so the electrical resistance will fall. The direct effect of this will be a drop in the potential difference across the microphone as a whole. In other words the reading on the voltmeter will drop.

If we were to suck the membrane outwards, the carbon granules would become less closely packed and the resistance would be increased. The voltage would therefore go up, above the normal value when the membrane is in its rest position. Although the voltmeter would not be able to respond fast enough, the effect of a sound wave impinging on the membrane will be to compress and draw out the granules in quick succession to cause the voltage in the circuit to oscillate in an almost identical manner. There is a bit of a problem here, though, in that we have not quite got a proper electrical analogy of the sound wave. The fluctuations which occur in atmospheric pressure occur above and below the normal pressure, so the values of the sine wave alternate from being positive values when the pressure is above atmospheric, and negative values when the pressure fluctuates to below normal atmospheric pressure. Our electrical signal, the oscillating voltage

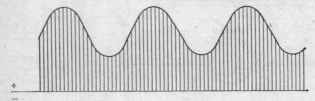

Figure 47

in the circuit of the carbon-granule microphone, is just a pulsating direct current, and does not alternate from positive to negative, which it must do to represent the sound wave correctly. (See Figure 47.) How do we turn a pulsating direct current into an alternating current?

There is a surprisingly simple way of doing this: by using a small transformer. Remember that the lines of electromagnetic force around an induction coil swish back and forth as the current flowing through the coils changes in value. Although we have been mostly interested in the voltage oscillations in our circuit, do not forget that if voltage oscillates, so does current. If another induction coil is placed alongside a primary coil wired into the microphone circuit, the fact that the lines of force around the primary coil are swishing back and forth as the current oscillates means that they keep cutting across the coils of the secondary coil. When wires cut lines of force and vice versa, current is induced.

As the lines of force swish outwards, the current in the

124

secondary coil, in Figure 48, will be induced to flow from A to B; as the lines swish back again, the current will be induced to flow in the opposite direction. Now we have our truly alternating signal in the output from the transformer. Even now, this signal is not going to be a lot of use, because if we transmit it through a long cable, the resistance of the cable will soon cause it to peter out, and any microphone with a reasonable frequency-response will not give a big enough voltage to overcome this. We are going to need some means of amplifying the signal by increasing its voltage.

To help us think how this might be done, suppose that the

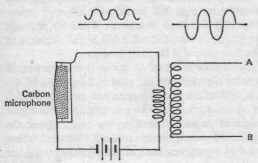

Carbon
microphone

A

B

Figure 48

sound wave had not in fact been converted into an electrical signal in a wire, but into pressure waves in a fluid other than air, say water in a pipe. Suppose also that the signal that we had in the water was not big enough, and we wanted to turn it into a bigger one by increasing the amplitude of the pressure waves. It would not in fact be very difficult to do.

Let us imagine that our weak signal travels along a $\frac{1}{4}$ inch diameter pipe, and that at maximum it reaches 5 pounds per square inch. Let us take another pipe and connect it to a pump capable of raising the pressure of the water in the pipe to 50 pounds per square inch. Now the thing is to transfer the low-pressure signal in the original pipe into the new high-pressure pipe. The way to do this will be to fit a valve in the high-pressure pipe capable of being continuously varied between being completely closed and completely open.

When the valve is open, the pressure in the new pipe will be relatively low, because the pump has not got very much back-pressure to work against and the water can flow along it easily. When the valve is completely closed, the pressure will go up to the maximum value the pump is capable of delivering. Now if the value is made so that it is controlled by a pressure-sensing device in our low-pressure pipe, we will achieve just what is wanted. As the pressure in the low-pressure pipe controls the amount by which the valve in the high-pressure pipe is opened, this will mean that when the pressure is at its highest in the low-pressure pipe the valve in the high-pressure pipe will be fully closed, and consequently the pressure will also be at its highest. When the pressure in the former pipe is at its lowest, the valve will be fully open, and the pressure in the new pipe will be at its lowest.

You can now see that the effect of all this is to cause an exact replica of the pressure signal in the old pipe to be created in the high pressure pipe, and as the peak pressure has gone up from 5 to 50 pounds per square inch the device has amplified the signal 10 times. If we wanted to go still further, we could repeat the performance with the 50-pound-per-square-inch pipe controlling a valve in a pipe fed by a pump capable of 500 pounds per square inch.

Since you don't have to top up the telly with water, applying this analogy to electronics obviously means finding an electrical equivalent to the controllable water valve, in other words an electronic valve. If you think about it, an electronic valve would have to be a resistor of some kind whose value could be changed easily and at high speed merely under the influence of the fluctuations of a weak signal in another circuit. All the variable resistors we have met so far would clearly not respond anything like fast or sensitively enough, and so we must be looking for a completely new device.

The new device is called a thermionic valve (Figure 49). It is a glass tube out of which the air has been pumped or, in some cases, which contains some other gas. (In the U.S.A. valves are in fact known as tubes.) At one end, usually the base, is a small metal cathode, incorporating a filament by which it can be electrically heated. At the other end is a metal anode. There are several other parts in it as well, but for the moment it will be best to see just what functions the anode and cathode perform. We will put the valve in a circuit by connecting a battery across the anode and cathode, and for reasons which will soon emerge, the negative terminal of the battery is connected to the cathode. This battery is in fact the equivalent of the 50 pounds-per-square-inch pump. Another connection must also be made to the heating element in

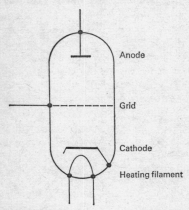

Figure 49

the cathode, and for simplicity we will bring in another battery to do this.

When the metal of the cathode is heated, the electrons in the metal become very much more agitated, and in leaping about are less influenced by the atomic forces keeping them within the metal. The cathode anyway has a negative charge, which means that it will tend to have an excess of electrons as the battery is trying to pump them in all the time.

The anode on the other end has a positive charge. This means that it exerts an attraction towards the cathode. This attraction is enough to draw electrons away from the cathode, and since there are no air molecules to bump into on the way, a good many of

127

them find it quite easy to travel across the intervening space and land on the anode. A current therefore flows through the valve.

As it stands, this device will not work as an amplifier, but it is in itself a useful component known as a diode. The function of a diode is to permit current to flow in one direction only; for instance if you have an alternating current and want only the positive halves of the alternating cycle to get through, you can use the diode as a means of getting rather lumpy direct current (Figure 50). This is possible because if you try to reverse the flow of current by making the anode negative and the cathode positive,

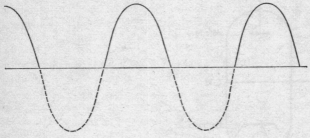

Figure 50

you will not make a circuit. Only the cathode is heated, so it is only from the cathode that electrons are really willing to depart. Nor will the electrons on the cathode be in the least bit inclined to travel to the anode because it is negatively charged and repels them. This prevents current-flow in the reverse direction.

Now suppose a lattice-work grid were inserted between the cathode and the anode. On its own, the only effect it will have will be that some electrons will bump into it on their way past. But what if it is given a negative charge, or a negative bias as it is called? 'Opposite charges attract; like charges repel.' The grid will tend to repel the electrons on the cathode and prevent them crossing over to the anode. Let the weak signal to be amplified be superimposed over the negative bias on the grid. As the signal oscillates into a positive value it will partially offset the effect of the negative bias and let more electrons pass; as the signal

128

switches to a negative value it will increase the total negative charge on the grid and even less electrons will get through than before. This is an identical situation to the one with the water valve; here is our electronic amplifier, known as a triode.

Here we are going to leave thermionic valves, almost as soon as we have met them, and turn to another way of doing the same job. Valves will pop up again throughout the rest of the book, but it is only fair to give due prominence to the diminutive device which has revolutionized not only the world of electronics but almost the world itself, the transistor.

Transistors are of course best known to most people as miniature substitutes for radio valves; they have become so popular in the manufacture of portable radios that they have even given their name to the whole radio and not just to the essential components which they in fact are.

Chambers's Twentieth Century Dictionary * defines a transistor as an 'amplifier with crystal and two cat's whiskers': and adds, 'later development of this, able to perform many functions of multi-electrode valves'. Crystal sets featured very prominently in the early days of radio, generations before the modern transistor came into being; the term 'cat's whisker' is in fact a nickname for a fine tungsten wire.

The crystal in a crystal set was usually a piece of silicon, which belongs to a family of materials which have some most peculiar characteristics. Silicon (along with other materials including germanium) in the form it is used in electronics, is neither a conductor nor an insulator. You will remember that the definition of a conductor is a material which offers a low resistance to the passage of electricity; and an insulator, one which offers a very high resistance indeed, often of several million ohms. Silicon and germanium in their pure forms are mediocre insulators, but in a special, slightly impure form they become neither insulators nor conductors; they become semiconductors.

The significance of this will not become apparent until we have been into the peculiarities of these materials rather more deeply, and to do this, it will be necessary to call up some of the information in the first chapter about the nature of atoms and electricity.

* Revised Edition.

129

In Chapter 1, we went into the reasons why and how atoms combine with one another to form molecules, and in so doing we discovered that the electrons in orbit round an atom reside in shells of varying potential energy. Each shell was prone to containing a particular number of electrons, and when it had that number it was full: if it had less than that number it was deficient. The outermost shell of an atom, other than hydrogen, is full when it contains eight electrons, and if it has any less it will bag any other electrons it can lay claim to. The valence of an atom is the number of electrons by which the outer shell is deficient.

Silicon and germanium atoms, although very different in the total number of electrons they contain, both have only four electrons in their outer shells. Since in this respect they are the same, we will confine our attention to germanium, which is the most commonly used semiconductor.

In a pure germanium crystal, the atoms form a lattice and position themselves so that each one of the four electrons in the outer shell of an atom can conveniently form a pair with one of the electrons of another adjacent atom. In this way, by sharing each other's electrons, the outer shell of each atom has, at least for some of the time, eight electrons to satisfy its need.

Now let the plot thicken, and let the germanium crystal be doped with arsenic. Arsenic has five valence electrons. When a few arsenic atoms are mixed in with the germanium atoms they too will form pairs between their valence electrons and those of neighbouring germanium atoms. However, for every arsenic atom there is going to be one electron left over, an odd man out, and this electron will be left fairly free (Figure 51). In fact, a single arsenic atom to ten million germanium atoms is enough to cause a large number of free electrons to occur, because there are more than 10,000,000,000,000,000,000,000 germanium atoms in a cubic centimetre.

It will not be difficult to see that the doping with arsenic will cause there to be enough free electrons to turn the germanium crystal into a conductor of electricity. It will still have a very high resistance though, and is better suited to the name of semiconductor. If, however, an electric field is placed across the crystal by connecting the terminals of a battery to opposite sides of it, the positive terminal of the battery will attract the negatively charged free electrons and a current will flow. The lost electrons will of course be replaced from the negative battery terminal.

Suppose, instead of arsenic, atoms with only three valence electrons had been used to dope the crystal; what would have happened then? Take indium as an example, although several

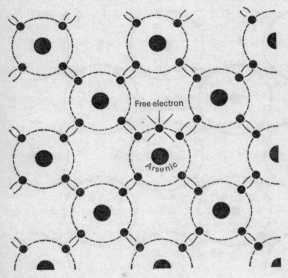

Figure 51

other elements like aluminium have only three valence electrons. Around each indium atom each one of the electrons will form a pair with one of the electrons of a neighbouring germanium atom, but because there are only three, one of the germanium atoms is going to be left short, without a pair for one of its electrons. You could call this a hole, because if a spare electron did appear from anywhere, it would be snapped up by the germanium atom with the unpaired valence electron. What effect does this have?

Each of these unpaired electrons is keen to find a partner. Since all electrons are negatively charged this is tantamount to saying

131

that the hole has a positive charge. If a battery is connected across a germanium crystal doped with indium, the positive holes will be attracted towards the negative terminal, where there are plenty of single electrons available. Now unfortunately, these electrons will not form very stable partnerships because the electron which fills a hole will not, like all the others, belong to an atom. Although

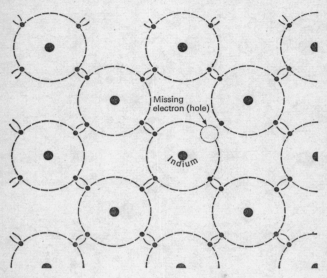

Figure 52

there will as a result be four pairs of electrons around the indium atom, only three electrons actually belong to the atom.

At the other end of the crystal, near the positive battery terminal, an electron from a fourth pair round an indium atom will fairly easily be enticed away by the attractive opposite charge of the terminal. The result is again conduction of current, although in this case it is not done by a flow of free electrons from the negative terminal to the positive terminal as in the case of the arsenic-doped crystal, but by a transfer of electrons resulting from the movement of holes towards the negative terminal. You may say that it amounts to the same thing, and you would be right in so far as all electric current consists of electrons passing from negative to positive. However, the way it takes place with the aid of these holes in the indium-doped germanium is important when you come to make things like transistors.

Because the indium-doped crystal carries its current by virtue of the positively charged holes it is known as P-type material, and

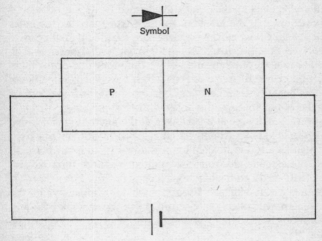

Figure 53

the arsenic-doped germanium, since its current flows by virtue of the free (negatively charged) electrons, is known as N-type material.

Now to get down to business; how do semiconductors perform the same duties as valves? In a thermionic triode valve, fluctuations in a weak current were induced in an identical fashion in a much stronger current, achieving amplification of the original signal. How is this done with semiconductors?

To answer this question, the first thing we must look into is what happens when a piece of P-type germanium is fused with a piece of N-type. What sort of current-flow does that produce?

Figure 53 shows the semiconductor equivalent of the diode described on p. 128, and consists of a P-N junction produced by changing the impurity in the germanium as a crystal is 'grown' from the molten material. The two ends of the double crystal have wires soldered to them, and the P-type material is connected to the positive terminal of a battery, the N-type to the negative terminal.

In the N-type material, there are a good many free electrons which are repelled by the negatively charged battery terminal and drift over towards the junction. In the P-type material, the holes which virtually have positive charges are repelled by the positive battery terminal and they too drift towards the junction. The holes are in need of electrons, and what do they find at the junction but a crowd of free electrons which have been pushed over from the negative terminal. They combine, and the free electrons from the N-type occupy the holes in the P-type.

However, each time a hole is filled at the junction, the positive terminal manages to syphon off an electron from the weak pair, thus creating another hole. What this amounts to is current-flow across the crystal: electrons are emitted from the negative terminal, drift across to the junction, occupy positive holes (in other words make a fourth pair around an indium atom), while the positive terminal collects up electrons by breaking weak pairs and makes more holes. There is a net flow of electrons round the circuit.

Now change the battery round and see what happens. The terminal soldered to the N-type material becomes positive, and attracts the free electrons in the material towards it. The terminal on the P-type material is negative, and attracts the positive holes. Apart from attracting the electrons and the holes away from the junction, nothing more happens. A few electrons may be drawn into the positive terminal, and a few holes may be filled with electrons from the negative terminal, but it will stop there, and no electrons will cross the junction. No current flows.

In actual fact, a tiny bit of current does flow, because heat causes thermal agitation in the material, and some valency bonds break down causing what is called reverse current. This is a small amount of current which barely increases even when the voltage is increased considerably, within limits. You may have been wondering what happens in a diode when the circuit is broken, and there is no battery connected across it either way. Do holes and electrons combine spontaneously at the junction? The answer is in fact the reverse. The effect of a P-N junction is that a small internal e.m.f. or voltage is generated causing the holes and electrons to drift away from the junction. One has to bear this in mind when one considers what happens when you connect an external e.m.f.

Now to the transistor. Since the transistor is to the semiconductor diode what the thermionic triode is to the thermionic diode, to make a transistor we have to put in some semiconductor equivalent to the grid in the triode. However, the way a transistor works is not quite analogous to the workings of a triode.

A semiconductor diode has only one junction, between the P- and N-type materials. A transistor has two junctions; it consists either of P-N-P materials fused together, or of N-P-N materials. Either way, it amounts to a piece of one type of semi-conductor with a wafer-thin centre barrier of the other type. In a P-N-P transistor, most of it is material like the indium-doped germanium, containing positive holes, but across the middle is a wafer of material like the arsenic-doped germanium, containing a supply of free electrons. In an N-P-N transistor it is the other way around.

Figure 54 shows a P-N-P transistor which has been connected up into a simple circuit. (It is necessary to have two cells for reasons which will soon be clear.) Let us first look at it as two P-N diodes stuck together: the left-hand junction is connected up in a way that will allow a fairly free flow of current across it; the right-hand junction is connected up in a way that will allow only a trickle of reverse current to flow.

The way the batteries are connected is called the bias and in correct terminology the left-hand junction is said to have a forward bias, and the right-hand a reverse bias. To get the nomenclature absolutely right, we should call the left-hand bit of P-type material the emitter, because the holes appear to emit from that side, and the right-hand piece of P-type material the collector. The centre section of N-type material is called the base.

135

What, then, happens to the holes, the electrons and everything else when you make up a circuit as in Figure 54? Holes are going to drift away from the positive battery connection at the emitter, and meet the emitter/base junction. This junction has a forward bias, so the holes will accept electrons from the base region with open arms. But alas, the base junction is only a wafer, and there cannot possibly be enough free electrons in it to satisfy all the holes that arrive from the emitter. All but about 5 per cent of the

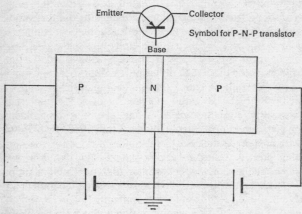

Figure 54

holes will have to press on into the P-type material on the other side of the base, the collector region, and be attracted to the negative battery terminal at the end where their thirst for electrons can finally be slaked. This means that the collector current will be about 95 per cent of the emitter current, the missing 5 per cent being swept up in the base region.

How does this give you any amplification, which is what this is all about? The collector current is *less* than the emitter current. However, we are not trying to amplify current, but voltage. The resistance across the emitter/base junction which has a forward bias is small, say 200 ohms; but the resistance across the reverse-biased collector/base junction is surely very high, because this junction is like a diode through which current is trying to flow the wrong way, the very thing diodes are designed to prevent. The resistance of the collector/base junction will tend to be about 200,000 ohms.

Now Ohm's Law tells us that voltage is equal to current multiplied by resistance. The voltage across the emitter/base junction, the input voltage, is going to be current, say 1 milliamp, times resistance, 200 ohms, which gives:

$$0.001 \times 200 = 0.2 \text{ volts.}$$

The output voltage will be current, 0·95 milliamps, multiplied by resistance of 200,000 ohms:

$$0.00095 \times 200,000 = 190 \text{ volts.}$$

This makes the voltage gain across the transistor:

$$\frac{190}{0.2} = 950$$

In other words if the emitter voltage were 1 millivolt, the collector voltage would be 0·95 volts.

Now sometimes we want a power amplification, not just voltage amplification. If you remember that power in watts is equal to voltage times current you find that the emitter voltage of 0·2, multiplied by the current of 1 milliamp, gives power of 0·0002 watts. At the collector the voltage of 190 multiplied by the current of 0·95 milliamps gives 180·5 watts. The power gain is therefore:

$$\frac{180.5}{0.0002} = 902,500$$

This terrific amplification is only theoretical however, because the rest of the circuit has to be taken into account in the calculations; but it still gives a good idea of the sort of things a transistor can do.

There is no fundamental difference between the transistor just described and the other sort, in which the emitter and collector are made from N-type material and the base is P-type. Figure 55 shows this set-up; the emitter/base junction still has a forward bias and the collector/base junction a reverse bias. The main difference is that the current carriers in this case are not holes, but electrons.

We will not deal with them here, but there are also transistors with three junctions, i.e. P-N-P-N transistors, and even P-N-I-P transistors, where the I-type material is intrinsic germanium con-

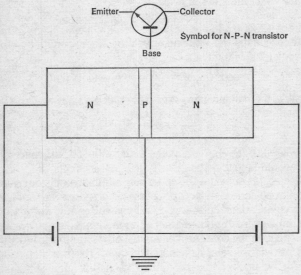

Figure 55

taining equal numbers of both types of impurity. When it comes to the ultimate stages in sophistication, there are yet more variations on the theme; but, for the time being, the P-N-P and N-P-N transistors will cope with our needs.

P-N junctions alone, however, possess a capability which has implications far beyond the world of amplifiers and transistors. When light strikes a P-N junction in a silicon semiconductor, energy from the light is available to give a boost to some of the

138

valence electrons of silicon atoms. Light energy can be broken down into tiny, discrete 'lumps' known as photons, whose energy content depends on the frequency of the light. A photon of light at the infra-red end of the visible spectrum can be just the right amount to boost a valence electron in a silicon atom so that it jumps out of the valence band. The effect of this is to create not only a free electron, but also a hole where it came from.

If a reverse-biased P-N junction is exposed to light, the newly liberated electrons resulting from the radiation will all congregate in the N region, because the positive potential given it by the bias voltage will attract them over. Similarly, the new holes will nip over to the P region. The result is that, whereas a reverse-biased P-N junction normally allows little or no current through because electrons go one way, holes the other, the creation of new holes and free electrons causes a steady flow of electrons to arrive at the positive terminal and a supply of holes at the negative terminal. The holes are immediately filled by electrons from the terminal. The flow of electrons out of the negative terminal into the new holes and of newly freed electrons out by the positive terminal is of course an electric current, plain and simple.

The power output of a photo-electric cell is proportional to the intensity of light falling upon it, and the cell will go on delivering electricity as long as the light shines. Satellites sent up in 1958, using solar cells for power, are still sending back information about the tests they are carrying out. The thing which limits the power output of a single cell is the practical size of the silicon crystals, which is seldom more than about 250 mm.^{2} The maximum power output is about 200 milliwatts, at about 0·6 volts. Consequently a large number of single cells have to be connected together to increase the output to anything useful.

7 The Anatomy of a Circuit

Simple amplifiers

You need only take the back off a radio to see clearly that there is rather more to an amplifier circuit than just a transistor out there all on its own. Even the simplest amplifier, used for instance to raise the output signal from a microphone to something suitable to drive a loudspeaker in a public address system, has to have quite a few components to make it work properly. We had better have a look at just such a case and see what is wanted.

We came across a simple microphone in the last chapter, consisting of a pot of carbon granules. Unfortunately the fidelity of sound reproduction with a microphone like this is not good enough for anything much better than a telephone, and before we can embark on the amplifier for the loudspeaker, we will need to bring in a more sophisticated microphone.

There are certain types of crystal, of which Rochelle salt (sodium potassium tartrate) is but one, which are affected by mechanical deformation of the crystal in a way that produces electrical charges. This is called the piezo-electric effect, and you can imagine that if you design a microphone so that the fluctuations in air pressure due to a sound wave can be made to impinge on a piezo-electric crystal, voltage fluctuations in the crystal will occur which, by being proportional in magnitude to the degree of deformation of the crystal, give an electronic replica of the sound wave. Of course the amount by which the voltage fluctuates will be small, and there will be negligible power, because the only source of energy for the piezo-electric crystal is the sound wave itself which may, in all, involve only a fraction of a milliwatt. Because loudspeakers are inefficient things, and because we also want to raise the volume of sound in our amplifier, both the voltage and the power in the signal have got to be increased.

Before going any further, we need to know something else about sound. Every time that a sound you hear doubles in loudness, the intensity, i.e. the amount of energy in it, has to go up very nearly ten times. Now since very many doublings of loudness have to take place to cover the range from the quietest sound you can hear to the loudest you are ever likely to put up with, it is clear that the range of intensities that the ear can cope with is phenomenal. In fact the energy actually entering the ear when you are listening to the very quietest sound is only 0·0000000000000001 watts, and when you are wincing at the screech of a jet at the end of the runway, your ear is picking up about 0·0001 watts.

If you wanted to amplify the former sound to the level of the latter you would need to amplify it a million million times. Ratios like this take a bit of dealing with, and so to simplify matters, it is easier just to count the noughts. The number of noughts are then expressed as a value on a scale of units called 'Bels', and to give the scale a bit more flexibility the Bels are divided into ten sub-units called decibels. A ratio of a million million involves 12 noughts, so the jet noise is 12 Bels or 120 decibels above the quietest sound. In practice a standard 'reference' sound is always used, and all others expressed as a number of decibels above it. A doubling of loudness (a tenfold increase in intensity) means putting on another nought, or an increase of ten decibels.

You can see that we are in for some pretty large amplification factors to get our public address system to work. We may have blinked in the last chapter at the sight of a theoretical power amplification from a transistor of the order of 1,000,000 to 1 but we can now see that this is going to be the sort of thing we are after.

Let us now go back to our piezo-electric microphone and start wiring it up. We know that across the two terminals are voltage oscillations, mimicking the air-pressure changes which the sound is causing.

Voltage or potential difference can in fact only be developed across a resistance (or an impedance), so the first thing we must do is to connect a resistor across the output from the microphone. Now if each end of the resistor is tapped with a piece of wire, we can start thinking about connecting these to a transistor.

Problem number one arises when you discover that the transistor has to have the appropriate bias voltages. In the P-N-P transistor in Figure 56a the emitter/base junction needs a forward bias, and the collector/base junction a reverse bias. Let us therefore produce a 12-volt battery and try to achieve this state of affairs. You could conceivably just connect up the positive terminal to the emitter and the negative terminal to the collector, but

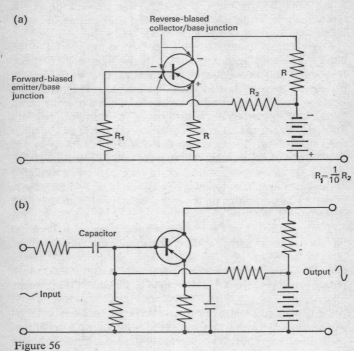

(a)

Reverse-biased collector/base junction

Forward-biased emitter/base junction

R_2

R

R_1

R

$R_1 = \frac{1}{10} R_2$

(b)

Capacitor

Input

Output

Figure 56

then the only resistance in the circuit would be the internal resistance of the transistor and when the rest of the circuitry problems materialized, you would be in difficulties.

A good way to do it is to connect what is called a voltage divider across the battery. This consists of two resistors in series, one of ten times the value of the other. A wire connected between

142

the two resistors is then connected to the base of the transistor. The emitter is connected via a resistor to the positive battery terminal, and the collector also through a resistor to the negative terminal. With this arrangement, the base is going to be mildly negative with respect to the emitter. Looked at another way, the emitter is mildly positive with respect to the base, and this is just what is wanted to provide the forward bias. The collector being connected via a load resistor to the negative battery terminal, this furnishes the collector/base junction with its reverse bias.

(To make circuitry easier, it is usual to connect the positive terminal of the battery to an 'earth' wire, which acts like a sort of general purpose drainpipe, and carries electrons from all parts of the circuit back to the positive terminal. This wire is shown in diagrams as a straight line running along the edge, with various wires connected to it, and forming one terminal of any output or input connection.)

We are now almost ready to connect up the microphone. One wire can go on to the base connection of the transistor, and the other to the earth wire. In order not to upset the bias voltage on the base by creating a D.C. path through the microphone, a large-value capacitor is included in series with the microphone. The capacitor allows an A.C. signal of audible frequency to get through, but no D.C. current can flow.

Now what happens? As the A.C. input signal oscillates, electrons are pushed to and fro in the emitter/base circuit, and this amounts to an A.C. current. We have already discovered that current variations in the base/emitter circuit cause similar variations in the collector circuit, but because of the high resistance of the reverse-biased collector/base junction, the voltage of the output is greatly increased.

There is still a slight problem, though. The load resistor at the output in Figure 56b has a D.C. potential difference across it at all times, caused by the battery in the circuit. This makes the resistor negative at the bottom, positive at the top. However, electrons flow from negative to positive, and when the input fluctuations are amplified in the collector circuit, they are manifested as variations in the flow of electrons from the collector. This means that the collector current, albeit a fluctu-

143

ating signal, is in opposition to the steady D.C. current from the battery.

The total voltage in the collector circuit at any instant is therefore the battery supply-voltage minus collector or load voltage; consequently the total voltage in the collector circuit is at its minimum when the load voltage is at its maximum, and vice versa. On top of this, the load voltage increases directly as a result of an increase in the input voltage, with the consequence that the total voltage in the collector circuit does, in amplified form, the exact opposite of what the input voltage does. The technical description of this behaviour is that the output signal is 180° out of phase with the input signal.

You might not think that this mattered very much, until you realized by looking at the circuit diagram that the emitter is connected via a resistor to the positive or earth lead, which is common to both input and output circuits. This means that since the output signal is an amplified replica of the input signal 'upside-down', the input signal is going to be cancelled out by the opposing output signal.

To overcome this problem, it is necessary to put some device in the lead to the emitter which prevents an A.C. signal from getting through. This is done by putting a by-pass capacitor across the resistor in the emitter connection. The capacitor has a large value so that all frequencies down to the lowest in the audio range can get through with very low impedance. Since a voltage only exists (for A.C.) across an impedance, this effectively attenuates the output signal from the emitter current, leaving only D.C.

The effect of cancellation of the input signal by an opposing output signal is known as degenerative feedback. In some circuits the output signal is in phase with the input signal and then regenerative feedback occurs. When transistors are connected up as in the above example, because the emitter is connected to both input and output circuits, the set-up is technically termed a 'common-emitter' connection.

Usually, a single transistor like this does not give enough amplification, and the output is connected as the input of another similar circuit. There are in fact four different ways of connecting

144

the two, but for our purposes a method known as resistance-coupling will do. Figure 57 shows that resistance-coupling in a transistor circuit merely amounts to joining up the output of the first stage to the input of the second through a coupling capacitor. The capacitor is necessary to prevent the flow of D.C. current from the battery of the first stage. The second stage is then identical to the first, and you can in fact connect up quite a number of stages to form what is known as a cascade.

However, no matter how many stages of transistor amplifiers are resistance-coupled together, you still will have great difficulty in driving a loudspeaker from the output. You have got yourself

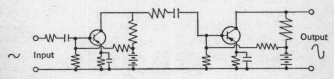

Figure 57

plenty of voltage amplification, but you have not yet got the required power.

One of the most important factors in the transfer of power from one circuit to another concerns the impedances of the circuits. Impedance in a circuit carrying an alternating current, as we have seen, is the combined effect of straightforward resistance, and the opposition to current-flow presented by capacitors and induction coils. To transfer power efficiently from one circuit to another, the impedances of the two circuits should be matched. Impedance matching is in fact a subject which will crop up again and again.

In the case of an audio amplifier, the main problem is that the impedance of the transistor–amplifier circuit will be high, and the measly few turns of wire stuck to the cone of the loudspeaker will have a low impedance. Power equals current times voltage, and precious little would be extracted from the amplifier across the very low impedance of the loudspeaker.

A power amplifier circuit is basically similar to a voltage amplifier, except that the components are rated for higher currents; the transistor is a rather beefier affair, and designed to get rid of as much of the heat generated by the large currents as possible. In order to match the output impedances, audio amplifiers are usually coupled to the loudspeakers by means of transformers. We have seen in previous chapters that the changing electro-magnetic flux round a coil caused by alternating or fluctuating current flowing through it induces a similar fluctuating current in another coil placed alongside. The voltage in the secondary coil is proportional to the number of turns in the coil compared with the primary coil. You can probably see that this is a rather good way of impedance matching. The primary coil to which the output

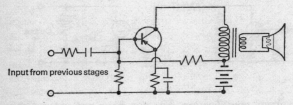

Input from previous stages

Figure 58

from the power amplifier is connected has a large number of coils so that its impedance is nearly the same as the amplifier im-pedance, and through the induction process it transfers the elec-trical signal across to a small number of turns in the secondary coil, which is well matched to the low impedance of the loud-speaker (Figure 58).

A power amplifier designed on the principles we have so far come across is called a 'Class A' amplifier, and has the following disadvantages to offset its very low distortion. Firstly it is wasteful of current when there is no input signal; secondly its efficiency as a power amplifier is limited by the fact that the maximum voltage of the input signal must not go above the point which would make the base positive with respect to the emitter, because then no current would flow at all.

These problems arise from the characteristics of transistors themselves. Remember that we went to some lengths in designing the simple voltage amplifier to get the biasing of the emitter, base

146

and collector terminals correct. The emitter was connected through a resistor to the positive terminal of the battery; the collector through a resistor to the negative terminal; in addition, the base was biased to be mildly negative with respect to the emitter.

The effect of the input signal on the base is to make it either more or less negative with respect to the emitter as the signal fluctuates. In a P-N-P transistor, the more negative the base is, the more electrons there will be in the base at the base/emitter junction to combine with holes arriving from the emitter. The base becomes more negative with respect to the emitter and the emitter current increases. Because the base is wafer-thin, only a very small proportion of the holes drawn from the emitter by the negative base voltage are actually mopped up in the base region. As well as increasing the emitter current, the rise in base voltage also increases the collector current; the great majority of holes go charging across the base region into the collector region to be filled in by electrons from the collector terminal. However, if the base becomes positive, it will attract no current from the emitter at all; it will repel holes back towards it. So when the base becomes positive it passes through the 'cut-off' point.

In a Class A amplifier, the negative bias of the base with respect to the emitter is such that the input signal is never great enough to drive it to positive. Even when the input signal rises to a positive peak, the combined effect of the bias voltage and the input voltage still leaves the base slightly negative. Consequently, collector current flows at all times. Even when there is no input signal, for instance if the amplifier is just switched on but not being used, the negative bias of the base draws current from the emitter and thus gives a collector current, albeit a D.C. current.

A power amplifier will be more efficient if you can put a bigger voltage signal in at the input. Now suppose the base of the transistor is biased so that only the negative cycles of an alternating input cause current to flow. Emitter current only flows when the base is negative with respect to it; if the biasing is organized so that with no signal at the input the transistor is at cut-off, then current will only flow during negative portions of the input signal.

One way of doing this is to make the collector negative with

147

respect to the emitter, and to apply no bias voltage to the base. This is a 'Class B' amplifier.

The input signal is applied across the base and the collector; it consists of a fluctuating or oscillating voltage, sometimes positive, sometimes negative. When the input fluctuates to a negative condition, it will make the base region negative with respect to the emitter, draw current from the emitter and hence cause collector current to flow. When it fluctuates into a positive condition, it will repel holes away from the base/emitter junction and no current will flow. The amplified output signal in the emitter–collector circuit will look like Figure 59, with all the positive

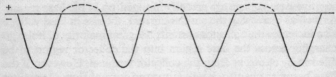

Figure 59

sections decapitated. This provides extra efficiency, because the whole of the operating range of voltages allowable for the base is available for only half the amplitude of the input signal, whereas in Class A operation the whole peak-to-peak amplitude of the signal had to be fitted into the same range. But what about the other half of the signal?

If only our transistor could cope with positive instead of negative input signals, we could perhaps amplify the missing positive half of the signal with another transistor and fit the two together at the end to reconstruct an amplified version of the original signal.

What we need to do is to design a complementary set-up in which everything has the opposite sign, and where better to begin than by taking an N-P-N transistor instead of a P-N-P one? Once again, we bias the base to near cut-off, but the effect will be the opposite of that with a P-N-P transistor. The emitter will be negative this time, since current conduction is done with electrons, not holes, and to repel electrons towards the emitter/base junction the emitter must be negative. Therefore, to get current to flow

148

from the emitter, the base must be positive, likewise the collector. If the base becomes negative with respect to the emitter, no current will flow, and in this circuit only the positive sections of the input signal will be amplified.

All that remains is to piece together again the two halves of the signal to get our amplified version of the input (Figure 60). This

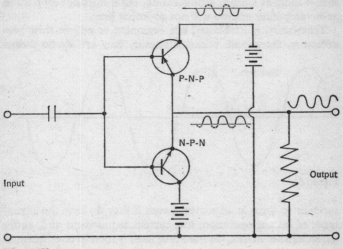

Figure 60

is done simply by joining the emitters of the two transistors. In this circuit the collectors are earthed, making it a common-collector circuit; the input is applied between the base and the earth, and the output extracted across the emitters and the earth.

This sort of circuit is called a push–pull circuit, and the use of two different transistors is called complementary symmetry. One of the effects of using a common-collector configuration is that there is no phase reversal at the output as there is with a common-emitter connection. In addition, the output impedance is low, and no transformer is necessary to match the output to a loudspeaker.

149

The input impedance on the other hand is high, and suitable to accept the high impedance output of a preceding voltage amplifier.

Class B operation, as we have seen, can be more efficient, but it can give greater distortion than Class A, mainly because of the imperfections occurring at the point where the two halves of the signal are separated and joined up again (Figure 61). There is also such a thing as Class C amplification, but it does not crop up in audio amplifiers and we will not go into it here.

Transistors, quite clearly, are beginning to eclipse their predecessors, thermionic valves. However, they are by no means

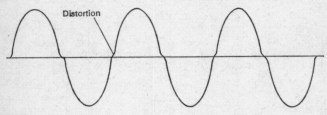

Figure 61

superior to them in all respects, even if they do have the advantages of instant operation, low current requirement and, above all, small size. In fact, the transistor itself is soon to be eclipsed, at least as a single, self-contained component that is soldered into a circuit. When the transistor was invented, everyone involved realized its potential for reducing the size of electronic equipment, but frantic efforts had then to be made to reduce the size of the other passive components which go with transistors, such as resistors, capacitors and inductances. Meanwhile came the introduction of the printed circuit. Printed circuits, apart from anything else, greatly tidy up the whole business of circuitry. The circuit is designed on paper, and drawn out with 'paths' of varying widths representing wires. The drawing is then transferred photographically to a coated copper film deposited on an insulating backing, and etched so as to leave only the conducting paths. The board is perforated in appropriate places so that the wires of

150

the various components can be inserted through and soldered into place.

It was the next step that really broke with tradition: integrated circuits. An integrated circuit can be a wafer only a few millimetres square which intrinsically contains an entire circuit: transistors, diodes, resistors, capacitors, inductances and all. One type is formed entirely on a single crystal chip of semiconductor. The construction process is started with a P-type silicon layer on

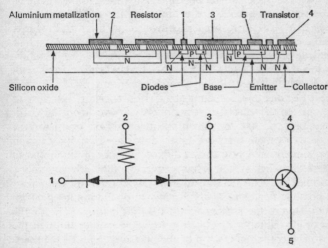

Figure 62

which is grown a layer of N-type silicon. This layer eventually becomes the collector region for all the transistors in the circuit and one element of the diodes. Next comes a silicon oxide coating. After this a series of masking, etching and diffusion processes is performed. 'Windows' are etched into the oxide coating to allow the material to be diffused through into the layer beneath, and complex islands of P-, N- and P-type material can be produced through the diffusion process.

Transistors and diodes are formed by diffusing in such a way as to produce either P-N-P and N-P-N sandwiches or P-N junctions

151

(Figure 62). For resistors, the resistance of the P-type base can be used, and capacitors can be formed using the silicon oxide as the dielectric, with heavily doped N-type silicon on one side and an aluminium coating on the other as plates.

The next stage in the miniaturization game is even more extraordinary. The idea is not to bother with innumerable hordes of electrons charging like football crowds round the circuits, but to manipulate electrons almost individually. Films of material only a few atoms thick can be deposited on the base and electron beams are used as tools for etching out the circuitry. By this means it is possible to get the equivalent of more than twenty circuit elements into a space of a cubic millimetre.

In spite of extraordinary advances in electronics like those just mentioned, you will still find in places good old valves being used. This is because they do have some important points in their favour. For one thing, when dealing with transistors you have to look out for the effects of temperature. Above about 85°C for germanium, and 200° for silicon, the junctions in a transistor, the very heart of their function, break down irretrievably. Even at lower temperatures, heat causes the conductance of the emitter to increase, although silicon is less susceptible than germanium.

Another drawback to transistors is the fact that the amplification possible decreases as the frequency of the input signal increases. One of the reasons for this is that it takes time for the holes or electrons to travel across from the emitter through the base to the collector. On top of this, the resistance of the semiconductor material combined with the capacitances of the components creates a sort of filter which blots out the highest frequencies. Finally, in order to speed up the time it takes for the holes or electrons to cross from the emitter to the collector, the base area is made extremely thin. The result is that the junctions break down at rather low voltages, and the current is limited by the maximum operating temperature.

It therefore seems that valves still have their uses ; they are not much affected by temperature changes, and can have better frequency response as well as being able to cope with high voltages. We ought to have a quick look at some valve circuits before passing on.

You will see from Figure 63 that there is not a great deal of difference between a basic valve amplifier circuit and a transistorized version. The input signal is connected directly to the grid of the valve, which has a negative bias. This is necessary because if the grid is ever allowed to become positive with respect to the anode, current will actually flow from the grid to the anode; this not only distorts the signal but also requires power from the input circuit which will often be too weak to supply it.

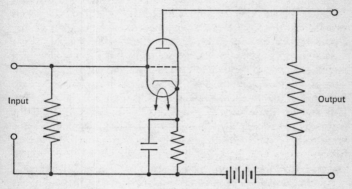

Figure 63

Voltage amplifiers of this type are always operated so as to draw no power from the input, and to do this the grid is given a negative bias. This means that, if the bias is −6 volts, instead of an alternating input signal jumping up and down between, say, +1 volt and −1 volt, the input voltage will oscillate between −5 volts and −7 volts. It is in fact one of the advantages of valves that they are purely voltage operated, whereas transistors are current operated.

The output or anode circuit of the valve amplifier is very similar to the collector circuit of the transistor set-up, including the fact that the output signal is 180° out of phase with the input signal. Figure 64a shows an amplifier with a second stage, and again you can see the strong similarities to the transistor equivalent. It is when you come to things like push–pull valve amplifiers that the differences creep in. You will remember how with transistors it was possible to get two inputs out of phase with one another by using one N-P-N transistor and one P-N-P transistor; you cannot do this with valves.

In order to obtain two input signals 180° out of phase with each

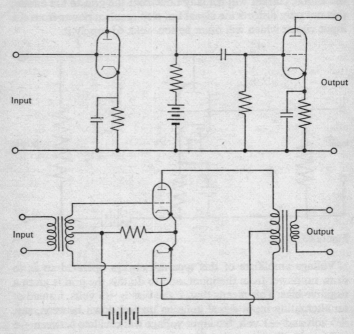

Figure 64

other in a push–pull valve amplifier, you have to have a transformer-coupled input and output. We have met transformers in this kind of role already; we found them rather useful for impedance matching, for instance at the output of an amplifier circuit for a loudspeaker. The microphone could also be connected to the primary coil of a transformer, and the input of the amplifier to the secondary coil. This way you get a spot of im-

154

pedance matching thrown in, if you want to use a microphone with a low impedance.

Splitting the input signal is done by tapping the centre of the secondary coil of the transformer, and wiring this up as the 'earth'. Then, if the grid of one valve is connected to the top of the coil and the grid of the other to the bottom, we will get what we want. What happens is this: as the voltage in the input circuit oscillates, it induces the voltage in the secondary coil to oscillate in a similar manner. The voltage across the secondary coil will switch from one polarity to the other, and when the top is negative, the bottom will be positive. By tapping it in the middle, when the top is positive, the bottom will be negative with respect to the middle, and vice versa. Connect the top to the grid of one valve and the bottom to the grid of the other, and here is our sought-after phase opposition.

The outputs of the two valves will also be in phase opposition, and by connecting them to the top and bottom of the primary coil of another transformer and earthing the centre tap, the same sort of thing happens as at the input transformer. The top will be negative with respect to the centre when the bottom is positive, and so on. The effect is to combine the two output signals and get twice the amplification of a single valve. The name 'push–pull' is really rather apt; it is like two people operating a saw which is oscillating across a log. One person is moving his arms 180° out of phase with the other, but at the log, the 'centre tap', the efforts of the two combine to put twice the elbow-grease into cutting through the log.

This sort of push-pull circuit can be operated in either Class A or Class B; because of the transformer-coupled output the complete anode signals of both valves, operated in Class A, can be combined together. In fact transistorized push–pull circuits using transformer input and output are common in Class A operation in addition to the Class B complementary-symmetry circuits we have already looked at. In these cases both the transistors are of the same type because the phase splitting is done by the input transformer with its centre tap.

So much for simple circuits, but how much do we know about

their performance? All amplifiers are designed to operate over a particular range of frequencies known as a band; you will find that good amplifiers have their bandwidth quoted in terms of the upper and lower limits of the frequency range which they will amplify without falling off by more than three decibels. If the high-frequency response of an amplifier is poor, it will cut off the higher overtones of voice and musical instruments. As it is the

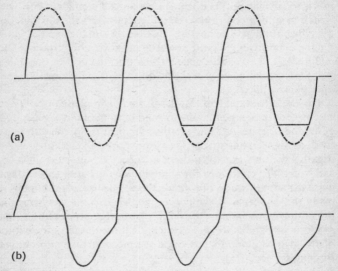

(a)

(b)

Figure 65

overtones which give sounds their quality or 'timbre', the loss of high-frequency response means that flutes and oboes sound the same, and it is more difficult to identify individual speakers. On top of this, an uneven response to the frequencies which are in the range of the amplifier will mean that sounds of one pitch are given greater amplification than sounds of another. This can give rise to a rather 'hollow' sound.

However, even if an amplifier happens to cover the range of frequencies you are interested in, it does not necessarily mean to say that any signal within the range will automatically be amplified perfectly. If you are not careful, distortion occurs. Distortion is really any adulteration of the shape of the input signal as reproduced at the output. The signal can be virtually decapitated (Figure 65a) or non-linearities in the performance of circuit components can cause distortion in the shape of a signal; Figure 65b shows an example. This happens when a given small change in the amplitude of the input signal does not produce proportionately the same change in the output signal.

A rather useful way of reducing distortion is to use negative

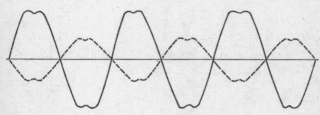

Figure 66

feedback. Negative feedback has already reared its head, where it was not wanted, in the case of the simple amplifier; it was necessary to put a by-pass capacitor in the emitter connection in the common-emitter amplifier to overcome the problem of the output signal reducing the input signal. By contrast, positive feedback also occurs in public-address systems when the microphone is held too close to the loudspeaker, or the gain of the amplifier is turned up too high. This makes the amplifier operate as an oscillator, causing the thing to howl.

However, the sort of feedback that is useful in amplifier circuits involves feeding the output signal back into the input after having 'turned it upside down' (Figure 66a). Negative feedback will of course reduce the gain of the amplifier, because being 'upside down', the feedback signal tends to cancel out the input signal. The point is, though, that getting adequate gain out of an amplifier is seldom a very great problem, it is distortion that takes a bit of coping with.

Negative feedback can reduce distortion because any kinks in the output signal are fed back into the input upside down, and consequently partly offset the output distortion (Figure 66). The reduction in distortion achieved by negative feedback is roughly proportional to the loss of gain. Feedback also makes an amplifier rather more stable and less affected by changes in the supply voltage. A typical transistor amplifier circuit incorporating negative feedback is shown in Figure 67. A voltage divider across the output is tapped between the two resistors, and a reduced part of

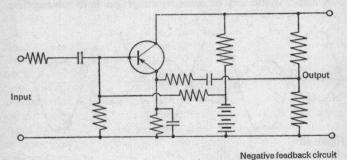

Negative feedback circuit

Figure 67

the output signal is fed back through a blocking capacitor and a resistor to the emitter of the transistor. Because of the 180° phase shift in the output of a common-emitter amplifier, the signal is automatically negative.

A really good amplifier should be able to cope with frequencies ranging from 30–40 Hz at the bottom end, to cover big organ pipes and bass drums, to at least 15,000 Hz at the top end, if not right up to 20,000 Hz. Admittedly, many people cannot hear sound of a frequency much higher than about 15,000 Hz but there are plenty of young people who can hear over 18,000 Hz and the presence of a full range of overtones or harmonics in a sound gives it a remarkable quality of realism and 'presence in the room'.

This same high-quality amplifier will be almost completely linear both in the behaviour of the transistors and in its relative response to different frequencies. It will be stable as far as its gain is concerned, and not be over-susceptible to ill-effects if the supply voltage changes.

There is something about amplifier circuits, though, which has so far been left out. Almost all amplifiers allow the user to control the volume, or gain, and also to adjust the response of the set to upper and lower ranges. How is this made possible in the circuitry? First of all, the volume, or gain control, needs some explanation. The gain of a basic amplifier circuit is normally constant; often, however, we do not want a constant output and so some means is included in the circuit to enable rather less than the full output signal to be taken if required.

To achieve this, a variable resistor known as a potentiometer is connected across the output from the last stage of the amplifier. There is a problem in doing this, though, because the object of the exercise is to control loudness. We saw earlier in the chapter that the ear does not respond in a linear manner as far as loudness is concerned, and in fact it takes a tenfold increase in sound intensity to give the subjective impression of a doubling of loudness. If the loudness control were to reduce the output voltage in direct proportion to the amount by which the knob was turned, then you would have to turn it a very long way indeed to keep lowering the voltage to one tenth of its amplitude each time a halving of loudness was required.

To overcome this, the resistor in the volume control is made so that the electrical resistance along its length increases logarithmically. This simply means that if you measured the resistance 1 mm., 2 mm., 3 mm. and 4 mm. along its length, instead of it reading something like 1,000, 2,000, 3,000 and 4,000 ohms, it would be 1,000, 2,000, 4,000 and 8,000 ohms. To take another example, the readings might be 1,500, 4,500, 13,500 and 40,500 ohms. What is happening is that each millimetre along the resistor the resistance is increased, in the first example by a factor of 2, and in the second by a factor of 3, instead of in direct proportion to the length.

Our volume-control potentiometer therefore consists of a logarithmic resistor, often in a sort of doughnut shape, with one connection at one end, and the other on a sweeping pick-up arm which is traversed along the resistor by turning the control knob. If we want to get, say, five doublings of loudness in the whole range of the control and the resistor were 10 mm. long, the resistance along the first 2 mm., 4 mm., 6 mm., 8 mm. and along the whole length would be: 10,000, 100,000, 1,000,000 and 10,000,000 ohms.

One of the most important controls of an amplifier is the tone control. The response of the amplifier to different frequencies in the audio range determines the tone quality of the sound that comes out. Consequently it is possible to vary the tone of the sound by altering the frequency response of the amplifier.

Tone control is usually achieved by having a means of independently attenuating frequencies above about 3,000 Hz and below about 300 Hz. The response to frequencies between 3,000 and 300 Hz will stay constant while either one or both of the treble and bass controls is altered.

To understand how a tone control works you have to think back to some of the basic characteristics of circuit components, in particular, induction coils (sometimes called 'chokes') and capacitors. A capacitor allows absolutely no D.C. current to pass, because once the electrostatic potential across the plates has built up to its peak, nothing further happens. The effect is similar for very low-frequency A.C., but as the frequency increases, a capacitor starts to conduct rather better and at high frequencies it offers little impedance at all.

With this information in mind, you can appreciate that if you connect a capacitor across the output from an amplifier, it will present a very much higher impedance to low frequencies than to high frequencies, and the latter will therefore find an easy way across. You will remember that a large-value capacitor in the emitter circuit of a transistor was used to provide a by-pass route for A.C. which had such a low impedance that no significant voltage was developed across it. Similarly, in the amplifier output, a smaller-value capacitor allows an easy, low impedance, by-pass route for high frequencies, so for them there is very little load to develop a high voltage. Low frequencies will still meet quite a high impedance and so will still give decent voltages across the load resistor.

160

Figure 68 shows how this principle can be utilized to make a variable tone control. The bass and treble circuits are basically the same thing, looked at from opposite viewpoints. The capacitor is wired in series with a variable resistor: with the resistor turned to a low value, the by-pass path for high frequencies is good, and high frequencies nip across without having to do their work across the output terminals. This therefore has the effect of giving the bass frequencies more prominence. If the variable resistor is turned to its maximum resistance position, then the impedance of

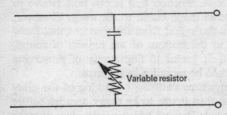

Figure 68

the by-pass route will be so high to any frequencies, that the high frequencies will reach the output full strength.

If it is necessary to attenuate low frequencies rather than just play around with high frequencies, then induction coils instead of capacitors may be used. The effect of an inductance is the opposite to that of a capacitance: it passes low frequencies without hindrance, but as the signal frequency speeds up, the impedance of the coil increases. The effect of shunting an induction coil across an output is to provide an easy by-pass for low frequencies, so that they do not develop much in the way of voltage at the output.

But more about audio amplifiers in the next chapter.

8 Sound Storing

*Sound recording
and reproduction*

Some sounds that are made can last for as long as a quarter of a minute; in specially constructed laboratories with heavy, hard walls there is so much reverberation that it can take twelve to fifteen seconds for a sound made inside to die away. However, most sound is gone in a flash, and from the moment that Isaac Newton started to get to the bottom of the physics of sound, scientists have racked their brains to find a way of preserving sound the way sights could be recorded in pictures.

Nobody really got anywhere until the beginning of the nineteenth century, and even then it was to be many decades before anything workable emerged. They all had the right idea, though: sound is a series of waves of pressure-changes in the atmosphere, and whenever it meets a surface it tends to 'suck and blow' on the surface, making it vibrate. If the vibrations could somehow be recorded, for instance by engraving them as a wavy line on a plate, then a basic sort of record of the sound could be achieved.

Early attempts all involved attaching a needle to a membrane vibrating in sympathy with sounds made in front of it, and allowing the needle's sharp point to score a plate moving across it at constant speed. However, they never tried to replay the sound they had thus recorded; they were merely trying to enrich the science of acoustics by examining in detail the physical differences between the sounds emitted by different sources, usually musical instruments.

An Irishman residing in France, F. L. Scott, developed in 1857 a fascinating machine called a 'phonautograph'. This device embodies almost all the elements of a gramophone but no attempt was made to play back the sound that was recorded on it. It was a Frenchman, Charles Cros, who twenty years later made a reversible recorder called a 'paleophone'. This simply enabled the scored plate to be moved past the needle which in turn vibrated the membrane to reproduce the pressure-waves of the original sound.

But the man who really started it all was Thomas Edison, an American who, independently of Cros and at about the same time, invented an almost identical instrument. The difference was that Edison was the first man to reproduce the human voice, and he called his invention 'The Phonograph – The Ideal Amanuensis'. He thought that his brilliant invention was worth nothing more than to find a role as a dictating machine!

The instrument was regarded as a novelty; famous singers sang into it at the Great Exhibition at the Crystal Palace, and then amused crowds heard 'grinding from the interior, sounds supposed to be a reproduction of their most sweet voices', to quote the *Musical Times* of November 1887. A decade later, the same paper replied to a correspondent, 'In reply to your question as to the newest Edison phonograph, we can say from practical knowledge that it is a very wonderful instrument. The tone qualities of various musical instruments are reproduced with remarkable fidelity, though the various gradations of tones are, perhaps, not so marked a feature, though they are by no means absent. You ask, "does it reproduce music (orchestral music, principally) in a manner that would satisfy a musical ear?". That question is a little difficult to answer. There is naturally a ventriloquistic character about the reproductions, but by no means sufficient to be offensive to the ear. There will probably be improvements in the construction of the instrument, whereby the most delicate effects will be absolutely reproducible, though it is almost too much to expect that the results obtained will be equal to the original sounds. But, as we have already said, it is a wonderful invention, and one whose use will give much pleasure and not a little amusement. The cost is six guineas; but a large metal bell, which amplifies the sound and effectively disperses it in a large room, would cost about fifty shillings more.'

The instrument had clearly advanced considerably in the twenty years since its invention, but to a modern ear it would sound awful. Distortion was described in the last chapter, and although produced mechanically and not electrically, the sound

163

from an early Edison phonograph was strongly distorted, mainly by mechanical and acoustical resonances.

Edison's instrument used a revolving cylinder of wax, which was inscribed by the recording needle. This method was greatly improved upon by Emile Berliner, who devised the more modern method of using a disc instead of a cylinder, so that the needle scores spiral grooves, and the vibrations are recorded by the needle oscillating from side to side instead of up and down. Berliner also made the whole process much more permanent by developing a method of producing a master from the original wax disc, from which any number of durable copies of the record could be made, moulded in a shellac mixture. Berliner, incredibly, had even less foresight than Edison, and far from thinking his invention was only a dictating machine, he thought its future lay in the construction of talking dolls! He even started producing them.

Now, the number of gramophone records, electrically produced, runs to inestimable numbers. The invention has had the most profound effect on the history of music, and later developments in sound recording and even television recording have dominated the entertainment industry of the twentieth century.

What, then, are the technicalities of a modern gramophone record? We start, once again, with a microphone, and the one described in Chapter 7 will do admirably. Next, we need an amplifier, and in most commercial recording processes this is in fact the first stage of a highly elaborate tape recorder. However, it would be jumping the gun to start talking about tape recorders now, and as it is perfectly possible to make records directly from the original sound, we will feed the output from the amplifier straight to the record-cutting process.

The heart of the process is a beautifully smooth, blank, aluminium disc which is coated with a mirror-like finish of cellulose lacquer. This blank disc is fitted to a machine which is mechanically designed to rotate the disc as smoothly and as evenly as possible. The disc is the counterpart of the turntable of a record player, and the counterpart of the pick-up head is a finely constructed cutting tool. Basically it is a tiny heated chisel which when lowered on to the lacquered blank cuts a V-shaped groove to very close tolerances. If no attempt were being made to record sound on the disc, the cutter would cut, on a 300 mm. diameter, long playing record, a spiral groove over half a mile long. The distance between the grooves would be about 0·05 mm. and the depth about 0·003 mm.

The cutter, however, is fitted into an electronic head which is capable of 'modulating' the groove so as to record the required sound. The modulation is achieved by fitting the cutter on a pivot. On the pivot is a coil which is free to swivel in the field of a

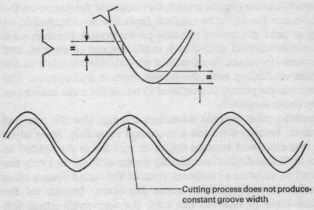

Cutting process does not produce constant groove width

Figure 69

permanent magnet. We have seen in previous chapters that the effect of passing an electric current through a coil in a magnetic field is to produce a rotational force on the coil. This was in fact the principle on which a galvanometer was designed, and so you can see that if the coil on the cutter pivot is connected to the output from the amplifier, it will swivel from side to side in direct proportion to the amplitude of the voltage in the output signal. For example, if the sound being recorded were a simple tone, a sine wave, then the modulated groove would look like Figure 69.

The blank disc is then coated with a thin deposit of silver to make it conducting, so that it can be electroplated with nickel.

165

The electroplating is then carefully separated from the blank, and consists of a negative master disc, with ridges instead of grooves. This master is used to produce a positive matrix from which any number of negative discs can be made from which the finished discs are pressed in a vinyl-type plastic.

Replaying a finished disc is then the reverse process to that of cutting one. The pickup stylus is usually of sapphire or diamond, made to finely controlled dimensions so as not to damage the groove. This is mounted on a hinged cantilever which is coupled to a ceramic piezo-electric crystal. Deviations in the groove on the record cause the stylus to oscillate from side to side, and in so doing to exert alternating pressure on the crystal. Pressure on a piezo-electric crystal generates a small amount of current, and from there on we are faced with a very similar situation to the problem of dealing with the output from a microphone. The signal from the pickup is amplified in much the same manner as in any audio amplifier.

However, most records nowadays are not like the one just described, because that was a monaural recording. Most of us have two ears, and because sound in real life is distributed in space, both ears do not hear exactly the same thing. Not only are the relative volumes of different parts of the sound source often dissimilar in each ear, but more important, because of the physical distance between our ears, the very same sound will arrive at one ear at a slightly different time from the other. The result is that the sound arriving at the left ear is often out of phase with the same sound arriving at the right ear. If this phase difference and the other differences in the sound arriving at the ears can be reproduced, then the end result will have much more realism, restoring much of the directional characteristics of sound and thus giving it an extra dimension. This is what stereophonic sound is all about.

In order to reproduce stereophonic sound, it is necessary to record two tracks entirely independently, and to do this in one groove on a gramophone record looks, at first glance, rather impossible. Some people think that somehow there must be two grooves, and the pickup stylus has to have two parts, but this is not so. One groove and one pickup stylus are capable of dealing more than adequately with two entirely independent signals. How is it done?

The groove on a gramophone record is, as we have seen, V-shaped, and in mono-recording it is modulated by wiggling it from side to side. In a stereo recording the groove is not wiggled from side to side; instead, the cutter making the groove is made to oscillate in two directions, one diagonally upwards to the right, the other diagonally upwards to the left. This way, the groove can be modulated twice over, once by wiggling the right-hand wall of the V-shaped groove, the other by wiggling the left-hand wall. The cutting-head must therefore have two degrees of freedom, and two electromagnetic coils, one to move the cutter one way, the other to move it the opposite way.

To illustrate this, Figure 70 shows how a replay stylus in a stereo groove would move in response to the two signals. Figure 70a shows the direction the stylus would move in a mono groove; Figure 70b if the right-hand stereo track only is modulated; Figure 70c if the left-hand stereo track only is modulated. If both tracks are modulated 'in-phase', the stylus will move vertically up and down, and if both tracks are modulated anti-phase, then the stylus simply moves from side to side.

Stereo records can of course be replayed on a mono record-player. When this is done, the stylus is free to move from side to side only; the whole pick-up arm can move up and down, but only side-to-side movements produce an electronic signal. This is no great problem, since a modulated sidewall also pushes a stylus to one side as well as upwards (that is what diagonal move-ment is). A mono stylus therefore gets pushed from side to side by the two walls in various combinations, thus picking up part of the signal from each track. It is only when both tracks carry signals which are 'in phase' that the groove has no sideways movement at all, and, in practice, this state of affairs occurs only momentarily.

The pickup head on a stereo reproducer must have two piezo-electric crystals, one responding to movements in one diagonal mode, the other to movements in the other diagonal mode. The two signals are then separately amplified in isolated circuits of their own.

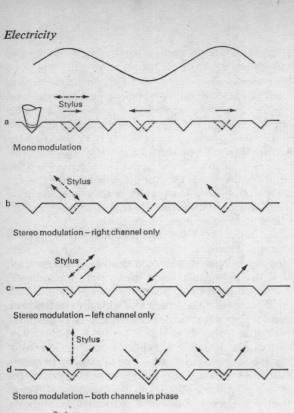

a

Mono modulation

b

Stereo modulation – right channel only

c

Stereo modulation – left channel only

d

Stereo modulation – both channels in phase

e

Stereo modulation – both channels anti-phase

Figure 70

Tape recording, on the other hand, is rather more involved than recording on gramophone records. It is not surprising, therefore, that high-quality tape recording came on the scene rather later in history. The very basic principles are the same however; sound is converted into a fluctuating voltage, which in turn is used to cause a permanent equivalent fluctuation in another medium by a reversible process.

The obvious difference is that whereas the fluctuations in a gramophone record are physical deviations in a groove, in a tape recorder, the magnetic tape is magnetized to a varying degree along its length. To achieve this, and at the same time retain good fidelity of the recorded sound, takes quite a bit of doing. There are four essential elements to a tape recorder:

1. A magnetic tape capable of being magnetized with varying degrees of strength and polarity.
2. A recording head that impresses magnetic oscillations on to a magnetizable medium.
3. A playback head that can detect magnetic modulations on the tape.
4. A magnetic eraser to wipe all magnetic signals from the tape and leave it ready for re-use.

In addition there have, of course, to be suitable recording and playback amplifiers.

First of all, then, let us look at the tape and see just how it is capable of being magnetized. The tape itself (usually P.V.C.) is coated with a thin layer of ferrous oxide which consists of a multitude of tiny magnetic particles, each with their own north and south poles. In a new, virgin tape, these particles are distributed in a random manner, and so their own individual magnetic fields cancel each other out. However, if an external magnetic field is brought close to the tape, the particles in it will be polarized so that they all face the same way; the result is that the tape itself becomes locally magnetized in the region of the external magnetic field. If the magnetic field is then removed, the tape stays magnetized, but only in the local area that was originally subjected to the magnetizing force.

The recording head consists of a circular ferromagnetic core, having a small break or insulating layer. The core is wound with a coil, and capable of being electromagnetized by current in the coil. Consequently when the core is magnetized, a magnetic field, complete with our old friends the lines of force, is produced across the insulating gap, against which the tape is made to pass (Figure 71).

If you are jumping to the conclusion that the next step is to put the recording signal across the coils of the recording head – hold it. It can be done that way, but in the interests of quality the whole process is often rather more complicated.

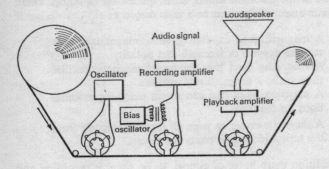

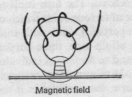

Magnetic field

Figure 71

The first thing we have to consider is tape biasing. We have already had trouble with biasing transistors in order to make them operate within the required part of their range; similarly, in order for the magnetic tape to respond in direct proportion to the applied magnetization, it, too, has to be biased.

It could be biased, like a transistor, with a D.C. signal, but improved linearity, less distortion and lower tape-noise result if the bias is a high-frequency A.C. signal. The bias has to be of

170

ultrasonic frequency so as not to upset the audio signal, and so usually has a frequency of between 30 and 150 kHz.

This high-frequency bias signal is therefore the base which is recorded on the tape, and corresponds to the unmodulated spiral groove on a disc blank when no signal is being recorded. As a result of the bias signal being applied across the coils of the recording head, the magnetic flux across the gap varies sinusoidally in strength. The tape goes past the head and is similarly magnetized as a result.

To record an audible signal on to the tape, the bias signal has to be modulated, and there are two ways of doing this. The most

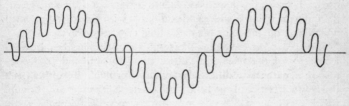

Figure 72

common way is simply to superimpose the audio signal over the bias signal, with the result that the mean value of the bias signal is modulated in direct proportion to the instantaneous voltage of the input signal (Figure 72).

However, in some sophisticated tape recorders, the frequency of the bias signal is modulated. To do this requires a special circuit which is frequency-sensitive, and variations in the voltage of the input signal cause variations in the frequency of the 'carrier-frequency'. We shall be looking at this process in much more detail in the chapter on radio transmission.

Now, having recorded the signal on tape, all that remains is to play it back. The playback head is similar to the recording head, and in fact some cheap recorders make the same head do double duty. Instead of the head being an electromagnet, however, it is inert. It is thus capable of being magnetized by the tape as it passes by. Magnetization in the cores of the playback head in-

171

duces a weak voltage in the coils, which is then fed into the input of the playback amplifier, and so on.

What about the erase head? How do you get rid of a signal if you want to use the tape again? You can do it with a permanent magnet, and many a valuable tape recording has been damaged by being placed on an instrument containing a magnet or, in some other way, accidentally coming into a magnetic field. However, to erase the tape on a tape recorder with a D.C. magnetic field would leave a rather noisy tape, and so the erase head is again fed with a high-frequency signal. It may in fact be the bias signal, boosted to a higher voltage, or it may be a strong signal of even higher frequency. At all events the erase signal must be above the audible range. Because the erase-head has to produce a diffuse magnetic field, it usually has a wider gap compared with the recording head which has to confine its magnetic field to a very fine strip.

Tape recorders have amplifiers and so, of course, they are subjected to all the usual difficulties of distortion and frequency response, with the addition of a few more problems resulting from the characteristics of the heads and the tape. Two words, though, which you hear in connection with tape recorders especially, are 'wow' and 'flutter'.

Wow and flutter are basically the same phenomenon, and result from uneven movement of the tape past the recording and playback heads. Wow is in fact a deviation from constant tape speed, resulting in a slow oscillation and therefore variation in the frequency of the recorded sound. In extreme cases a wowing sound is the result. If the speed deviation results in an oscillation above about 20 Hz, then the fault is called flutter, and it can in fact occur up to as high as 200 Hz.

Both wow and flutter are governed by the mechanical design of the tape deck, the mechanism which transports the tape and turns the spools. Whereas in a record player the turntable can be made like a heavy flywheel to smooth out its rotation, in a tape recorder there is little rotational inertia in the spools. It is not in fact the turning of the spools which governs the tape speed; the tape is advanced by being gripped between a capstan and a roller, and the capstan is mounted on the spindle of a flywheel. The flywheel is in turn connected to a good-quality motor by means of a very flexible elastic band to avoid transmission of motor vibrations to the flywheel.

We have now covered microphones, amplifiers, record players and tape recorders, but they will all be precious little use without the most vital link in the chain, the loudspeaker system There is no point whatever in spending large sums of money on hi-fi equipment if you neglect to install a well-designed speaker system. Even below the realms of hi-fi, the ultimate performance of an audio system will be judged by most people on what it sounds like, and what it sounds like will be greatly dependent on the means of turning the electronic output signal into sound.

No loudspeaker system, even in the most sophisticated stereo set-up, can exactly reproduce recorded sound as the recordist heard it. The spatial distribution resulting from the sizes, shapes and positions of the original sources of sound can never be exactly reconstructed, although stereo sound gives vastly more satisfying results than mono recordings.

Basically, what a loudspeaker has to do is to push and pull the air around it (in response to an oscillating electrical signal) in such a way as to send out pressure waves in the air of the appropriate frequencies and amplitudes. In the early days this was done by vibrating a small mica disc at the end of a large metal horn, and although horns are still used as an efficient way of producing sound, for instance in public address systems, they are now electrically operated. You will not, however, find horns used in hi-fi systems except for radiating very high frequencies.

A modern loudspeaker consists of a cone of paper, with a means of moving it to and fro. Since the paper is in the form of a cone, it is mechanically remarkably stiff, and of course exceedingly light. The result is that it has very little inertia indeed so that it can be vibrated at high frequencies. The edges are corrugated and adhered to the frame, so that there is plenty of scope for free movement fore and aft. The business end of the thing is at the apex of the cone.

A small cardboard cylinder is fixed to the apex of the cone around which is wound a fine coil of wire. It is across this coil that the output signal of the amplifier is applied. At the rear of the speaker is a specially shaped permanent magnet: this consists

173

basically of a cylindrical magnet, having one pole at one end of the cylinder, the other pole at the other end. One end of the cylinder has an annular ring fitted to it, and the other end a complete disc; in the centre of the disc is fitted a core which extends through to the hole in the centre of the annular ring. There is then a narrow circular air-gap around the core and magnetic flux is developed across the gap between the ring which is one pole, and the core which is the other (Figure 73).

The cardboard cylinder on the back of the loudspeaker cone on

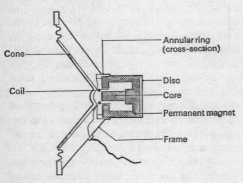

Cone

Coil

Annular ring
(cross-section)

Disc
Core
Permanent magnet

Frame

Figure 73

which the coil is wound fits neatly through the gap between the core and the ring. Once again, we avail ourselves of the fact that when you pass a current through a coil you turn it into an electro-magnet, and if you place the coil in the field of a permanent magnet of opposite polarity, you will have an opposing force between the coil and the magnet. So when current flows through the loudspeaker coil in a direction which makes it magnetic in opposition to the magnet, the coil and the whole loudspeaker cone will be pushed away from the magnet. If current flows through the coil in the opposite direction, then the coil will be magnetized in the same direction as the magnet, and the cone will be pulled towards the magnet.

The result is that as the current in the coil is made to flow back and forth as the output voltage from the amplifier switches from positive to negative, so, in direct proportion, will the loudspeaker cone oscillate. In moving to and fro, the loudspeaker cone will compress and rarefy the air around it, and thus our long-awaited sound will have been reproduced.

But the story does not end there. You can never hope to reproduce high-fidelity sound with just one all-purpose loudspeaker, and in fact many people spend large amounts on hi-fi systems and neglect this most important link in the chain. The main problem is one which does not occur to many people, but is really quite simple. We have talked about loudspeakers pushing and pulling the air around them, but we did not stop to think that while the paper cone is pushing on the air in front of it and compressing it, it is simultaneously pulling on the air behind it and rarefying it. Now for fairly high-frequency sounds, all this means is that the loudspeaker beams sound to the front and the rear (the two sides being anti-phase), but with low-frequency sound, with wavelengths several times the dimensions of the loudspeaker, the effect is for the rarefactions at the rear to cancel out compressions at the front, and vice-versa. For this reason, a loudspeaker all on its own will give very poor low-frequency response.

As if this were not problem enough, most large speakers are bad at radiating very high-frequency sound. Since much of the quality of hi-fi is due to accurate reproduction of high-frequency sound, it is essential that the speakers are able to cope with it. One of the difficulties is that a large cone will be difficult to vibrate at the very fast rate required, and that it will not move as one single unit; parts of it will be going inwards while other parts of it are going outwards.

Let us therefore start by trying to overcome the bass problem: the simplest thing to do is to fit the speaker in an aperture in a large wooden baffle board. This means that the sound waves created at the rear have a long way to travel to get round to the front. To save space, the baffle can be replaced by an enclosure, which as well as keeping the sound generated by the two sounds from interfering with one another, can also improve problems caused by acoustic resonances. As this book is about electronics and not acoustics, suffice it to say that the complexities of speaker enclosure design are not to be trifled with, and successful doing-it-yourself requires considerable research into the technicalities.

The high-frequency problem is sometimes partially overcome by fitting a little rigid cone to the centre of the main cone, but for best results, the high-frequency end of things should be separately dealt with by a specially designed 'tweeter'. In contrast, the large speaker is then left to cope only with the low and middle frequencies and is given the splendidly apt name of 'woofer'.

Tweeters vary considerably in design, but are all small in size. Some are like miniature woofers, working by the moving coil principle, but having rigid plastic cones with domed central diaphragms; others use small horns working on the principle of Edison's machine.

An elaborate speaker system will have, all contained in the same cabinet, a woofer and a tweeter and even an intermediate mid-range speaker as well. However, the desired effects will in no way be achieved by feeding the whole output signal into each of the three speakers, and here we must now return to pure electronics. Systems incorporating more than one speaker unit have to have circuitry to divide up the frequency spectrum on the output signal so that only those frequencies which a particular speaker is designed to handle will be fed into it.

Assuming for the time being that we only have a woofer and a tweeter to cope with, we shall have to feed the output signal through two filters. One filter will have to be a 'low-pass' filter, meaning that only frequencies below a certain cut-off frequency will be allowed through without attenuation; the output from this filter will then be supplied to the woofer. The filter for the tweeter will be a 'high-pass' filter, allowing all frequencies above the cut-off frequency through to the tweeter. How do you design these filters?

You will by now be turning straight to thoughts of capacitors and induction coils as being the agents for coping with different frequency ranges. Figure 74 shows a typical crossover network used for dividing up the frequency range: the wires leading to the bass speaker have a capacitor shunted across them, and there is an induction coil in series with one of them. As capacitors offer a low impedance path for A.C. of high frequency, the high-frequency components of the signal will be short-circuited across the shunt capacitor and will not develop any voltage at the speaker. On top of this, because inductances will only let low frequencies through with low impedance, and since the induction coil is in series with the output lead, high frequencies will be

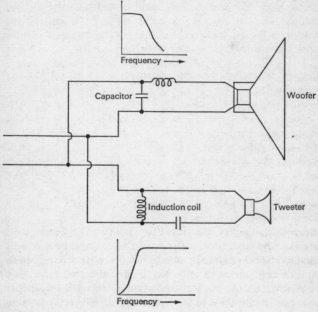

Figure 74

attenuated on their way through. The combined action of the two components forms a low-pass filter.

The high-pass filter, on the other hand, has exactly the opposite configuration. An induction coil is shunted across the output, which offers a low impedance path for low-frequency parts of the signal, thus allowing them to by-pass the output. In addition, there is a capacitance in series with the output, allowing high frequencies through, but offering a high impedance to low frequencies.

177

In this case, the cut-off frequency of both filters is the same, but had there been a mid-range speaker to feed also, there would have had to be a band-pass filter to attenuate both the top and bottom ends of the scale. This would consist of a low-pass filter with a cut-off frequency at the top of the speaker's range in series with a high-pass filter with a cut-off frequency at the bottom of the speaker's range. No filter, though, suddenly gives totally efficient attenuation immediately the cut-off point is reached, and the efficiency of a filter is looked up in terms of the rate at which the response curve falls off above or below the cut-off.

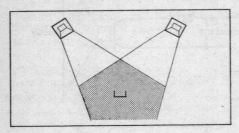

Figure 75

Even with a mono system, it is often worth having more than one speaker, but of course with stereo there has to be a pair of matched loudspeaker systems, and they have to be correctly positioned for the stereo effect to be worth having. In most domestic environments, the scope for really good stereo is somewhat limited; one of the reasons is that once you are some distance from a speaker, you hear not only direct sound from the speaker, but also reflected and reverberant sound caused by the reflectiveness of the walls of the room. It is easy, therefore, to get into a position where you hear so much reflected sound from both speakers that they cease to have their individual effects on the ears. Figure 75 shows a good arrangement of speakers, where the best listening area is just behind the apex of the shaded area. Speakers should not be put in the corners of a room, because this excites room-resonances which will be extremely undesirable.

A way of keeping both channels of a stereo recording completely apart until they reach the ear is to use stereo headphones. The effect is quite extraordinary; one gets the weird sensation that the sound is being generated somewhere inside one's head. However, stereo records are not recorded with the intention that they should be listened to with headphones, and the complete isolation of the two channels can sound rather artificial. To overcome this, part of the left signal is sometimes leaked over to the right earphone, and vice versa, to give more of the sort of effect you would have in a room. However, the sound you hear is subject only to the acoustics of the recording room, whereas with loudspeakers, the acoustics of the listening room colour the sound as well.

It should be pointed out that some people who listen for extended periods to stereo through headphones report rather undesirable physco-physical after-effects. One or two disc jockeys have found the effect to be disturbing.

Let us end this chapter by taking a look at how earphones work. First of all, it is a good thing to provide ear-cups which exclude as much as possible of the ambient sound going on around you, and for this reason good earphones are based on a pair of plastic, foam-lined cups with fluid or other flexible sealing-rings to make the seal around the ear as airtight as possible.

Early earphones consisted of electromagnets positioned close to metal diaphragms; changing current in the winding of the electromagnet attracted the diaphragm in proportion to the current, and the vibration of the diaphragm created the sound. The quality of these earphones is poor, mainly because of diaphragm- and cavity-resonances. Hi-fi headphones today are all of the moving-coil type, and really each earpiece contains a tiny moving-coil loudspeaker.

The small dimensions of the earpieces do not necessarily render their low-frequency response poor, because the cones of the speakers are close to the ear canal, and the pressure fluctuations are fed straight into the ear. Poor-quality earphones, though, have resonances at the high-frequency end of the scale, and the twenty-fold difference in price between the best and the worst earphones is usually reflected in a very marked difference in frequency range and linearity.

179

9 Ethereal Dances

*Radio waves;
their transmission
and reception*

There is still, even to this day, something science fiction-like in the phenomenon of radio waves. What extraordinary things they are: where you are sitting right now you are surrounded by radio signals from scores of transmitters, some not even on this planet. Some radio waves are reaching us from unthinkable distances in the universe, others are coming from just up the road. Some signals carry pictures as well as sounds, others carry coded information and the very existence of radio waves from celestial bodies is information in itself.

Radio waves are just part of a vast range of similar types of wave known as the electromagnetic spectrum. We are fairly familiar with other sorts of waves; we have talked a little about sound waves in this book, and most of us have stood idly watching the ripples caused by tossing a stone into a pond. To help us try to sort out the nature of electromagnetic waves, let us ponder on the causes of waves of any sort.

If it is possible to attribute the general phenomenon of wave motion to any one basic thing, one may say that waves happen because of the existence of time, and because everything we know about takes a finite time to happen. In many types of wave motion, other physical factors come into it as well, such as elasticity, inertia, density and so on, and although they are often essential ingredients to particular types of waves, they are not essential to the basic concept of wave motion.

Think of a line of cars waiting at the traffic lights. When the lights change to green every single car in the queue is, in theory, free to move forward and proceed on its journey. Does every car immediately move forward? No, because it takes time for the message to get back along the line. The first car sees the lights go green, and a second or so later moves forward; the car behind sees the car in front move forward, and a second later moves forward itself, the car behind does likewise. It can take several seconds before a car way back down the queue gets going, by which time the lights will have changed back to red. The car at the front of the line stops at the red light, then the one behind, the one behind that, and so on. In a long line of traffic there are always some cars moving forward while others are stopped, and there is a finite speed of propagation of the effect of the lights turning green; a wave of car-movement travels back down the queue.

If you could make everyone move forward instantaneously when the lights go green, there would be no wave. The time factor is the sole cause of the wave motion; elasticity, mass or density do not enter into it. From time springs velocity, the amount of distance covered in a given time: when elasticity, mass and density are essential to wave motion, as for instance in sound waves, it is only because they determine the velocity at which that type of wave is propagated. If for some reason the velocity is otherwise determined, they do not have to come into it at all.

Until somebody successfully debunks Einstein, modern science will be based on the theory that nothing can travel faster than light. This is rather less important than the fact that light takes a definite time to travel over a given distance. It does not take long, and in fact in one second it can cover 299,780 kilometres. There is nothing very special about light, and it is not the only thing which travels at that speed; light consists of electromagnetic waves just like radio waves except that the wavelength of light is very much shorter. However, the speed of light must be looked upon as the sort of ultimate in velocity: one must imagine that there are two boundaries to the range of velocities, zero and the speed of light. Zero velocity is no velocity, and the speed of light is 'absolute' velocity.

The point is this: because nothing can travel faster than light, news of any change cannot travel faster than light. However quick the drivers of those cars had been, the appearance of the green light would have taken a tiny fraction of time longer to reach the chaps at the back of the queue than those at the front, and there would still have been an infinitesimally small time-lapse

Electricity

between the first car getting off the mark and the cars further back
starting to move.

Now, think about an electron, all on its own. What properties
does it have? It has mass. It has a negative charge of electricity.
Because of this it will exert a force on another electron and repel
it, or attract a particle having an opposite charge, such as a
proton. An electron is surrounded by force, and the area in
which the force exists is an electrostatic field. This force is equal
in strength in all directions round the electron, but as you get

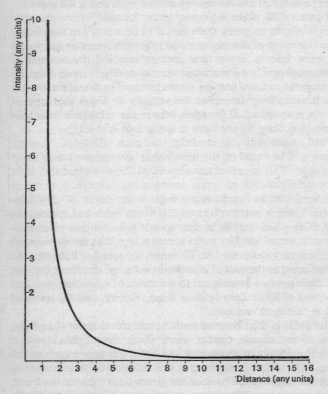

Figure 76

further away from the electron, the force is diluted over a larger area. The area we are talking about is the surface of a sphere; its centre is the electron and on its surface is our measuring position. The further away from the electron you get, the larger the sphere round the electron at that point. Now the area of a sphere increases four times each time the diameter is doubled: if the diameter is trebled, the area goes up nine times. In other words, the area of a sphere is proportional to the square of the diameter. This leads us to say that since the force round the electron gets spread over a larger area the further away you get, the force is *inversely proportional to the square of the distance*.

This fact is called the 'inverse square law', and it has interesting consequences. For instance, it explains why the electrostatic force round an electron has comparatively little effect at more than a very close proximity: Figure 76 shows how the force falls off sharply as the distance is increased. However, although the force round one electron is tiny, even quite close to it, we must not overlook the fact that, however tiny, it extends outwards from the centre of the electron for an infinite distance. The distance can never be so great that

$$\frac{1}{\text{distance}^2} = 0$$

If two electrons come within range of one another, they will push each other apart along a straight line, because each is exerting its force in straight lines away from its centre. Now, suppose you accelerate an electron from rest or from uniform motion, what effect will this have on the field surrounding it? Think of a measuring point some distance from an electron (Figure 77) and consider the direction of the force exerted by the electron on that point. When you accelerate the electron, you are going to alter the direction of the force slightly, since you are changing the position from which the force radiates, and this is the crux of the whole problem. News of the changing position of the accelerated electron has to travel outwards from it to the measuring point, and it can only travel at the speed of light. In all directions at right angles to the way the electron travels, news of its changing position will travel outwards at 299,780 kilometres per second. The news will

183

Electricity

in fact be a kink in the lines of force round the electron. This kink is none other than an electromagnetic wave.

The wave does not travel away from the electron in all directions, because in the direction the electron is moving, there is no change in the lines of force (Figure 78). The biggest change is at right angles to the direction of travel, and the wave is more cylindrical in shape than spherical. Now the area of a cylinder is directly proportional to the diameter, and not to the square of the diameter as

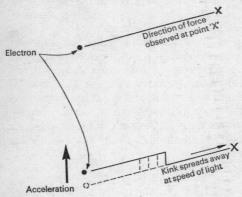

Figure 77

in the case of a sphere. This means that the intensity of the wave is inversely proportional to the distance from the electron, not to the square of the distance. The consequences of this are highly important.

Figures 79 and 80 show how different are the effects of intensity decreasing inversely with the *square* of the distance, and decreasing inversely with the distance. A long way away the difference is very great indeed, and in fact the kink in the force round an accelerated electron makes itself felt incomparably greater distances away than the actual force itself.

Let us now stop thinking of one electron in isolation, but as one of a myriad in a length of copper wire. Around the wire on its own there is no net electrostatic field, because the negative charges of the electrons are balanced out by the positive charges in the

184

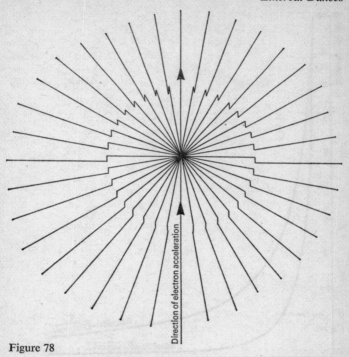

Direction of electron acceleration

Figure 78

atoms of metal. However, connect the wire suddenly to a powerful battery, and the electrons in it will be abruptly accelerated forward. Remember that it is only electrons that are accelerated, the atoms with their positive charges stay put. As a result, the kink still occurs, and there is no opposite kink of any kind to balance it out.

On top of this, you ought to be remembering that electrons moving along a wire are surrounded by a magnetic field; that is how electromagnets work. This field is similar to the electrostatic field, but its force acts in a different direction. Remember the right-hand-wire rule? The lines of force round a current-carrying wire are circular, around the wire, and if you wrap your hand round the wire with the thumb pointing in the direction of

185

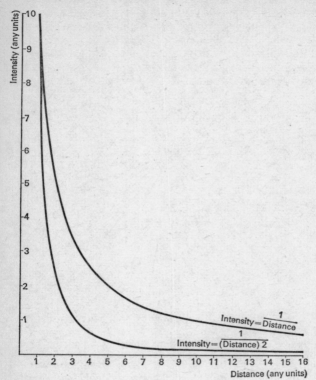

Figure 79

conventional current-flow, the lines of force will go in the direction of the fingers.

You can probably appreciate that when the electrons in our copper wire are accelerated, they build up a magnetic field, and news of this change also travels out as a kink or wave. The wave is in fact a dual affair, representing the change in the direction of the electrostatic force and the creation of a magnetic field. Both kinks are joined in one, but they are at right angles to one another, and both at right angles to the direction of travel.

186

Now let us imagine: wo theoretical copper wires, a few feet apart. One is capable of being switched into the circuit of a powerful battery, and the other, totally isolated from the first, has an extremely sensitive galvanometer connected across it. Neither wire exerts any sort of force on the other because they are in all respects electrically neutral. However, close the switch in the circuit of the first, and a kink will whip away from it at the speed of light. This kink will have two effects on the second wire. From

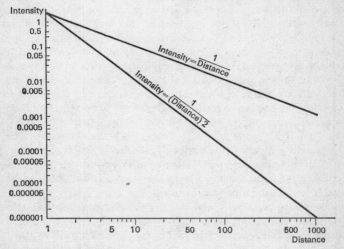

Figure 80

the electrostatic point of view, it is a wave of electrostatic force at right angles to its direction of propagation, and it will therefore exert a force on all the electrons in the second wire in the direction the wire runs. Secondly, the magnetic part of the kink will have a similar effect, the reverse of the occurrence that caused it, and the net result will be that all the electrons in the second wire will move a little. This is another way of saying that a little electric current will be induced in the wire, and the galvanometer will register momentarily. We have our first radio transmission!

The important point is that it is not the movement of electrons in the transmitting wire, but the acceleration of them, that causes the phenomenon. The speed of light is so great that news of the changing position of electrons moving at constant speed will not cause a detectable wave, because they are moving relatively slowly. It is only when they are sharply accelerated that a wave occurs. Of course, to keep on transmitting a wave, after the initial production of the kink, would not be possible by continuing to accelerate the electrons down the wire. The only practical way to keep on emitting waves is to oscillate the electrons to and fro, then instead of a kink we will get a series of ripples.

If you apply an alternating current to a conductor, the effect will be to push and pull the electrons in it, and in pushing and pulling them you are accelerating them. If you drive a car forwards and backwards you will be constantly accelerating it and decelerating it (or giving it negative acceleration). The acceleration given to electrons by the ordinary alternating current of the mains is nothing like enough to transmit radio waves. To do this you need an alternating current of a frequency in the region of 1,000,000 Hz (1 MHz), compared with a measly 50 Hz of the mains. The higher the frequency, the higher the acceleration. To prove this, pick up a heavy object and wave it from side to side. Start increasing the speed you are waving it at, and you will find that the faster you go the more hard work it is.

Before we can start, then, we need to be able to apply a high-frequency alternating current to the transmitting wire or aerial, in order to be able to keep on accelerating electrons enough to maintain a steady stream of electromagnetic waves. We will come to the means of producing this current later, but for the time being, let us look a little closer at the effects.

Alternating current, we know, has a waveform like a graph of the trigonometrical function, the sine or cosine. The current in Figure 81 rises and falls from a maximum positive or forward value to a maximum negative or reverse value; this is in fact caused by the voltage oscillating in a similar manner. When the voltage is at its greatest positive value, electrons are moving forward at their greatest velocity, under the influence of the electromotive force; when voltage reaches its greatest negative value, the electrons are moving backwards at their greatest velocity. They receive the greatest acceleration at the point when they are being turned from going forwards to going backwards, that is, when the velocity curve is passing through zero, and they will get the least acceleration when they are in the middle of their forward or backward journeys, when the velocity curve is at its peak.

The strongest wave is going to be produced when the electrons are getting the most acceleration; no wave at all will be radiated

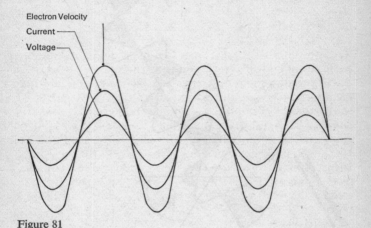

Figure 81

for the instants of nil acceleration as the graph reaches its peak. Consequently, a detector, some distance away from the aerial, will measure electrostatic force which also oscillates like a sine wave at the same rate as the voltage graph. The polarity of the force will swap round completely, twice every cycle, but the direction in which it is felt will always be at right angles to the direction in which the wave is travelling.

The magnetic part of the wave will be slightly different. The magnetic field round the aerial will be greatest when the electrons are moving the most, and least when they are suffering peak acceleration, because at that time they are just turning round and barely moving. However, it is the change of magnetic field that is propagated as a wave, and the greatest change occurs at the same

189

time as the greatest acceleration of electrons. Consequently the magnetic field is in phase with the electric field. The difference is that the direction in which the magnetic force acts, although at right angles to the direction of propagation of the wave, is also at right angles to the electric field (Figure 82).

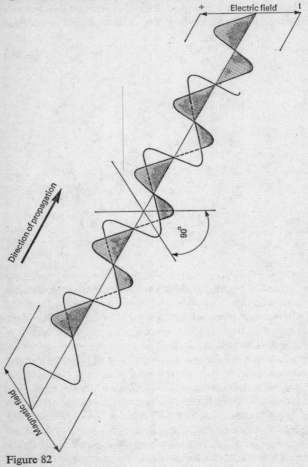

Figure 82

The really interesting thing about electromagnetic radiation is not so much the existence of these fields, but the way in which they are transmitted over such great distances. The main reason for this is to be found in the fact that the intensity of the wave is only inversely proportional to the distance from the source, not inversely proportional to the *square* of the distance, as we have seen for the intensity of electrostatic force. Because of this, aerials by no means radiate spherically and, in fact, to get them to work well the design can be quite critical. However, before we can understand

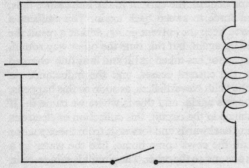

Figure 83

this, it will be necessary to go back to the problem of producing our required high-frequency oscillation, which is, after all, the heart of the process.

To find out what is needed for an oscillator, we must go back to some circuitry. The simplest electronic oscillator is called a tank circuit, and as with most oscillators it consists basically of capacitance and inductance. Figure 83 shows a tank circuit, and let us imagine that the capacitance has been charged up, and there is an excess of electrons on one plate, a deficiency on the other. The capacitor cannot discharge because the switch in the circuit is open. The other end of the circuit is an inductance, and the moment the switch is closed, electrons from the negative plate in the capacitor will rush round the circuit towards the positive plate. In rushing round, which they take a short but very precise time to complete, they amount to a current flowing through the inductance. It will not be a constant current, since there is only a given number of electrons to come from the negative plate before it becomes neutral again.

While the current is flowing through the inductance it builds up a magnetic field around the coils. This means that the lines of force round the coils cut through the turns of wire and in doing so they induce a voltage in the reverse direction of the current. This voltage tends to slow down the rate at which the capacitor discharges. However, as the discharge nears its end and the plates of the capacitor become neutral, the current in the inductance falls, causing the lines of force to sweep back again. This induces a voltage which helps to keep the current going, and as a result the capacitor is charged up again, but this time the other way round.

As soon as the capacitor has taken its fill and is as fully charged as its size permits, the current ceases, and the inductance no longer has a magnetic field. Nevertheless, as soon as this happens, the capacitor discharges again, and this is where we came in. If there were no resistance in the circuit, this collection of electrons would go on swishing backwards and forwards from the capacitor to the inductance till the cows come home, like the water in a bath slopping from one end to the other. The circuit is said to be in resonance.

It takes a very definite time for the water in a bath to slop from one end to the other, and so it does for the electrons to travel from the capacitor to the inductance. Depending on the values of these two components, the circuit will oscillate at a fixed frequency. Unfortunately, there is resistance in the circuit, if only in the wire itself, and the effect is to remove energy all the time. Thus the amplitude of the oscillation steadily falls and eventually dies away, as all free oscillations must. To keep it going we have got to think of a way of feeding energy in to replace the energy removed and turned into heat by the resistance.

What more suitable means of doing this than some form of amplifier? Our problem is to provide steady amplification of a waning oscillation, and provided we can connect an amplifier to the tank circuit in a way that will not affect its capability of resonating, we should be able to ensure a hefty amplitude of

192

oscillation at the output. There are a great many ways of connecting an amplifier to a tank circuit, and to cut a long story short, we will look at just one way of doing it. The secret of it all is our old friend, feedback. If we can tap the tank circuit and take the oscillating signal from it to the base connection of a transistor, we will get an amplified replica of the oscillation across the collector and the emitter (in a common-emitter connection). All we have

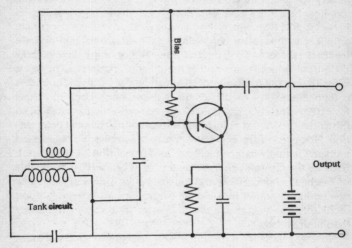

Figure 84

now got to do is to feed back some of the output signal at the emitter to the tank circuit in order to keep giving it a boost.

You will remember that the tank circuit's two basic components are an inductance and a capacitance. Now induction coils are also the components of transformers: we can treat the inductance in the tank circuit as the secondary coil of a transformer, and put the primary circuit in the output from the transistor. The effect will be that the amplified output signal will oscillate in the primary coil on its way out, and induce the secondary coil into greater oscillation, thus pumping up the amplitude of oscillation in the tank circuit. All we now need are some refinements like a bias resistor to make the base of the transistor negative with respect to the emitter, a coupling capacitor to prevent D.C. current being drawn from the tank circuit, likewise in the output circuit.

I mentioned earlier that there were several ways of producing resonant circuits and oscillators, although we are not going to look at them in detail. However, you may remember the undesirable effects that we found in Chapter 7 if positive feedback occurs in an amplifier. One of those effects was to make the amplifier howl, and in fact the howl is just the result of oscillation in the circuit! Consequently all you have to do is to connect up an amplifier with suitable phase-shifting circuitry to obtain positive feedback; the output will then reinforce the input, which reinforces the output, which reinforces the input again and so on. The result is oscillation at a frequency determined by the values of the circuit components. Some oscillators make use of piezo-electric crystals for extremely stable results. We have only met these crystals in so far as they produced voltages as a result of mechanical deformation. However, the reverse also happens: an applied voltage across a crystal actually causes mechanical deformation of the crystal. Because the crystal, like most materials, is 'elastic', it is capable of mechanical resonance, and the associated electrical behaviour can be incorporated in a circuit to produce an extremely good oscillator, less susceptible to changes in its resonant frequency than many others.

Now we can return to the business of transmitting radio signals. We have got our oscillator, and indeed any of the types mentioned can be designed with suitably sized capacitors and inductances to make it oscillate at a frequency high enough for the production of electromagnetic waves. Let us pick a frequency of 1 MHz, or one million cycles per second, and connect the oscillator to a power amplifier of the kind described in Chapter 7: from there we can connect to the aerial. Here we meet our next complication.

Any length of wire conducting alternating current possesses capacitance and inductance of its own, even without coils in it or anything like that. How can this be? If you think about it, because current takes time to travel along a wire, the whole wire is not going to switch its polarity from positive to negative as the current oscillates, all in one go. At any instant, part of the wire will be switching from positive to negative while another part is doing the reverse. Remember the cars at the traffic lights. At any instant, some cars were moving off from rest while others were pulling up. The effect is that lines of force are going to be swishing about with the now familiar inductive effect, and on top of this, the parts of the wire which are negative at any instant are going to have a capacitive effect with those parts of the wire which are positive at the same instant, and vice-versa. Electric charges do not have to be placed conveniently opposite one another on the plates of a capacitor for you to get some form of capacitance.

Now, we know that inductance and capacitance are the ingredients of a resonant circuit, and so surely the aerial itself will resonate at a certain frequency. To find out at what frequency the resonance occurs, we have to find out the distance along the aerial between the points, at any instant, where maximum negative and positive voltages occur. The whole phenomenon is the result of the time it takes for the wave of current to travel along the wire, so if we divide the speed of travel of this wave by the number of oscillations per second we will have the wavelength of the oscillations in the aerial. This wavelength is twice the distance between the points of maximum positive voltage and maximum negative voltage, or the distance between one point of maximum negative voltage and the next. We can say that, because of the characteristics of the metal of the wire, the speed at which the wave of current will travel along the wire is about 80 per cent of the speed of light, which works out at about 240,000 km./sec. The frequency of our oscillator is 1 MHz, so an aerial

$$\frac{240,000}{1,000,000} = 0.24 \text{ km.}$$

or 240 metres, long will be resonant at that frequency.

This will not be much use to us, because as Figure 85 shows, when a full-wave aerial is resonating, one half is carrying current in one direction while the other half is carrying current in the other direction. This is no use, because the radio waves radiated by one half will cancel out the waves radiated by the other half.

195

To overcome this, we must use only a half-wave aerial, which will also resonate at that frequency, but which has only one point of maximum current – in the middle.

Figure 85 shows the voltage and current variations along a half-wave aerial in resonance. The voltage reaches its maximum and

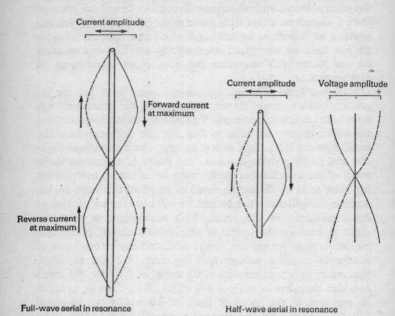

Full-wave aerial in resonance Half-wave aerial in resonance

Figure 85

minimum at the ends, and the current reaches its greatest in the middle. You can regard the ends as the capacitative part of the resonator, since one end will be positive when the other is negative, and there will be electrostatic attraction between the two ends (remember that electromagnetic waves are caused by current, and not voltage, changes). The middle part of the aerial is the inductive part, since the changing value of current in the middle causes lines of force to swish past the ends and induce the voltages there.

196

However, even this half-wave aerial for our 1 MHz signal is going to be 120 metres long, and that is no small aerial. There has to be an easier way of doing it. For much higher frequencies, the aerial will come down to a manageable size, but if you think what would happen with frequencies as low as 100 kHz, the Eiffel Tower would not be big enough.

For medium frequencies, we can halve the length of the aerial again, and have a quarter-wave aerial, but in order for it to work, the bottom end has got to be earthed. What happens is that the current in the aerial induces currents in the earth, and produces a

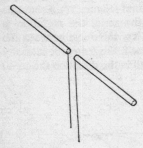

Figure 86

sort of image of the aerial in the ground. Even this, though, is not going to give a short enough aerial for many frequencies, and another way has to be found of cutting down on the length. One method is to turn the aerial over at the top so that it runs parallel with the ground, and its capacitance with the ground is increased. In fact, a 'shortening' capacitor can actually be included in the aerial.

An earthed aerial, one quarter of a wavelength long, is sometimes called a Marconi aerial, after one of the several people involved in the invention of radio. The half-wave aerial, not earthed, is called a dipole, and is often constructed in two halves as shown in Figure 86. Since the greatest current occurs in the centre of a half-wave aerial, it makes sense to place the input there. These aerials are sometimes called Hertz aerials.

Before leaving the aerial, we must have a look at the way in

197

which it radiates electromagnetic waves. We have already discovered that it does not do so spherically, and we talked about radiation patterns which were more cylindrical than spherical. In practice, the radiation pattern of a dipole is much more complex than this, although the cardinal fact, that the intensity decreases in inverse proportion to the distance and not to the square of the distance, of course applies. If you draw lines round a Hertz dipole in the direction in which waves are radiated, and make the length of the lines equivalent to the strength of the radiation in their own direction, you can draw the directivity pattern on paper. If you then draw an 'envelope' of the ends of all the lines, you will get a shape like a doughnut (Figure 87). From this you can see that at right angles to the aerial the radiation is strongest, as you would expect. The less the angle between the direction of radiation and the aerial itself, the lower the intensity of radiation. There is no radiation at all in the direction the aerial itself is pointing.

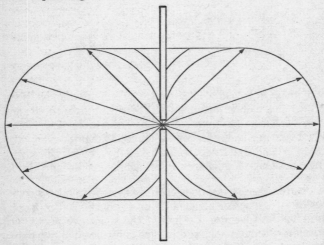

Figure 87

What use, you may ask, is the transmission of the signal oscillating at 1 MHz that we have gone to such lengths to achieve. The object of the exercise was surely to transmit sound, for a start, and even bats cannot begin to hear anything that high-pitched. Well, now that we have mastered the subject of waves, aerials and oscillators, we can get down to the serious business of transmitting information in our radio signal.

We cannot transmit sound waves simply by feeding amplified electrical versions of them straight into an aerial because, for one thing, the frequencies involved would require an aerial thousands of kilometres long; and for another, the great range in frequencies would cause extraordinary things to happen to the waves in as far as their propagation is concerned. The 1 MHz wave, or whatever frequency it may be, is only the carrier wave, and what we have to do is to modulate it somehow in such a way that it is encoded with all the information necessary to enable a meaningful signal to be extracted by the receiver.

A simple and early example of the 'modulation' of a carrier wave was the intermittent interruption of the signal, usually with the use of morse code. Obviously it is no longer remotely practical to send radio messages by morse code except in rare circum-stances, and some way of impressing a much more complex signal onto the carrier wave is necessary.

There are two ways of doing this; the original and simpler way is to make the amplitude of the carrier wave vary in direct proportion to the waveform of the signal to be transmitted. Figure 88c shows a carrier wave which has been subjected to amplitude modulation in this way, together with the sound wave with which it has been modulated. The second method of modula-tion involves no variation in amplitude of the carrier wave, but instead, its frequency is varied in proportion to the amplitude of the transmitted signal. Figure 88d shows the same sound wave as in Figure 88b 'encoded' on the carrier wave by means of frequency modulation.

Amplitude modulation, which is normally used for low- and medium-frequency transmissions, is not quite as easily achieved as you might think. If you just mix together the output of the audio amplifier and the oscillator, all you get is a carrier wave whose amplitude does not vary, and only the polarity of the signal changes (Figure 72, page 171). In order to achieve proper

199

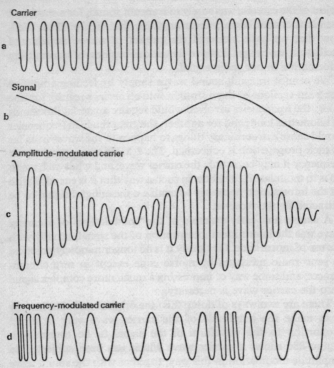

Carrier

a

Signal

b

Amplitude-modulated carrier

c

Frequency-modulated carrier

d

Figure 88

amplitude modulation we must end up with a carrier wave that looks like Figure 88c in which the peak-to-peak values of the wave are altered by the modulation. To do this we will have to have a suitably designed modulating amplifier, and the most usual and convenient method of bringing about the desired result is to use a 'choke-modulation circuit', as shown in Figure 89.

The principle is that instead of the collector of the transistor in the oscillator being supplied with a steady negative voltage from the power supply, it is connected to the output of the audio-frequency amplifier which contains the waveform of the sound to be transmitted, and so the emitter–collector voltage is amplitude modulated; the collector voltage varies in proportion to the audio signal as well as oscillating at the radio frequency of the carrier wave. To minimize distortion it is usual to use only about 80 per cent of the amplitude of the carrier wave for modulation.

Here, an unforeseen problem crops up. We have tacitly assumed that because we are in the field of amplitude modulation and not

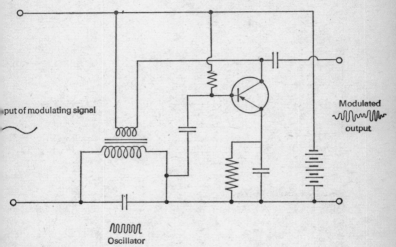

Input of modulating signal

Modulated output

Oscillator

Figure 89

frequency modulation we are coping with just one fixed-frequency carrier wave. Unfortunately, mathematics rears its ugly head, and we find that if you modulate a fixed-frequency carrier wave with another fixed-frequency audio wave you in fact end up with three waves in one. Where the devil did the third one come from? Have you ever driven away from the traffic-lights alongside a noisy lorry, and heard the noise of your car-engine and the lorry-engine interact to give a beat between them? If you have not, get two people to sing a steady note one just out of tune with the other; you will hear a fast beat in the resulting discord. The reason for the beat is that the two notes, of slightly different frequency,

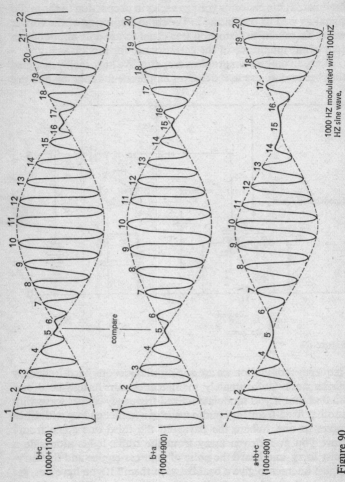

b+c
(1000+1100)

b+a
(1000+900)

a+b+c
(100+900)

compare

1000 HZ modulated with 100HZ
HZ sine wave,

Figure 90

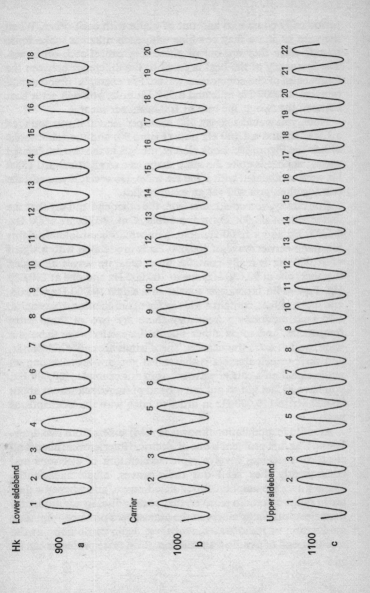

Hk   Lower sideband
900   1 2 3 4 5 6 7 8 9 10 11 12 13 14 15 16 17 18
a

      Carrier
1000 1 2 3 4 5 6 7 8 9 10 11 12 13 14 15 16 17 18 19 20
b

      Upper sideband
1100 1 2 3 4 5 6 7 8 9 10 11 12 13 14 15 16 17 18 19 20 21 22
c

periodically come into and out of phase with each other. When they are in phase they combine with each other to make more sound; when they are out of phase they cancel each other out. The frequency of the beat is equal to the difference between the frequencies of the component waves. For example, if you sound together a 1,000 Hz note and a 900 Hz note, you will get a beat between the two at the rate of 100 beats per second.

Now, you would also get 100 beats per second if you sounded a 1,000 Hz and a 1,100 Hz note (Figure 90) and the result looks rather like Figure 88c. Look closely, though, at the two modulated waves: neither is quite the same shape as a straightforward 1,000 Hz wave modulated with a 100 Hz wave. However, if you add the two together, you will get an exact replica.

Conversely, you could start from the other end and say that the ingredients of a 1,000 Hz note modulated at 100 Hz are a 900 Hz, a 1,000 Hz and a 1,100 Hz note. You would be absolutely right; if a radio carrier wave of 100,000 Hz is modulated with a signal of 10,000 Hz it really contains three separate waves all added together. one at 90,000 Hz, one at 100,000 Hz and one at 110,000 Hz. Few radio broadcasts consist of a single 10,000 Hz whistle, and most, in fact, contain a wide range of modulating frequencies. For each modulating frequency there are two of these extra frequencies, and so on either side of the carrier wave there is a wide band of extra frequencies. These bands are called sidebands, and their principal effect is that when you are broadcasting an audio signal on a carrier wave of, as in our example, 100,000 Hz, you have in fact got to put out a band of frequencies from about 90,000 Hz to 110,000 Hz in order to cope with the sidebands as well.

Amplitude modulation (known as A M) suffers from two drawbacks. The first problem is one of electrical interference: almost all electrical machines involve rapid acceleration of electrons and consequently they send out radio waves, albeit inefficiently. These waves are amplitude-modulated waves, and whenever they are in range of a radio receiver, they cause noise. In addition, random electrical disturbances in the atmosphere produce amplitude modulation of radio waves, and these again cause noise at the receiving end of a radio transmission. Both these problems can be overcome by increasing the power of the transmitter, but this remedy does not make for an efficient system. The other drawback is that it is impossible to transmit high-fidelity audio signals in an AM system. This is because of the sidebands. For hi-fi radio reception, you need to be able to broadcast all the components of audio signals right up to 15,000 Hz, if not 20,000 Hz. The 'airspace' allotted to AM radio channels is usually only 20 kHz wide, and most broadcasting stations use only 15 kHz of a channel to avoid interference with neighbouring stations. This means that you cannot modulate the carrier wave, whatever its frequency, with a modulating frequency higher than 7,500 Hz, and this severely restricts the quality of reproduction. The unfortunate thing is that this drawback to AM is purely arbitrary and man-made. It dates from the days when electronics was so primitive that broadcasting was only practical using frequencies from about 300 to 15,000 kHz or, as AM stations are usually designated, wavelengths from 1,000 metres to 200 metres. Consequently, the bandwidth assigned to each station had to be deliberately restricted in order to cram as many transmissions as possible into the available airspace.

To overcome the problems of AM, the other method of modulation we have already mentioned briefly, frequency modulation, was introduced just before the Second World War. Frequency modulation, or FM, is a highly effective way of getting over the interference and noise problem since the receiver is insensitive to amplitude variations. On the other hand, the bandwidth problem is in some ways made worse, since FM requires a leeway of up to 150 kHz around the carrier-wave frequency. However, FM came into use at about the time that it was becoming possible to broadcast at frequencies as high as 300 MHz, and the whole of the VHF band from 30 to 200 MHz was available. A band from 88 MHz to 108 MHz was assigned to FM broadcasting, and each station is normally allotted a channel width of 0·2 MHz. By this means, 100 FM stations can operate in the same area.

In an FM signal, as we have already discovered, the amplitude of the carrier wave remains constant. When modulated, the frequency of the carrier wave is made to swing up and down, and the number of times it swings up and down per second is equal to

205

the frequency of the modulating signal. Before we can go any further then, we have got to find a circuit which will do this.

In the old days, it was common to achieve frequency modulation by including in the oscillator circuit a valve which acted like a capacitance whose value was controlled by the grid voltage. The latter was connected to the modulating signal, and so the resonant frequency of the tank circuit was varied in proportion to the amplitude of the modulating signal. However, if you are using a crystal oscillator, you cannot do this since the frequency of the oscillator is dependent on the properties of the crystal. Consequently it is more common to use phase modulation instead of frequency modulation.

Phase modulation in effect amounts to frequency modulation. If you look at Figure 91, which shows a frequency-modulated carrier wave, you can see that what is involved is the moving of the crests of the wave either to the left or to the right, by varying degrees. Is that not what phase alteration is? At points 3, 8, 13 and 18, curve (a) in Figure 91 is 180° out of phase with curve (b), and the only difference between the two is that the waves in (b) have been pushed to one side. If, therefore, by means of some fiendishly clever circuitry, we can get the individual waves of the carrier pushed to the left or to the right, in proportion to the amplitude of the audio signal which we want to impress on the carrier, we will have our FM signal.

To do this we must go back to the AM state of affairs, and those sidebands again. The effect of adding the two sidebands to the carrier is to produce the modulated carrier (Figure 90). Let us see what happens if we put the carrier constantly 90° out of phase with the sidebands. We lose our amplitude modulation altogether, and gain phase modulation! All we need to do this is a device called a balanced modulator to suppress the carrier wave from the output of an AM modulating circuit, and to replace the carrier with another which has been through a circuit to shift it 90°. The refinements include a frequency inverter which reduces the amplitude of the modulating signal in proportion to its frequency, to overcome the difficulty which arises in phase modulation due to the frequency deviation of the carrier being proportional to the frequency of the modulating signal as well as to the amplitude.

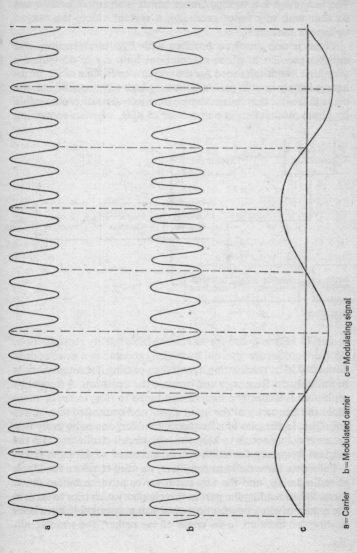

a = Carrier   b = Modulated carrier   c = Modulating signal

Figure 91

The final stage is a voltage limiter which is an amplifier designed so that with any input exceeding a certain value, the output voltage is constant.

There is one unsolved problem with FM broadcasting, and another peculiar to phase modulation; both are to do with the very high frequencies used for the carrier waves. One of the problems is simply how to generate the very high-frequency signal, the other is the fact that the maximum frequency deviation obtainable by phase modulation is only about 25 kHz, whereas something

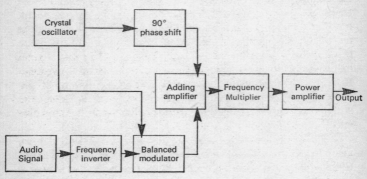

Figure 92

nearer 75 kHz is called for to achieve high-fidelity reproduction. Both difficulties are resolved by initially generating a wave of only about 200 kHz, modulating it, and then passing it through circuits to multiply the frequency and increase the deviation. A frequency multiplier is basically a tank circuit tuned to two, three, or more times the frequency of the input signal and connected to a power amplifier. In the case of a frequency doubler, one pulse every two cycles is quite enough to keep the tank circuit oscillating, and the original frequency deviation will be increased at the same time.

Before we leave radio transmitters, we need to take a final look at radio aerials, and the way radio waves are transmitted down them. When reading the part in this chapter which tries to explain the nature of electromagnetic waves, you may possibly have been waiting for mention to be made of the aether, the strange, all-pervading medium in which these waves travel. Well, it does not exist. It was invented in the days then they thought the waves were a deformation of an elastic medium, as sound waves are of air, but this is now known not to be the case. Although radio waves do not travel in a medium of their own, this does not mean, however, that they are unaffected by any other medium through which they may happen to pass.

Our radio waves leave the aerial, travelling at the speed of light, and as far as we Earth-bound mortals are concerned, they will most of the time be travelling through air. They will also travel through other things, like bricks and mortar, to a certain extent, but they will not get through electrically active materials, such as metals. On setting off from the aerial, some waves will be able to travel directly from the aerial to the receiver. However, a great many waves will travel downwards and be reflected off the ground. In fact at low frequencies, depending upon the nature of the ground, there is an odd effect where the waves travel along the surface at higher frequencies, ground-absorption reduces this effect.

Some waves travel up into the sky and are reflected down again by the ionosphere, where there are electrically ionized layers to provide a sort of radio mirror. It is this effect that makes it possible to transmit signals of high frequency over long distances, such as across the Atlantic. However, the ionosphere is rather unstable, since it is the result of intense radiation from the sun at altitudes of up to 250 miles, and is subject to all sorts of disturbances of the sun and the atmosphere.

All forms of wave propagation are subject to a phenomenon known as diffraction. In acoustics, diffraction is the mechanism which enables you to hear round corners when there are no reflecting surfaces to help. Exactly the same happens with electromagnetic waves, even with light. Indeed, the reason you cannot see round corners is because the wavelength of light is so short that the effects of diffraction are difficult to detect, but with radio waves of long wavelength the effects are large. Wavelengths, we have already found, are calculated by dividing the speed of propagation of a wave by the number of cycles per second. Our 1 MHz wave, once it has left the aerial, will have a length of

$$\frac{299,780}{1,000,000} = 0.299,780 \text{ kilometres, or } 299.780 \text{ metres.}$$

The effects of diffraction are greater with increasing wavelength and since we know how great they can be with sound, where wavelengths are of the order of only a few metres at the longer end of the scale, you can appreciate that the effects with radio waves can be very much greater.

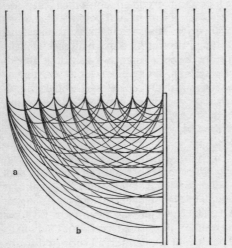

Figure 93

Why does diffraction occur? What happens is that all waves when propagated from their source have a natural tendency to spread out in all directions; were it not for a phenomenon called interference, they would always radiate in all directions, and round the sharpest corners you would get perfect reception. However, the shorter the wavelength, the less are waves able to do this because for geometrical reasons they tend to cancel each other out at angles away from the principal direction of travel (Figure 93). Consequently, low-frequency radio waves can travel quite long distances by bending over the horizon, but very high-frequency

210

signals (VHF) behave much more like light, and ultra-high-frequency signals (UHF), of frequency up to 3,000 MHz and wavelength down to the order of 100 millimetres, really only travel along lines of sight.

Frequency Range	Wavelength Range	Application
30–300 kHz	10,000–1,000 m	Marine and broadcasting (Long Wave)
300–3,000 kHz	1,000–100 m	Broadcasting (Medium Wave)
3–30 MHz	100–10 m	General communication (Short Wave)
30–300 MHz	10–1 m	VHF television and radio, radar, air and marine navigation
300–3,000 MHz	1–0·1 m	UHF television, radar, microwave communication
3,000–30,000 MHz	0·1–0·01 m	Radar and navigation

Frequencies above and below this range are also, if rarely, used.

Table 3. The radio spectrum

Table 3 shows the range of frequencies used for radio transmission, and you can see that the range with which the man in the street comes into contact is very large. Propagation of long-wave transmissions is no great problem, because diffraction occurs to a considerable extent, and the direct wave from the transmitter to the receiver will carry long distances. At the other end of the scale, great difficulties can arise with UHF transmissions because of screening, either by the horizon, hills, or buildings. The problem is made slightly easier by the fact that the atmosphere does tend to scatter UHF waves, but many people who have suffered bad UHF television reception will know that it can be a difficult business to ensure that the waves reach all the areas around the transmitter.

Let us now leave the transmitting end of things and look at the reception. This is, after all, where most of us come in, and what more natural point from which to start the story of radio reception than the receiving aerial. This end, the aerial has not nearly such an exacting task to perform as it had when it was transmitting. It does not have to discharge into space a sizeable amount of power in the form of electromagnetic radiation; it has merely to lie back and be titillated by the caresses of passing radio waves, and let the receiver set sort out the meaningful signal it requires.

As radio waves pass a conductor, they induce in it voltages which are proportional to the length of the conductor, and for our present purposes, a simple length of wire will suffice for our aerial. Radio waves are a form of energy, and you might think that if you use a big enough aerial you ought to be able to put the energy picked up by the aerial to direct use. This you can indeed do, with the aid of some simple circuitry, and many will know that you can listen for hours to AM broadcasts by means of a crystal set relying purely on the strength of the power in the radio waves themselves.

The first problem to be overcome is that the aerial will of course pick up a whole cacophonous confusion of signals, and we only want one signal borne by a carrier wave of one frequency. Let us therefore connect the aerial in series with the primary winding of a transformer, and earth the end that is not sticking out into space. The secondary winding of the transformer becomes the inductance in a tank circuit, and the very weak current induced in the aerial contains, among other things, a component at the resonant frequency of the tank circuit. It will set the tank circuit oscillating, and the amplitude of the oscillations will follow the amplitude modulation of the carrier wave imparted to it at the transmitter. The capacitor in the tank circuit will be variable so that the circuit's resonant frequency can be tuned in to match the carrier frequency. The tank circuit can be tuned to select any carrier frequency within a 'band' permitted by the range of variability of the tuning capacitor. If necessary, another higher, or lower, band can be selected by switching in induction coils of higher, or lower, fixed values. Before we go any further, we should remember that the design of the tank circuit must not make its tuning so sharp that it will not pick up the sidebands as well, because, as we know, it is thanks to them that we have any modulation at all.

What has to be done now is to turn the modulated carrier back into a replica of a sound wave. This calls for a detector circuit. In its simplest form, a detector will consist, first of all, of a rectifier. You will remember that an amplitude-modulated carrier wave is symmetrical top and bottom, and if we somehow extract just the carrier, we will not be left with the modulation, because the top half will cancel out the bottom half. A rectifier will stop the bot-

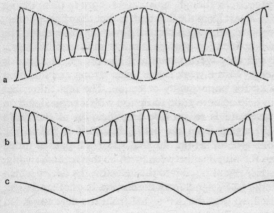

Figure 94

tom half from getting through, because it is a device which allows current to flow in one direction but not the other. This is where the crystal in a crystal set comes in.

Crystals and cat's whiskers were the forerunners of semiconductor diodes, and current was able to pass from the point of the tungsten cat's whisker into the crystal, but not back again, just as current can pass across a forward-biased N-P junction, but not in the reverse direction. This rectifies the signal from the aerial and the tank circuit so that it looks like Figure 94b. All that remains is to get shot of the carrier wave and we will be left with only the modulating sound wave. This can be done providing a low-impedance by-pass route for the high-frequency carrier, leaving only the lower-frequency modulation signal to develop a voltage across the output load. We therefore shunt a capacitor across the output with a low enough value to offer a very high impedance path to audio frequencies only. We are finally left with an audio signal with just enough power in it to drive the coils of a pair of headphones. In the old days many a schoolboy made his own crystal set, and even now the cost of the headphones would be the only reason why making a radio with a semiconductor diode instead of a crystal costs pounds and not pence.

Most radio receivers, though, have rather more to them than a crystal set does. Apart from the fact that, rather than headphones, they have loudspeakers, which require power to drive them, the detection and amplification process is rather more sophisticated. A crystal set will only work passably if the broadcast signal is good and strong. With a weak signal, even strong amplification cannot make up for poor-quality detection. The first thing that can be done to help achieve good reception with a weak signal on a crowded waveband is to provide amplification of the radio frequency (RF) signal from the aerial, before it is fed to the detector. In one type of set-up, the first stage is a pair of tuned circuits with an RF amplifier between them, so that a good, strong, modulated carrier signal is fed into the detector, the device which extracts the audio (AF) signal from the carrier. In another design, feedback is used, so that the AF signal from the detector is fed back to the RF amplifier which is made to do double-duty and re-amplify the AF signal as well as the RF signal. The AF output is then fed to a power-amplification stage and then to the loudspeaker. Alternatively, the output from the detector can be fed right back to the input, to the tuned circuit, through a phase-changer to achieve regenerative feedback.

The feedback process is done in a rather neat way, making use of the type of aerial that is used in modern portable radios, the ferrite rod. Ferrite is a relatively recent innovation; a chemical compound incorporating ferric oxide (of which lodestones are made up) the molecules of which have had one of their iron atoms replaced by one of a metal such as copper or zinc. The material is then strongly magnetic, but has a resistance which is thousands of times greater than pure iron. The compound is made (for our purposes) into rods by a sintering process which produces an extremely strong crystalline structure.

A ferrite-rod aerial will consist of the basic rod, about 200 mm. long at most, and up to 8 mm. in diameter. Tuned coils are then wound around it, over a paper sleeve; in a radio capable of receiving both medium and long wavebands, the medium-wave coil may be at one end and the long-wave coil at the other. In acting as an aerial, the coils on the rod are sensitive to the magnetic field of an arriving radio wave, and because of the ferrite's extremely high susceptibility to magnetism, the oscillating magnetic field set up in the coils produces a high flux density (p. 64) in the rod. In other words the coils are rendered much more inductive.

We can now answer the question why you have to twiddle transistor radios round before you get good reception: in order to get the greatest strength of magnetic field in the ferrite rod, it must be turned so that it is at 90° to the direction of the signal approach. Not only is this sort of aerial extremely compact, but also we can use the inductance of the aerial coil and rod as part of our tuned circuit. All we need to do is to connect the ends of the coil to a variable capacitor or, in rarer cases, to a fixed value capacitor when tuning will be achieved by sliding the coil up and down the ferrite rod.

When feedback is required, it can be very tidily achieved by feeding the output from the detector and phase changer to a coupling coil on the same ferrite rod as the aerial coil. Whereas the aerial coil may have as many as 80 turns, the coupling coil can have as few as 5, and the changing magnetic field round the coupling coil will induce a stronger replica in the aerial coil.

Now let us leave these plebeian receivers and move on to the élite of the radio world, the 'superheterodyne' receiver. Almost all the most expensive commercial radio sets are this type, because in just about every respect the performance is superior to any other design of receiver; its performance is about as impressive as its name.

This is how a superheterodyne receiver works: the aerial signal is fed into a tuned circuit in the usual way, but after that it is mixed with another signal, generated locally within the receiver. You will remember that when we were discussing sidebands we saw that when two sine waves were mixed, a third wave was produced, of frequency midway between them, which was modulated, or had superimposed upon it, a beat of frequency equal to the difference between the component frequencies. In just the same way, if you mix with a carrier wave received from the aerial, a locally-generated signal of slightly different frequency, you will find yourself with a third wave of frequency equal to the difference between the two. The third wave will still be encoded with the original modulation so that an audio signal can eventually be extracted.

By producing a beat-frequency, you can overcome a great many of the limitations of amplifying incoming radio signals. The first point is that the tuned circuits in the set can all be of fixed frequency, since the locally generated oscillation can itself be varied in frequency to ensure that the beat-frequency is always the same. Because the tuned circuits do not have to be variable, they can be made much more efficient. The amplification of a tuned RF stage varies with the tuning capacitor owing to the resulting change in the impedance of the circuit. This difficulty is eliminated with superheterodyning, and the result is uniform gain and selectivity at all frequencies; an extremely useful advantage.

After the beat-frequency, or intermediate-frequency (IF), signal has been produced by the heterodyning process, it is passed to an IF amplifier, and then to a detector, in order to extract the AF signal, or demodulate the IF signal. Superheterodyne circuits often incorporate an automatic gain-control device to keep the volume of the output in constant proportion to the strength of the input signal. This is achieved by feedback from the detector to the IF amplifier.

So far we have only talked about radio receivers capable of dealing with amplitude-modulated transmissions such as are used on long, medium and short waveband broadcasts. However, as the last chapter showed, the fidelity of sound reproduction possible with AM is restricted by the cramming of too many stations into too little airspace. Anyone buying a new radio, even if he does not want high-fidelity sound, should almost always go for an FM set, sometimes just called a VHF receiver, because not only is the quality so much better, but interference is greatly reduced. In addition, some broadcasts are now only available on VHF.

The biggest difference between an FM and an AM receiver, apart from the very much higher frequencies of the carrier waves, is in the design of the demodulating circuit, or detector. It is no longer just a simple matter of a rectifier and shunt capacitor, because in FM the amplitude of the audio-signal wave is proportional not to the amplitude of modulation of the carrier, but to the degree of deviation of the carrier signal from its centre-frequency. We have therefore got to have a sort of frequency-measuring circuit. How is it done?

The carrier wave, as we have said, is of very high frequency, even up to 100 MHz, and the first stage after amplification of the RF signal from the aerial will be to use our friend the super-heterodyne. By this means, the carrier frequency will be brought down to something more manageable, like 10 MHz. The frequency deviations caused by the modulation will be within the range of 75 kHz on either side of the carrier, and will not themselves have been affected by the heterodyning.

The detection circuit will consist first of all of a resonant tank circuit whose frequency is that of the carrier wave after hetero-dyning, 10 MHz in our example. There will then be two more tank circuits (Figure 95), one tuned at a higher frequency than the carrier, the other to a lower one. They are known as 'detuned' circuits, and the whole set-up as a 'detuned discriminator'. Now, as we have seen before, the response of a tuned circuit is not so sharp that it resonates at precisely its centre-frequency, and not at all at a frequency 1 Hz higher or 1 Hz lower. The response-curve in fact falls off progressively at increasing or decreasing frequencies, to form quite a smooth 'hill' of a curve (Figure 95a).

It is the two detuned tank circuits that are of most interest. They are connected together in opposition, so that the response curve of one is 'upside down' with respect to the other; when the two curves are combined, the resultant response curve looks like Figure 95d. You can see that, as a result of combining the two response curves, we are left with a nice straight centre section

217

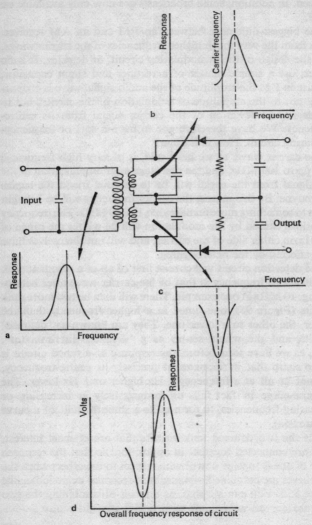

Figure 95

where the output voltage of the circuit increases directly in proportion to an increase in carrier frequency. This is just what we want.

Now we can put the discriminator together. The tank circuit tuned to the carrier centre-frequency is the first stage, and its job is, as with A M, to pick out the carrier wave we want from the jumble of broadcasts. Its response is such that the deviations in frequency are also picked up. The circuitry of this stage also includes a limiter to make sure that any extraneous amplitude-modulation which may have got in owing to atmospheric, or other interference, is removed by ensuring constant amplitude of the input signal. After this, the inductance of the first tuned circuit is used as a primary transformer coil, the two secondaries of which are the inductances of the two detuned circuits.

What happens is this: the constant-amplitude carrier signal with its frequency variations is picked up by the tuned circuit; the oscillation in the inductance of the first circuit tries to induce similar oscillations in the inductances, and hence in the tank circuits themselves, of the two oppositely-coupled detuned circuits. When the carrier wave is exactly at its centre-frequency, it excites both detuned circuits in an equally weak manner. Because they are connected in opposition, there is no net output. However, if the carrier signal deviates in frequency upwards, as it will to represent a rise in amplitude of the wave with which it is modulated, then the carrier will be nearer to the resonant frequency of one of the detuned circuits, and further away from the other. The result will be a stronger response in one circuit and a weaker response in the other. Figure 95d shows that this gives a rise in voltage at the output. On the other hand, if the frequency of the carrier wave drops, to represent a fall in the voltage of the modulating A F signal, then the oscillation in the detuned circuits will be closer to the other resonant frequency (the one which has been turned 'upside-down'), and further away from the former, with the result that there will be a drop in voltage at the output. Now you can see that as the frequency of the carrier wave sweeps up and down, so the voltage at the output from the joined-up detuned circuits oscillates in exactly the same manner as did the original audio signal before it was encoded into the carrier.

219

From here on, an FM receiver is very much like an AM receiver in that what is now required is amplification of the detected audio signal. The usual arrangements of feedback are often used, as is a circuit system for ensuring accurate and automatic tuning to the broadcast station, called an automatic frequency control or AFC. However, if you own an FM radio, you will have noticed that you cannot use a ferrite rod for an aerial; you either have to have an extending, telescopic antenna, or an outside aerial. The reason for this is that the coils in the ferrite rod have to be tuned to the frequency of the broadcast, and it is not possible to achieve frequencies as high as those used in FM this way. In the circuitry as a whole, considerably greater problems arise in avoiding losses in wiring, or distortion of the high-frequency oscillations.

You might have gathered from all this that to make a simple AM radio yourself would not be all that difficult, and indeed, once you have mastered the tricky business of using a soldering iron without burning the component you are soldering, yourself or the table, and still get the correct amount of solder in the right place, you could well get an urge to try making a crystal set. Still more, when your portable transistor goes phut, you will probably stare at the conglomeration which reveals itself when the back comes off, and wish you knew what to do. Unfortunately, the effort in trying to repair a cheap little set is very often just not worth it, and on a better set, you stand a chance of ruining it completely if you try yourself.

Faults usually range from dead silence, general crackling, or weak, distorted or interfered-with signals. Sometimes the cause is simpler than it seems. If you examine the printed circuit-board in good light with a magnifying glass you may find a hairline crack across one of the fine copper conductors, or alternatively you may find that the thin wires running from the ferrite rod have broken or come adrift. Leads anywhere may have parted and soldered joints come unstuck. If you look more carefully you may find a resistor that shows signs of scorching through overheating or a capacitor may have become distorted, causing a short-circuit through it.

Many faults are invisible though, and unless you are a real

expert you will not be able to get any further without a circuit-diagram for a start, and even after reading this book you could easily confuse many a circuit-diagram with the Paris Métro, and to set about systematically tracing a fault would prove impossible even if you had the equipment. Never tamper with a television, and take extreme care with a mains-operated radio.

10 Fictive Pictures

Television broadcasting

When you listen to a sound radio, in one second you will receive information in the form of up to 20,000 electronic oscillations. When you watch a television for the same length of time, it takes up to 5,500,000 electronic oscillations to bring the sight and sound to which so many millions of people are addicted. Think of the complexity of transmitting pictures by radio: not only has a picture got to be broken down into a single continuous signal, but the receiver has to put it all back together again in an intelligible form. Not only this, but the colour of the picture has to be split up, transmitted and reassembled with all the other information to produce as good a picture as a cine film in your own home, even though the broadcast may come live, in colour, from the moon.

Ask somebody how a television picture is made up, and he will probably say that on the screen are hundreds of horizontal lines, which each consist of a sliver of picture. This is not really true; in a monochrome set it may look as though there are a lot of lines, but in fact a television picture is really made up in exactly the same way as a newspaper photograph, with dots. The advantage a newspaper has over a television is that it can give you all the dots in a picture simultaneously. What a newspaper cannot do is give you a moving picture; a television can and does send you fifty newspaper pictures every second.

Most people know about the phenomenon of the persistence of vision. Move your finger fast across your field of vision and you will see it leave a ghostly trail behind it. Compared with your vision of the amazed expression of the person opposite you, the image of your finger has travelled quite quickly across the retina of your eye. Now your retina is also a bit like a newspaper picture, but instead of dots, there is a myriad of tiny sensors called rods. These are the things which give a sensation of brightness: there are corresponding sensors, called cones, which give you information about colour. When light falls on a rod, a chemical reaction takes place in order to stimulate a tiny lead from the optic nerve, and like all chemical reactions it takes time to happen. When the said light ceases, another chemical reaction occurs which stimulates the optic nerve to tell the brain that the light has gone; this too takes time. The time involved is about 80 milliseconds, or about one twelfth of a second.

If one rod in the retina receives a glint of light every twelfth of a second, the reaction from one will not have died away before the next occurs, and indeed any light which flashes more than about 15 times per second cannot be distinguished from a continuous beam. If you have a 'home-movie' projector, its normal projection speed will be 18 frames per second. You have probably noticed that this is only just fast enough to prevent the picture flickering as frame after frame come up on the screen; in fact, if the subject of the picture is changing fast, such as in a fast 'pan' of the camera, it will flicker, as it will with a small reduction in projection speed.

The dots on a television screen are brought to us one by one, and put on the screen by a ray of electrons from a gun. When the ray strikes the screen, it causes the phosphor-coating of the screen to glow, and this too involves finite time intervals. The ray of electrons (called a cathode ray) in a 25-inch television travels across the screen at a speed of nearly 15,000 miles per hour (10 times Concorde's top speed!). Or, put another way, it travels from left to right 15,625 times a second. At the end of each scan, it flies back to the left hand side and starts again. At the same time, the ray is being moved down the screen 50 times a second, and each time it gets to the bottom it flies back up to the top again. We shall see just how this is achieved later; for the time being we must just sort out exactly what it is that makes up the picture.

Although we cannot see them individually, on each horizontal line there is what amounts to a line of dots. In order to achieve the same degree of definition in both the vertical plane and the horizontal, each dot is as broad as it is long. Bearing in mind that a television screen, or 'raster' as it is sometimes called, is oblong in the ratio of 4:3, you will find that we are talking about a total number of dots of over 400,000. As we have said, what television boils down to is the transmission of a frame of dot-pictures once every fiftieth of a second. The process is not unlike the way you are reading this book, page by page, letter by letter, left to right, top to bottom. Your eye goes to the top of the page and scans the first line, flies back, scans the second, and so on. Each letter is analogous to a dot on the raster. At the bottom of the page you fly back to the top of the next, and the rate of horizontal eye-deflection is greater than the rate of vertical deflection in proportion to the number of lines on the page.

With television scanning, though, there is a big problem brought about by the sheer number of pieces of information to be conveyed in the time. To cover 400,000 dots, 50 times per second, would mean transmitting frequencies of over 20 MHz, which call for the use of astronomically high carrier-frequencies. This is not possible, and in an effort to bring things down to earth, the cathode ray is made to scan only every alternate line in each frame, covering the lines it has missed out in the next frame. If you have an acrobatic mind you will already have discovered this by dividing the frequency of the horizontal scanning-rate by the vertical $\left(\dfrac{15,625}{50}\right)$ and getting the answer of 312·5, half the number of lines in a 625-line set. In fact the bandwidth of a video signal is not even as high as half of 20 MHz, since good pictures result from a frequency of up to 5·5 MHz.*

Just as the dots in a newspaper picture are all of varying blackness, so the dots in a television picture are all of varying brightness, and we shall soon find out how the brightness is transmitted as a fluctuating voltage which controls the strength of the cathode ray and thus the degree of glow of the phosphor on the screen.

To get to the bottom of the workings of television, we must first take a trip to the beginning of the line, the camera in the

---

*You can appreciate why the changeover to the 625-line system also meant that the broadcast frequencies had to go up from the VHF band to the UHF band. As a point of interest, if age has not dulled your high-frequency hearing, you will know why the soft whistle from the inside of an old 405-line set has become a (to some people upsetting) very high-frequency singing noise. This is because the horizontal scanning-rate has gone up from 10,125 Hz to 15,625 Hz, and the vibration of the picture tube at this frequency radiates sound.

studio. Since all new television programmes are in colour, and because we have only one chapter to talk about it in, we are going to concentrate on colour from now on. If you have not got a colour set, you should spend less on the car and get one, because for most people colour television is to black-and-white as an old master is to a snapshot. You have the added sensation of colour and, with careful choice of set and good servicing, the colour can be as good as in a cinema; the picture appears completely free of lines, with vastly improved definition, and it somehow gains an extra impression of depth.

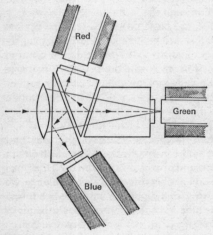

Figure 96

There are three primary colours: red, green and blue, and by adding together varying amounts of light in any of these colours, you can synthesize any colour you wish. If you shine a beam, of the right intensity, of each primary colour on to a screen you will have a white spot where they all converge. (If you add the colours by mixing paint instead of light beams you end up with a shade of mud because that way you are subtracting light, not adding it.) Conversely, the light reflected from any object can be divided up into its red, green and blue components.

225

After the light from the scene to be televised has passed through the lens of the camera, the first thing that happens is that it passes through 'dichrotic interference mirrors' which to you and me are just partial reflectors, often in the form of prisms, which only let through light of a certain colour. By this means, the image is divided into three – red, blue and green – and the three parts beamed to three separate camera tubes. In principle, each tube is basically the same as the single tube in a monochrome camera, and there are several types; the one most commonly used in modern television broadcasting is called a 'plumbicon', after the lead (Latin, *plumbum*) monoxide used in it. Two other types of tube are the 'image orthicon' and the 'vidicon'.

In all three types of tube, the basic process is that the optical image is focused on a small screen with special electrical properties, which is scanned from the other side by an electron beam in the same way as in a television screen. Before pressing on, therefore, we must take a preliminary look at what an electron-gun is. Let us think about the job required of it: to produce a fine stream of electrons in the form of a beam which falls on a screen or target and is capable of being deflected to and fro with great versatility. The first problem, though, is to achieve a beam of electrons, and to do this we have got to find a way of persuading electrons to take leave of a conductor and travel away from it. Does this sound familiar? Do you remember the brief acquaintance we made with thermionic valves? In a diode, for instance, we found that in an evacuated glass tube, a heated cathode could be given a negative potential with respect to an anode. The negative charge on the cathode would cause it to be bulging with electrons, which the heat would make highly agitated, so much so that, across the empty space between, the positive attraction of the anode was quite enough to make them stream off the cathode towards the anode and thus form a current between them.

Now, the electrons in a diode valve do not travel in a neat, controlled beam; this has to be achieved with a series of grids which have a positive potential and holes in the middle. Their action is to accelerate the electrons by exerting a powerful attraction, and then allowing some of them to stream on through the hole. The electrons emerging from the hole will still have a tendency to diverge, because they have a mutually repellant effect on each other. There therefore has to be a magnetic or electrostatic focusing-ring, which we shall look at in more detail later.

In a plumbicon camera tube, the light from the optical side of the camera is focused on a small glass sheet coated with a thin, transparent, electrically-conductive layer of stannic oxide, on which is deposited a layer of lead monoxide. The inner surface of the lead monoxide is doped to turn it into a P-type semiconductor, and the opposite side doped to make it N-type. The lead monoxide is 'photoconductive' which means that when light falls on it, the coated glass sheet (known as the 'target') offers a low resistance to current, whereas in the dark it is highly resistive.

The target is scanned on the inside surface by an electron beam, which is caused to sweep side to side and top to bottom under the influence of oscillations applied to the scanning coils just down-stream of the gun (we shall find out just how this happens later).

The photoconductive layer on the target, through the transparent conducting screen of stannic oxide, is connected into a circuit with the cathode of the electron gun across a load resistor. The circuit is arranged so that the target is at a positive potential with respect to the cathode. Now suppose the camera is pointed into a bright, even light. The lenses of the camera will cast bright light all over the target, making the whole of it conductive. Electrons will stream on to it in a beam from the gun and, since the target has a positive potential, it will attract electrons into it from the beam and cause a current to flow into the layer of stannic oxide and out into the circuit. This will result in there being a drop in voltage across the load resistor. At the other extreme, if you put the lens cap on the camera, the target will be in the dark, and highly resistive. This will cause a rise in voltage at the output.

Now let the camera operate in the normal way and an image, consisting of a host of patches of varying brightness and darkness, will be cast upon the target. The electron beam will scan the whole image at great speed. While it is passing over bright patches, the resistance will drop, current will flow and the voltage at the output will fall. However, as it moves across dark patches, the target will form a high resistance in the circuit causing a higher voltage across it.

You can see that as the electron beam scans the tiny picture which is focused on the target, the voltage at the output from the

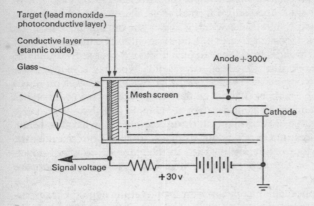

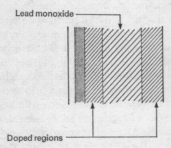

Figure 97

circuit will vary in inverse proportion to the brightness of the spot in the picture which the beam is traversing at that instant. This is just what we want, and it gives us the basis of an electronic signal which can be broadcast along with all the necessary synchronizing pulses to form a television picture at the other end.

Each of the three tubes in a colour camera analyses the three colour elements of the same picture at the same time. It is important that the images that they are scanning should be identical as far as positioning and registration is concerned. This calls for very great precision, both mechanical and electronic.

We now find ourselves with three electronic signals, one for blue, red and green, and somehow or other we have got to encode the information in these signals in a manner suitable for broadcasting. You could, in theory, attempt to broadcast each signal differently as if they were three different programmes, but this would be highly inefficient. Instead of this, it is better to redistribute the duties of the signals: the way it is at the moment, each signal represents the brightness of each colour-component at each spot on the television screen. However, if you think about it, why transmit information about brightness three times over? Brightness, to the eye, is one sensation, colour another, so why not transmit one brightness or 'luminance' signal, and another, or others, which simply indicate the proportions of primary colours which are necessary to reconstitute the picture in the correct colours. These other signals are called 'chrominance' signals. There is of course another very good reason why a luminance signal should be broadcast as well as the chrominance signals, which is that we must not forget all the poor, deprived owners of black-and-white sets. A colour broadcast must be of a sort which can be received by a black-and-white set without any modification being required of it.

The tubes in a colour camera are set so that when 'white' light enters the lens, each tube gives the same amplitude of signal at its output. White is in fact a matter of judgement, and there are agreed standards of the make-up of white light as far as colour television is concerned. However, the human eye has peculiarities as many other organs do, and it does not consider light at one end of the spectrum to be as bright as at the other. In fact, if you arrange beams of the three primary colours so that they converge on a screen into a white spot, you will find that the physical intensities of the beams are very different. The green will be the strongest, nearly twice as strong as the red, which will in turn be almost three times the strength of the blue. In precise terms, the relative luminosities of the primary colours are:

	%
Green	58·7
Red	29·9
Blue	11·4
Total:	100·0

You will not see pink elephants if we take the proportions as 11 per cent for blue, 59 per cent for green and 30 per cent for red. The consequence is that, since camera tubes are inanimate objects, they are not susceptible to the same nuances as our eyes, and if we are going to mix the outputs of the three tubes to make a luminance signal, they are each going to have to be attenuated by appropriate amounts to give us a subjectively correct, monochrome picture. The outputs from the three tubes therefore pass through an electronic matrix to produce the luminance, or Y-signal as it is called.

All we now need for the chrominance signals are what are sometimes called colour-difference signals, one representing the difference between the blue signal and the Y-signal, the other the difference between the red and the Y-signal. This gives us all the information we require, because information about green is simply obtained by combining the red and blue colour-difference signals: since any part of the intensity of the Y-signal that cannot be accounted for as blue or red must be green.

The most difficult part of the business is surely going to be transmitting all this in a practical way. The most important thing to transmit is of course the Y-signal so that, if nothing else, the monochrome boys will have an evening's entertainment. Let us concentrate on this to begin with. Figure 98 shows a typical monochrome video signal. As the scanning beam in the camera reaches the end of a line, a synchronizing pulse is transmitted, which is the moment when the beam has to fly back to the next line. These pulses are square in waveform and occur approximately every 64 microseconds, the time one line-scan takes to complete. Then, of course, it is necessary to synchronize the frames of the picture as well as the lines, which means there must also be 'field-sync' pulses. Each field consists of the alternate lines of a complete frame, since only half the total number of lines are scanned in one go and two halves are interlaced to make the complete frame. The two fields are called odd fields and even fields, since one scans all the odd-numbered lines, the other the even-numbered ones, and there is a different type of field-sync pulse at the end of an odd field from the one at the end of an even field.

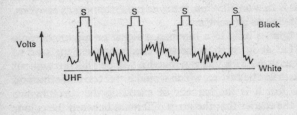

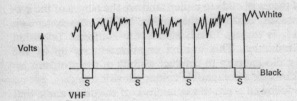

S=Synchronization pulses

Figure 98

If we now start on the means of generating the pulses we shall get rather bogged down, so let us take them for granted and move on to the modulation of a carrier wave with the composite video and pulse signal. There are two main differences between modulation of a video and an audio signal. The first and most obvious one is that the frequencies involved are very much higher for video. The second difference concerns the method of modulation: although video carriers are amplitude-modulated as with AM

231

radio broadcasting, with UHF the modulation is upside down (Figure 98). In other words, the carrier is subjected to negative modulation so that a peak in the video signal comes out as a dip in the modulation. The sync pulses are arranged so that they correspond to 'blacker-than-black' on the luminance scale, and therefore never show up on the screen. On the old 405-line system, positive modulation is used, and the main difference between the two signals is that on 405-line, the sync pulses appear as canyons, and on 625-line as skyscrapers.

All this applies only to a luminance signal or a monochrome system. What about getting the two chrominance signals on to the carrier as well? This you can imagine will be difficult, without using more than one carrier, which would be far too elaborate and clumsy. In fact it is the manner of encoding the chrominance signals on the carrier that the main difference between the colour systems occurs. You may remember at the time that Britain was chewing over the whole business of colour television, words like PAL and SECAM were bandied about. You may even have heard the initials NTSC used in this connection.

The first pieces of code to understand are the names of the systems themselves, and what they mean. NTSC, the system on which PAL is largely based, stands for National Television Systems Committee. This was an organization set up by the American radio industry to conduct a study of the problems involved in devising a compatible colour television system. Set up in 1950, it followed a pre-war committee of the same name that had formulated the monochrome television standard approved by the Federal Communications Commission in 1941. Its main job was to weigh up the relative merits of two systems, one developed by CBS,* the other by RCA.† In the end they recommended a system based on the RCA proposals; it was adopted in 1953.

Development of the NTSC system continued to progress, and a refinement was developed, mainly at the German firm of Telefunken, by W. Bruch. The principle involves alternating the phase of the two chrominance signals, and is known as PAL, for Phase Alternation Line. This is the system we are going to look at,

*Columbia Broadcasting System.

†Radio Corporation of America.

because it is the one adopted in the United Kingdom. However, many millions of viewers in France, East Europe and Russia enjoy programmes brought to them by the French SECAM system. Its name is derived from 'Séquentiale couleur à mémoire', and the fundamental difference between it and the other systems is that while NTSC and PAL both transmit and receive two chrominance signals simultaneously, the SECAM system transmits them separately, one at a time, on alternate lines. In addition, the chrominance carriers are FM modulated and not AM or phase modulated. It was developed from the original NTSC system by Henri de France in about 1956, although the modern version of it is somewhat different from its earlier forebears.

All three systems are capable of providing excellent pictures and, at a distance of about ten feet, under good conditions, it would be difficult to tell which system was in use. The NTSC system is reasonably simple to transmit and receive, but it is susceptible to distortion and requires a wide bandwidth to keep the chrominance signals well separated. PAL, on the other hand is complicated, and receivers expensive, but it is easier to transmit over long links and its recording on tape is better. There is less hue-distortion than with NTSC but colour resolution vertically is worse. SECAM is simple and relatively immune to distortion; phasing and mixing pictures is difficult and vertical colour resolution is reduced.

PAL certainly has given us a very good system in Britain as far as the quality of the picture and the colour is concerned, even if we have had to pay more for it; so how does it work? We are already familiar with the luminance signal and its modulation of the amplitude of the carrier; we have now got to add the chrominance signals.

The first thing that happens is the generation of a sub-carrier which is always operated at the critical frequency of 4·43361875 MHz. This absolute precision is essential in order that the chrominance signals do not get mixed up with the luminance signals. Consider the problem that faces us: the chrominance signals have eventually to be modulated on to the 'back' of the luminance signal, and yet they have to be kept entirely separate from one another and from the luminance signal. Now, although

Electricity

the video bandwidth is 5·5 MHz wide, the energy distribution of the video signal is by no means evenly distributed over the spectrum. In fact for most pictures, most of the video information occurs at low frequencies and reduces considerably at higher frequencies in the band. The dominating frequencies in the video

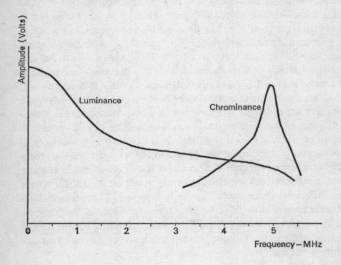

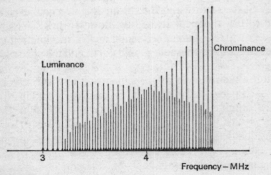

Figure 99

234

signal will be the line, field and picture frequencies which are due
to the scanning process. They, in addition to their harmonics –
frequencies equal to 2, 3, 4, etc. times the line (or field or picture)
frequency – will make up the bulk of the energy in the video
signal. In fact the multiples of the line frequency dominate, and
there are smaller groups at field and picture frequencies.

The reasons for this are not at first obvious, but look at it this
way: if a luminance signal is transmitting a plain, uniform, white
picture, then the lowest frequency in the video signal will be the
line frequency (15,625 Hz). The video signal for this picture will
be made up of square waves, and square waves are always made
up by the addition of a series of sine-wave harmonics to a sine
wave of the fundamental frequency. Therefore the frequency
spectrum for the white picture will be made up of harmonics of
15,625 Hz. Now put a normal picture on the screen: there will be
a large number of dots along each line which amount to varying
amplitudes of the luminance signal. However, even though there
may be a large number of dots on one line, there is an *integral*
number (no fractions). This means that all frequencies in the
video signal will be either at multiples of 15,625, even if the
multiple is many hundreds, or multiples of 25 (field- and picture-
frequency harmonics). The result of all this is that, all the way up
the spectrum between these harmonics, there is a series of 'slots',
which are in fact unused frequencies.

The thing to do is to slot the chrominance frequencies into
these vacant areas of the spectrum. To do this, we must ensure
that the frequencies of the chrominance information are precisely
arranged to fit in; the sub-carrier therefore has to be an odd
harmonic of half the line frequency. This and a number of other,
similarly critical requirements* create the need for the extra-
ordinarily exact chrominance sub-carrier frequency.

*The chrominance sub-carrier frequency has to be chosen so that it
is an odd multiple of half the picture frequency. It must be as high as
possible, while still allowing adequate bandwidth for the chrominance
signals to be fitted into the overall 5·5 MHz bandwidth. The sub-carrier
is raised above the 'odd multiple of half the line frequency', by a further
quarter of the line frequency, to prevent the dots from appearing to
move across the screen. To achieve interlacing of the dot-pattern,

To design, from scratch, an oscillator which is both stable to half a cycle per second and has a frequency as high as nearly 4·5 MHz would be extremely difficult. In fact, not only does the sub-carrier generator have to be an extremely stable crystal-controlled oscillator, but it has to be operated in a thermostatically controlled oven! You may also be wondering how different broadcast stations all over the country can all use a chrominance sub-carrier of 4·4336 etc. MHz. Surely we run the risk of getting the chrominance from the private lives of tropical fish mixed up with the luminance from hymn-singing in Aberystwyth.

The answer is that one does not broadcast the sub-carrier at all, nor even the sidebands from it, just as they are. Certainly, to start with, the sub-carrier is generated at that frequency but it is then modulated in a very special way to enable both chrominance signals to go onto one carrier. This is called quadrature modulation, and what it boils down to is that two sub-carriers are generated, both of the same frequency, but one being 90° out of phase with the other (90° is a right angle, hence the name 'quadrature'). Each sub-carrier is then amplitude modulated with one of the two chrominance signals, after which the two sub-carriers are added together. It is not necessary to go to the lengths of explaining why it happens, but you can probably now appreciate (if you have read Chapter 9) that the result of adding the two is one sub-carrier which is both phase and amplitude modulated. Remember what happened when the carrier of an AM signal was displaced 90° with respect to the sidebands. The result was phase modulation.

Next, the sub-carrier itself is suppressed, leaving only the sidebands. This is purely an economy measure; since the sidebands carry most of the information, the sub-carrier itself is only a sort of code-breaking mechanism which can perfectly well be regenerated at the receiving end. All that remains is to submodulate

---

another half-cycle per field is introduced by adding a further 25 Hz. The odd multiple is 567; so

$$\frac{567}{2} + \frac{1}{4} \times 15,625 + 25 = 4 \cdot 43361875 \text{ MHz}.$$

the chrominance sidebands on to the main carrier along with the luminance signal. Fortunately, the eye is much less discriminating as far as colour is concerned than it is with brightness, and a bandwidth only 1·4 MHz wide is plenty for the chrominance signals. Thus the sub-carrier sidebands are not directly broadcast at all, but are used to modulate the main carrier, using frequencies which slot in between those of the luminance signal.

At the receiving end, of course, the suppressed sub-carrier will have to be resurrected in order to decode the chrominance signals. While it can be easily generated in the receiver, it is

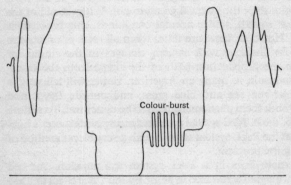

Colour-burst

Figure 100

crucial that it is generated in the correct phase-relationship to the sidebands. To ensure this, a thing called a colour-burst is broadcast at the beginning of each line (Figure 100). The beginning and end of the line-sync pulse are curiously called the front and back porches and on the back porch goes the colourburst, which consists of a few oscillations at 4·4336 etc. MHz, to set the correct phase for the locally regenerated sub-carrier with which the chrominance sidebands will be mixed after they have been demodulated from the signal as a whole.

So far, we have broken down colour pictures into only four components; the proportions of the three primary colours, and the brightness. There is, however, more to colour than the right mixtures of pure primaries. Technically, the colour of anything has three attributes: hue, brightness and saturation. Hue is what you or I would call the 'colour'; brightness is the amount of light – saturation is the one that is new to us. Saturation in a colour is its degree of freedom from added white. Since white is a mixture of the three primaries, then saturation simply means the degree of purity.

The amplitude-modulated part of a chrominance sub-carrier determines the saturation of the picture; the phase-modulated part determines the hue. Consequently, if the locally generated sub-carrier at the receiver is not accurately locked in the right phase-relationship, the hue will go all to pot. With the aid of the colour-burst signals, under normal conditions, this problem is overcome. However, there are times when all sorts of upsets can creep in, for instance with camera changes in the studio, or oddities in the propagation path of the signal from the transmitter. The result, as many an American viewer will tell you, is that you get red sea and blue grass, and outside Egypt and Kentucky both these phenomena tend to be unnatural. To restore some sense, the NTSC system receivers incorporate a user's hue-control, but the PAL system steps in with a very clever method of eliminating the problem.

On alternate lines in a PAL-system transmission, the red chrominance signal is reversed in phase by 180°. The effect this has is that in the resulting combined sub-carrier modulation, errors of phase in one line occur in the next line in the field (the next but one in the complete picture) as errors of exactly the opposite kind. In other words, if the picture is entirely blue for instance, some phase distortion half way along a line might cause the line to become greenish, since phase-angle determines hue. Now on the next line, the phase error will be reversed, and instead of the red line becoming greenish, it will become reddish. In simple PAL, the eye automatically averages out these errors, and since greenish and reddish mixed together make blue, and the eye is fairly insensitive to detail in colour, the colour distortion will be eliminated.

However, the PAL television sets in use in Britain at the moment are all rather more sophisticated than this, and do not rely on the eye doing the work at all. What they do is to store up the information in one line as well as displaying it on the screen, and then mix the stored line with the next (alternate phase) line and display the mixture. The newest part of that mixture is then delayed and mixed with the following line, and so on. The result is that the opposing phase errors cancel each other out, and any change of hue caused by phase distortion is automatically compensated for.

To achieve these clever results, it is of course necessary to find some way of storing the information in each line for a period of 64 microseconds before the next line comes along and the two can be mixed together. Now 64 microseconds is not very long. A car travelling at 100 miles per hour covers less than two thousands of an inch in the time, so we have not got to delay the signal all that much. The way it is done is to use a block of very special glass of critical dimensions. At one end is a tiny video-frequency loudspeaker, which turns the electrical signal into sound in the glass. Although the speed of sound in glass is pretty high, it does not need a very long block for it to take 64 microseconds to get to the other end where there is a very special microphone to turn it back into an electronic signal. Needless to say the length and stability of the glass is vital, and no distortion of the signal must creep in during the delay.

Not all transmissions, even if you have a colour receiver, are in colour. Until the vast stock of ancient films on both sides of the Atlantic is used up, many monochrome transmissions are yet to come. Consequently, when transmitting a monochrome programme which is going to be received in black-and-white on a colour set, the design includes a 'colour-killer' to tell the set to behave like a monochrome receiver. If this did not happen, spurious colour information might creep onto the picture. We shall be able to understand this process better when we have looked at the workings of receivers.

We now have a beautiful, distortion-free, colour picture on our delay-line PAL set, but what about the sound? The answer to this is simple: an entirely separate, FM, sound broadcast is made on a carrier frequency 6 MHz above the video carrier frequency. The sidebands of an audio signal are narrow compared with a video signal, and the gap of 0·5 MHz between the top of the video band is plenty. Figure 101 shows the complete spectrum of a television channel. You can see that it is 8 MHz wide. To save space, since both video sidebands carry the same information, the

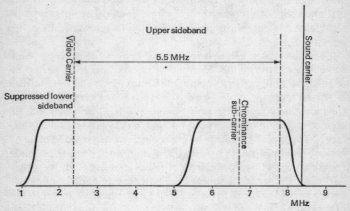

Figure 101

lower sideband is mostly suppressed, except for a vestige of it which it is not possible to get rid of completely.

*

A well-adjusted PAL colour picture on a good set, in many parts of the country, is as good as a photograph; if hi-fi sound accompanied it, the experience would be near complete. Until holographic* television comes we can ask for little better, and you can buy three colour sets for the price of a motor car. How does this miraculous machine work? We have heard a bit about phosphor dots, sub-carriers and sidebands. How do the cathode rays produce colour? What is behind all the controls? What makes for good reception?

Let us start with the question of reception, because this is clearly the first stage in the process, and some unfortunate

*Three-dimensional pictures produced with laser light

people cannot get good reception however hard they try, for reasons of topography. They have no doubt been enraged at the mellifluous descriptions of perfect pictures in this chapter, and if they have not by now thrown the book away in disgust, let us console them with some facts about their plight.

We discovered in Chapter 9 that although radio waves are the same phenomenon as light waves, their wavelength is so very much longer that they do not behave as light does in sticking very much to the straight and narrow when travelling from A to B. This is a great advantage in radio, particularly AM sound broadcasts, because the low frequencies employed mean that the wavelengths are up to two kilometres long. Diffraction, or spreading out of waves, occurs to a very great extent with such long wavelengths, and consequently one powerful transmitter can broadcast almost to a whole country. Not only is the ground wave strong, but the radio horizon is vastly further away from the transmitter than the visual one. However, as the frequencies of radio broadcasts rise, so the electromagnetic waves start to behave a bit more like light, until one reaches the VHF band where the ground wave disappears almost completely. The radio horizon is still fairly distant because some diffraction still occurs, and VHF television and radio broadcasts can be received in most parts of the country without difficulty, even though a greater network of transmitters is required.

The wavelengths in the UHF band, however, are very short. Although in the range of 300–600 mm. they are still nowhere near as short as light waves, but they behave rather more like light than like long waveband radio transmissions. This has two important implications; the first is fairly obvious, UHF television receiving aerials must be almost in line of sight of a transmitting aerial; the second is not so obvious at all, and concerns reflections. For rather complicated mathematical reasons, no wave of any sort can be efficiently reflected from an object whose dimensions are less than half the length of the wave. The sound waves of your voice can easily be reflected back at you from the side of a house, but you will not get much of an echo from a lamppost. (The wavelength of sound waves ranges from about 10 m to about 20 mm.)

The wavelength of most broadcasts is such that there are not many objects about which are big enough to reflect them to any great extent. However, once you get up into the realms of UHF you find that the place is littered with metal reflectors plenty big enough to cause all sorts of trouble. Most of the litter consists of aircraft because, of course, they vie with radio waves for airspace. Consequently those who are unfortunate enough to live near airports not only suffer from the noise, but also from 'ghosting' on their television pictures as the things fly over. In addition, sometimes there are fixed objects around which cause reflections.

The long and the short of it is that a very comprehensive network of transmitters is required to make sure that as few people as possible are in 'shadow', while nothing much can be done about reflections. Inevitably there are some people who are in sort of twilight areas caused by hills and if there are not enough of them to warrant a transmitter of their own, the best solution to their problems will be 'piped' television, brought to them by cable from a central receiving station with a suitably placed aerial. We will probably find piped television becoming very popular even in good reception areas in the future, because it means simpler sets and no need for a properly aligned individual aerial.

In the old days of VHF only television, all that was really needed for an aerial was a half-wave dipole, basically of the sort discussed in Chapter 9. This resulted in the conventional 'H' shaped aerial, or sometimes an 'X' shaped one. With UHF, though, it is not so simple. Still a dipole is used, and in spite of the Christmas tree shape of most UHF aerials, only one or two small pieces of metal at one end are in fact the aerial proper. They are just half-wave dipoles, and all the rest of the bits are called parasitic elements; they will usually consist of a long arm carrying transverse fingers, and a mesh plate at right angles to the arm at the same end as the dipoles. Only the dipole or dipoles are connected to the television; the fingers are in fact directors which are there to reinforce the signal, and the arm on which they are fixed points towards the station. The mesh plate is there to behave rather like a headlamp reflector in reverse, and again reinforce the signal. It also tends to reduce pick-up of signals from the rear, while improving pick-up from the front.

One of the effects of the array of directors is to lower the impedance of the aerial; in order to raise it back up to the impedance of the cable, to ensure efficient transfer of the signal down to the receiver, the dipole is usually folded (Figure 102). In areas with a very strong UHF signal, an indoor set-top aerial can be used, and it may be just a folded half-wave dipole, or in the form of a ring

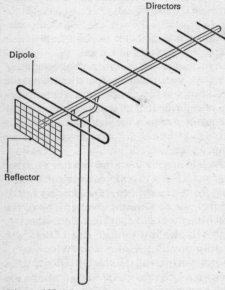

Directors

Dipole

Reflector

Figure 102

or square. However, it is very difficult to avoid getting multiple images due to reflections occurring inside the house.

Now let us set off from the aerial towards the set. We have to do this along some rather special cable, both to ensure minimal loss of signal, and to keep the impedances all the same to prevent reflection of the signal back along the cable. This consists of a central inner conductor surrounded by an accurately drawn sheath of thick plastic insulating material called the dielectric (as in a capacitor). Around this there is a layer of braided copper wire, which is then covered with an outer layer of insulation. This is called coaxial cable, and its impedance has a specific value; it also offers the lowest possible resistance to the passage of the aerial signal.

The television receiver itself is really two receivers in one; it is an FM receiver for the sound signal and at the same time an AM receiver for the video signal. In theory they could be totally different sets, but in practice the two signals are handled together in part of the circuitry. In principle, though, the idea of the television set should hold no great horrors for us, because we have talked a good deal about AM and FM in Chapter 9.

However, in addition there must be the circuits for generating the horizontal and vertical sweep signals for controlling the deflection of the electron beam in the picture tube. There is also the major complication of ensuring that all the lines of dots of the picture are put together again in exactly the right place relative to each other, so synchronizing circuits are required to time the scanning of the beam very precisely.

Both the AM and the FM signals from the tuner are heterodyned to bring the frequencies down to a more manageable intermediate frequency, which is them amplified. (The circuitry has to be capable of handling the wide bandwidths involved). Next, the video signal is separated from the audio signal in a video detector. The audio signal then goes its own way through an FM detection and amplification circuit to drive the loudspeaker. What we are left with is the video information plus all the synchronizing, blanking and colour-burst signals which are needed to reconstitute the picture. This is fed to a detector for demodulation, or removal of the signal we want from the carrier on which it has been broadcast. Now the luminance signal has to be separated from the chrominance signals; this is done with what is called a comb filter.

If you remember how the chrominance information was slotted into vacant bits of the luminance signal spectrum you can appreciate how we can reverse the situation by filtering out the 'slots' in which the chrominance signals were placed. A converse arrangement of a band-pass filter is used to get the chrominance signal on its own. It is interesting to note that if a colour broadcast is being received on a monochrome set, the chrominance signal is not separated from the luminance signal, and gets displayed on the screen as part of the luminance signal. The effect this can cause is to create a sort of latticework pattern of dots which crawl diagonally across the screen.

The chrominance signal is demodulated by two detectors to give us the two colour-difference signals, the sub-carriers being regenerated in the exact phase relationship to the ones that were suppressed at the transmitter. The colour burst sets the correct phase, and the two colour-difference signals then go to a matrix for turning back into a red, a green and a blue signal again, the reverse of the process in the transmitter.

The synchronizing circuitry centres round oscillators which are designed to generate not the smooth sine waves that we are familiar with, but sawtooth waveforms which will provide the forces to sweep the electron beam steadily across the screen, and then make it fly back at the end. The sweep oscillators, as they are called, are kept in step by the sync pulses in the video signal. Now we are ready to bring in the picture tube, and in a colour set the picture tube is the most precise and expensive part. A monochrome tube is child's play compared with a colour one, because all it amounts to is an evacuated glass tube with a flattish, phosphor coated screen at one end, and an electron gun with focussing and scanning coils at the other.

To start with, a colour tube has three electron guns, one to handle each of the primary colour signals that come out of the matrix. However, the electron beams which come out of them are all identical: there are no such things as blue or red electrons! The secret of the colour lies in the nature of the coating of the screen.

The inside of a monochrome screen is coated with a type of phosphorescent chemical which when it receives energy from a beam of electrons is excited into emitting white light. Now there are also phosphorescent substances which emit colours of light when bombarded with electrons, and in a colour tube three totally separate types of phosphor are used, one for each primary colour. However, they cannot simply be laid one upon the other in layers, otherwise the beam from each electron gun would excite all three primary colours and we would not have any colour television. The phosphors have to be placed on the screen as sets of individual dots. Groups of red, blue and green luminophors in dots about 0·42 mm. diameter, 0·72 mm. apart are arranged in triangular formation in lines across the screen (Figure 103).

Now we have a new difficulty. How do you make sure that the beam from one gun strikes only the dots of the colour it is dealing with, and hits the dots fair and square? To overcome this problem, a short distance away from the screen a perforated shadow mask is fitted which has one hole in it for each group of three

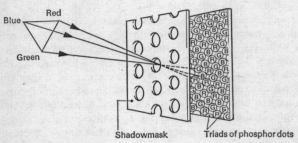

Figure 103

dots. Then if a beam of electrons can get through a hole in the shadowmask, it is sure to fall on the right dot for reasons of geometry (Figure 103). Because it is undesirable to have a very curved screen, it is necessary to include convergence magnets to aim the beams correctly right out to the corners of the screen.

You must be thinking what an incredibly complex job it is to manufacture a shadowmask tube. In fact it is not quite as difficult as it seems. The process starts with the manufacture of the mask which, from a large-scale drawing, is photographically etched to produce the holes. It is then pressed into its slightly curved shape. The screen is coated with a thin layer of say, red phosphor which behaves in a similar way to a layer of emulsion on a film. The shadowmask is fitted into position, and a beam of light is made to go through the motions that the eventual electron beam will. The phosphor emulsion is then 'developed' and fixed, so that the areas which remained in the dark are dissolved away, leaving only the dots.

Next a layer of one of the other phosphors is applied to the screen, usually by putting a blob in the middle and spreading it out with centrifugal force. The photographic process is repeated, leaving another set of dots, and since no light will fall on existing red dots, the developing process will clear the other phosphor from them. The whole thing is finally repeated for the remaining colour. It is therefore only because the dots are positioned with the use of the shadowmask in the first place that accurate colour reproduction is possible. It is extremely difficult to apply dots to the screen and then try to line up a shadowmask afterwards.

The three electron guns, which work on the same principle as the gun in a camera tube, are accurately aligned. Downstream of them there are a number of electrostatic plates, which are arranged so that the lines of force between them have the effect of focusing the electron beams. After them come the scanning coils which consist of electromagnetic yokes around the electron beams to which are fed the sawtooth waveforms generated in the synchronizing circuitry. The electrons in a beam are in principle no different from electrons travelling through a current-carrying wire. We have discovered in previous chapters what happens to a current-carrying wire when it passes through a magnetic field, because it is on this principle that electric motors work. In the same way the magnetic field produced by the scanning coils forces the electron beam to one side or the other, depending on the direction of the force.

All it remains to do is to modulate the strengths of the three beams so that they will excite the phosphor dots into radiating appropriate amounts of appropriate colours. To understand how this is done, we must have a slightly closer look at the design of the electron guns. We have seen that in principle they are like thermionic valves, in that they have a heated, negatively charged cathode, and an anode, and that electrons stream off from the cathode and whiz on through a hole in the anode. In reality, a picture tube gun has a considerable number of anodes, all with holes in them, so as to accelerate the electrons in the beam to the required extent. The final anode will have a potential of 25,000 volts in a colour set, and it is here that the special danger of television sets comes in. The electron guns also have a grid, as in a triode valve, and it is the grid which principally controls the intensity of the beam.

In a colour tube, each of the colour video signals is fed to the grid of the appropriate gun; variations in the grid potential caused by the fluctuating video signal will cause variations in the intensity of the beam and hence the colour on the screen. However, the luminance signal is fed to the cathodes of the guns, and this too controls the intensity of the beam. Thus, when a monochrome transmission is being received, there is only a luminance signal and no chrominance signals. The luminance signal is connected to all three guns; there are circuits to produce the appropriate intensity in each gun so that the red, green and blue phosphor dots give off light which appears as white in varying degrees of brightness. On the screen a monochrome picture appears. The colour-killer device which was mentioned earlier makes sure that the chrominance signals are cut off. The colour killer is in fact a bias voltage in the chrominance amplifier which prevents it from operating. When a colour transmission is received, the colour burst is rectified and fed to the chrominance amplifier to neutralize the bias. This is in addition to its duty of synchronizing the regenerated sub-carrier.

What about the controls of a television? On a modern colour set, problems like horizontal and vertical hold are considerably reduced, but on a monochrome set it is sometimes necessary manually to make fine adjustments to the frequencies of the saw-tooth oscillations in the synchronising circuits. Brightness and contrast, though, apply to both monochrome and colour sets. The contrast control is really a 'volume control' of the luminance signal. As the amplitude of the video signal is turned up, so its peak becomes comparatively greater than its low values, increasing the difference between bright and dark areas of picture. The brightness control, on the other hand, varies the D.C. bias between the cathode and the grid in the electron guns, and varies the intensity of the beam across the whole amplitude range.

Colour sets have several means of adjusting the saturation of the colour in the picture. This may be a sliding control for simultaneously reducing the intensity of the red signal and increasing that of the blue while the green remains constant. In some cases there may be an individual control for each colour, but usually this is done from inside the set. It is, however most advisable to get a set which permits saturation control from the front because many service engineers are capable of leaving a set poorly adjusted in this respect and it can make the colour of the picture unreal. Saturation can also be a matter of taste.

We have not yet seen the end of developments in the world of colour television. The three-gun picture tube, although excellent in performance, does have limitations, not least of which is sheer bulk and expense. It is, for instance, possible to design a colour tube using only one gun, in which a single beam scans all the different phosphor dots. However, extremely precise control over which dots are being scanned at any one moment is required so that the switching to the appropriate signal can be synchronized.

Eventually, we may see the end of cathode-ray tubes entirely in television. There is a strong possibility that some way will be found of transmitting holographic pictures which reproduce scenes not only in three dimensions, but also present an intriguing additional facility. Because the exact light-radiation pattern of the original scene is recreated, if you want to see something that is out of sight, you just move your head to one side and there it will be. No longer will it be possible to keep the camera cleverly positioned so that the girl in the bath is decorously screened by the edge. This is all a very long way off, but already laser beams have been suggested for use in television. Another possibility would be the development of flat screens faced with sort of woven matrices of conductors so that voltages can be fed to any specific crossover point to activate electroluminescent elements or mini-lasers. Finally, if it became possible to reproduce light with a predetermined spectrum as easily as it can be done with sound by a loudspeaker, great possibilities would be opened up.

11 Electronic Thinking

How computers work

The computer is hideously maligned. It is either blamed for charging us for more gas than an entire gasworks could produce in a decade (and for taking us to court when we have already paid for it), or it is regarded with sinister awe as a device which could dominate us in a new age of technical tyranny. Most books on computers start off by going to great lengths to persuade us how stupid computers really are, that they cannot in fact think at all, and the best they can do is to add 1 and 1, and even then they do not make 2 but 10. In so doing they are being almost as misleading as the science fiction writers. Make no mistake, computers are remarkable things. In the course of the next generation or so we shall probably find that the computer has had a more dramatic effect on mankind than the invention of the wheel and the atom bomb put together. It is still in its childhood; its gestation started in the seventeenth century and lasted until its birth in the Second World War; since then it has gone through three if not four stages of development and more are yet to come.

What, then, is this strange contraption? What exactly does it do, and how? First of all, let us realize that the word computer embraces a whole family of devices from an abacus to a slide rule, or from a cash register to an Atlas Computer. A computer is basically a calculator, and it can be one of two basic types: analogue or digital. The most basic digital computer is in two parts, and almost everybody has one: a set of fingers. The Latin word *digitus* means finger or toe, and man first began to count on his fingers, and still does. This fact has much greater significance than at first appears, and we shall come back to it later. An abacus is a digital computer; and it conforms to one of the basic requirements, that it deals in discrete quantities represented by single beads. A slide rule is an analogue computer because it deals with a continuous quantity, length, and length is used as an 'analogy' to some other quantity, such as pressure or velocity. Both forms of computer have their electronic counterpart, and it is these with which we are concerned in this chapter.

The computer which is really important, and on which we shall largely concentrate, is the digital computer. Analogue computers are really as different from digital computers as a speedometer from an adding machine. They are much less precise, and very often a job which could be done by an analogue computer is done on a digital computer by passing the data through an analogue-to-digital converter. Analogue computers never touch your gas-bill, and will never pose any sort of threat to anyone. Let us therefore deal with them briefly, first.

The key to the nature of an analogue computer is in its name. The physical quantity which is the basis of its computation is represented in the circuits of the machine not by numbers of any kind, but by electrical voltages, in other words the factors in real life are represented in the computer by electrical analogies. What sort of physical quantities and factors are we talking about? Typical ones are temperature, flow, speed, altitude and pressure.

The problem facing the computer can normally be represented as a mathematical formula, which shows how the value of one factor is dependent on another or others. Components have to be designed which respond in a way that is analogous to various parts of the formula. There are four basic components: amplifiers, potentiometers (voltage-control devices), multipliers and function generators. The amplifiers are really the heart of the machine; some large computers may have up to 1000 of them, and they perform quite a wide range of mathematical tasks, including addition and subtraction. Variable resistors called potentiometers are used in analogue computers to multiply by a factor of less than 1, such as 0·002 or 0·99. In combination with an amplifier (which has a constant amplification factor or gain of any number above 1) it is possible to scale a quantity up or down by any constant factor from say 0·001 to 1,000. Potentiometers are sometimes known as attenuators, and are among the most basic components of analogue attenuators.

Whereas multiplication by a constant is possible simply with an amplifier, a more sophisticated circuit is called for where it is necessary to multiply one variable with another. To do the job rather slowly, all you need is a potentiometer whose sliding contact is automatically positioned by an electric servo-motor which follows the voltage of the second constant while the first is fed through the coils of the potentiometer. However, this sort of thing is not nearly fast enough in many cases, and some crafty maths can be brought in to simplify the operation. We all know that $2 \times 3 = 6$, but we perhaps had not all appreciated that $\frac{1}{4}\{(2 + 3)^2 - (2 - 3)^2\} = 6$ also! This might look like a long-winded way of doing it, but it does in fact achieve multiplication merely by addition and subtraction, squaring and division by a constant. Addition and subtraction are then done by amplifiers, division by a potentiometer giving a gain of 0·25 and squaring by a function generator. A function generator is a circuit to generate a square, cube, square root, etc., of a variable input.

Analogue computers tend to be faster than digital ones, and to solve a typical problem, a time of 20 seconds would be nothing unusual. The sort of problems they deal with range from the calculation of the trajectory of a guided missile, to the design of airframes. All the factors affecting the calculation, such as velocity, gravity, wind speed and direction, aerodynamic drag and so on, can be represented in analogous electronic circuits, so that in the end, an answer such as a trajectory can be plotted out on an automatic graphic recorder.

For all the convenience of analogue computers in applications like these, they simply cannot compete in capacity and accuracy with digital computers, and very likely the output from an analogue computer will be a device to convert its answer into digital form so that it can be further processed and probably stored in a memory bank – so without more ado let us start to get to the bottom of the digital computer.

We really have to go back to square one. How do you count? One way is to make a mark for each item you are counting, so that the number of days in the week would be 1111111, the number of months in the year 111111111111. However, if you want to write down the number of days in the year, or hairs on your head, you will soon run out of whatever you are counting on. In fact, this problem never really arose in ancient times, because men began to use their fingers, so that they did not have to record every single item as a mark, but could record the number of times they had used up all their fingers. They developed a symbol for 1, 11, 111, 1111, 11111, and so on up to 9, and when they wanted to count higher than that they just wrote down the number of sets of fingers used up and started again. Logically the system would be:

0	1	2	3	4	5	6	7	8	9
10	11	12	13	14	15	16	17	18	19
20	21	22	23	24	25	26	27	28	29
30	31	32 . . .							

Computers of course do not have hands, let alone fingers, and consequently, there is no reason whatever for them to count as if they were using their fingers. In fact, a very good reason for not using the decimal system is that if you want to multiply two numbers together, you really need to know your tables. It would be much better to use a system where no such mental drudgery was called for. This simple system is the binary system.

Suppose man had no fingers, just two hands. How would we have coped with counting (assuming we survived at all)? We could have adopted the same philosophy and instead of counting on ten fingers, just have counted on two hands. It would not have been as economical in figures, but remarkably simple, and much more economical than marking every single item. First we would count the left hand, then the right, then we would note that we had used up both hands once and start again with the left hand. If the symbol for the left hand were 0 and for the right, 1, then the table equivalent to the decimal one above would be:

0
1
10
11
100
101
110
111
1000
1001

The numbers 0 to 20 in both binary and decimal are:

0	0
1	1
2	10
3	11
4	100
5	101
6	110
7	111
8	1000
9	1001
10	1010
11	1011
12	1100
13	1101
14	1110
15	1111
16	10000
17	10001
18	10010
19	10011
20	10100

just as 1000 in decimal equals 10^3, so 1000 in binary equals 2^3, or 8 and $10000 = 2^4 = 16$.

From this it is very clear that binary is not so economical on figures, and the decimal figure 67,108,864 is

$$100000000000000000000000000$$

in binary. What is the point, then? For one thing, whereas in a decimal calculating machine you need the equivalent of lots of little wheels each with ten positions on them, in a binary one, each indicator need only have two positions. When it comes to electronics, two positions can so easily be represented by a switch being either on or off. Suppose you yourself wanted to construct an illuminated sign to display numbers, in the decimal system you would find it very difficult indeed; in binary all you need is a row of torch bulbs, each of which is either off or on to represent 0 or 1.

The other advantage of binary is the ease of multiplication and division. To multiply 1011 by 1010, all you do is this:

$$
\begin{array}{r}
1011 \\
\times\,1010 \\
\hline
1011\ldots \\
0 \\
1011 \\
0 \\
\hline
1101110 \\
\hline
\end{array}
$$

which is exactly the same principle as in long multiplication in the decimal system, with the advantage that the addition is much simpler: $1 + 1 = 10$, $1 + 1 + 1 = 11$ and so on. Long division is made simpler too:

$$
\begin{array}{r}
1111 \\
\hline
110)\overline{1011010} \\
110 \\
\hline
1010 \\
110 \\
\hline
1001 \\
110 \\
\hline
110 \\
110 \\
\hline
\ldots
\end{array}
$$

Once again nothing is more complicated than $1 + 1 = 10$.

Almost all the calculating done in a digital computer is done in binary, and consequently just about the only major component is an electronic on-off switch. The switches must of course be controlled by other switches or electronic signals, but nevertheless, in the earliest computers electromechanical relays were used. Later, thermionic valves were used, and now the miniature transistor or its equivalent in an integrated circuit is used.

However, before we look into the ways in which transistors are used as switches, let us try to understand a bit more about the principles on which a digital computer operates. Computers perform two basic functions: they calculate, and they store information. A fully fledged digital computer is also equipped with several other sections, but these are all to do with getting data into or out of it, and since this is a book about electronics and not about computer programming, it will be necessary to talk of them in general terms. It is the calculating and memory elements that concern us here.

By far the most common type of computer is valued not so much for its powers of calculation, which may be very simple, but for its prodigious and highly accurate memory, from which it is possible to retrieve volumes of essential information in a very short time. These are the computers which control financial accounts, maintain stock control, act as vast filing systems and do simple processing on large amounts of complex information, such as producing a statistical analysis from a set of completed questionnaires.

The more romantic type of computer is the one which has only limited memory capacity, but is capable of long and complicated computations. This is the sort of computer that is used for scientific calculations in fields from particle physics to astronomy, or for solving complex engineering problems such as bridge or aeroengine design.

There is a third, intermediate type of digital computer which does a bit more thinking than the mere memory bank, which is used to control machine and manufacturing operations. It is basically programmed with electronic instructions to all the different parts of a process, and also has fed to it all the information about what is actually taking place in the process so that if something starts going wrong the computer will be able to send out modified instructions to keep the process on the strait and narrow.

Computers would certainly be little use without any calculating capability, so let us start with a look at how they do it. The circuits which do the work are broadly known as logic circuits; they fall into two categories, those which store information (temporarily) and those which perform logical operations on it. To understand the latter, it is necessary to understand some logic as well.

What electronic switches, such as transistors, in a logic circuit do is to answer questions. Questions in logic are usually of the 'true or false' type:

All dogs are animals	true
All animals are dogs	false
Some animals are dogs	true
Some animals are not dogs	true
No dogs are birds	true
Some dogs are birds	false

To the relationship between dogs and animals or birds, we can therefore apply four basic tests:

1. A is always B
2. A is sometimes B
3. A is never B
4. A is sometimes not B

As far as dogs and animals are concerned, 1 is the only proposition to which the answer is yes, but if animals are A and dogs B, then the answer to 2 and 4 is yes. A most important point is that the answer is never 'perhaps', it is either a definite yes or no.

Now we should put the animals away and get back to numbers. In the world of computer logic, the answer 'true' comes out as the binary symbol 1, and the answer 'false' comes out as 0. Let us start, therefore, by thinking up an electronic circuit which is capable of answering questions automatically. To do this, we need two basic 'connectives' which are known as AND circuits and OR circuits. Although the words *and* and *or* used in this connection started off in life as having the same sort of meaning as the words in ordinary use, here we have to give them special and precise meanings.

257

AND and OR circuits are really 'truth' devices which are applied to the classes A and B to see whether their relationship is such that the answer to one of the basic questions is 'true' or 'false'. The circuits are themselves switches, or gates. A gate, like a switch, allows current to flow when closed, not when open. After the gates have applied their lie-detecting mechanism to A and B, they answer 'true' or 'false' by allowing current to flow, or switching it off. What are the mechanisms of the two circuits? What attributes do A and B require to satisfy an AND gate?

If you come to think of it there are only two attributes that A or B can have: they can be either 0 or 1, since we are confined to the binary system of notation. An AND gate will say 'yes' and allow current to flow only when both A and B are 1. In some cases there may also be a C, which must also be 1 for the AND gate to close to allow current to flow. When the gate allows the current to pass, it is tantamount to an output of 1. When the gate is open and no current flows, the output is regarded as 0.

In terms of circuitry, an AND gate consists of two electronic switches in series (Figure 104a). Only when both switches are closed as a result of pulses or currents controlling them (which represent 1 in both cases) will the gate allow current to pass. If one switch responds to an input of 1, it will close, but if the other remains open in response to an 0 input, the AND gate remains open.

OR circuits also contain two switches, but they are ranged in parallel as in Figure 104b. From this you will see that the conditions which will make an OR gate close and pass current are: A = 1, B = 1; or A = 1, B = 0; or, A = 0, B = 1. The only time it will remain open is if both A and B inputs are 0. The OR gate will close if an input of 1 is present at either or both switches.

We are all very much more familiar with logic circuits than we realize. Somewhere in your house there is sure to be a system of light switches which allows you to switch the light on at one end of the room and switch it off at the other; you can then switch it on again at the first switch without touching the second. The circuit which permits this convenient state of affairs is shown in Figure 105. It consists of a light, from whose two terminals a circuit is made across the live and neutral wires of the mains, or across the positive and negative terminals of a battery. In the wire leading from the live terminal to the light is a pair of two-way switches in series. The switches have no 'off' position, they simply permit current to be channelled through one of two wires connected to their outputs and inputs.

Principle

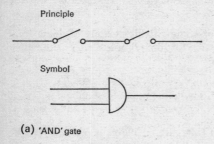

Symbol

(a) 'AND' gate

Principle

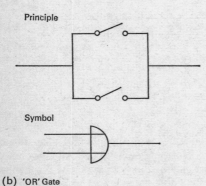

Symbol

(b) 'OR' Gate

Figure 104

Let us assume that when we switch a switch upwards we are giving it an input of 0, and when down 1. There are then four possible switch positions, which may either light the lamp (1) or extinguish it (0). We can tabulate the logic of the thing as follows:

259

Switch A	Switch B	Light
1	1	1
1	0	0
0	0	1
0	1	0

Now let us start to put some of this curious business into action, and use a circuit or two for some simple binary arithmetic. How about doing the sums:

$$0 + 0 = 0$$
$$0 + 1 = 1$$
$$1 + 0 = 1$$

All we need for this is an OR gate on its own, perhaps. It will certainly allow no current through with 0 at both its inputs, and

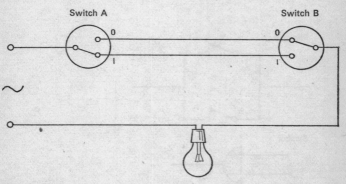

Figure 105

will let current pass with 1 at either of them. The trouble is that it will also answer 1 if both its inputs are 1, and we know that $1 + 1 = 10$, not 1. What do we do? The answer, as Figure 106 shows, is that we need not only an OR gate, but also two AND gates. As will be clear in a moment, we also need a device, an inverter, for transferring the output from one AND gate as an opposite input to the other AND gate. For instance, if the output from the first AND gate is 0, the inverter will feed 1 into the second gate.

What happens is this: the two inputs, A and B are fed both to an

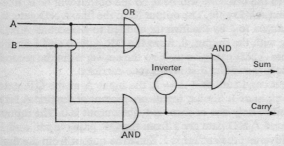

a Half adder

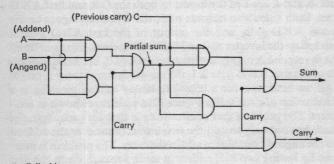

b Full adder

Figure 106

OR gate, and simultaneously to a parallel AND gate. The output from the OR gate is fed as one of the inputs to the second AND gate, the other input of which comes from the output of the first AND gate, through the inverter. If this were the end of the computation, and there were a binary read-out device like a row of lights (not that there would be in a practical machine), then the output from the second AND gate would be connected direct to the first light in the row, and the output from the first AND gate would be the 'carry' and fed into the next adding circuit along.

Now let us give this simple circuit the three sums: $0 + 0 = 1$, $0 + 1 = 1$ and $1 + 1 = 10$. Take the first one. Both A and B at the input to the OR gate will be 0, so the output will be 0, likewise the first AND gate. The output from the first AND gate, 0, will be changed to 1 by the inverter and fed to the second AND gate along with the output, 0, from the OR gate. 0 and 1 as the inputs to an AND gate give us 0, so the answer from the second AND gate is 0 and the first AND gate carries 0.

For the second sum, $0 + 1 = 1$, the input A at the OR gate gives an output of 1. Similar inputs are present at the first AND gate, but since only one of them is 1, the output is 0. The inputs to the second AND gate are 1 from the OR gate output, and 1 from the inverter; the answer is 1. Since the output from the first AND gate is 0, the carry is 0.

The third sum is the one with which we came unstuck before. Both A and B are 1 at the inputs to both the OR and first AND gates. Both gates give outputs of 1; the OR output goes to the second AND gate, and the output of the first AND gate is reversed by the inverter to 0 and fed to the second. Inputs of 0 and 1 at the second AND gate give an output of 0, but since the output of the first AND gate is 1, the answer is 0 and carry 1, or 10!

All we need now for a complete binary adding machine is a combination of circuits like Figure 106a which are known as half-adders. The problem that confronts us is that for each digit, the circuit has not only to add the two inputs (known as the addend and the augend), but also to add in the carry. The problem is overcome by having two half adders in series for each digit: the first produces the partial sum by adding the addend and the augend, and then the second adds any carry there may be to the output from the adjoining circuit. Figure 106b shows the result, a full adder.

So much for addition, what of subtraction? Subtraction can in fact be done by a circuit capable only of addition. This is because any subtraction sum can be turned into one of addition. If you are wondering whether there is something about arithmetic they forgot to teach you, let us leave binary for a moment and see how it

can be done in decimal numbers. Suppose we want to do the sum
659 − 293 = 366 in a way which was purely addition, we could
do it by finding the complement of 293 and adding it to 659. The
complement is the amount by which 293 is smaller than the
'modulus' of 1000, in other words, 707. Now 659 + 707 = 1,366
and since we took a modulus of 1000, we are really saying that our
adding machine only goes up to 999 and then starts again; we can
therefore disregard the 1 in the answer 1,366 because it would be
discarded by the machine. An easier method is to take what is
called the 9's complement, which is the difference between 293
and 999 and then add 1 to the last digit at the end.

Whatever use, you are saying, is all this? We have not achieved
anything at all because we need subtraction plain and simple in
order to obtain the complement. Ah! In binary, this part is
child's play; the complement of, say, −10101 with a modulus of
100000 is:

$$
\begin{array}{r}
100000 \\
- \ \ 10101 \\
\hline
01011
\end{array}
$$

However, the equivalent of using a 9's complement in binary is to
subtract not from 100000 but from 11111, as follows:

$$
\begin{array}{r}
11111 \\
-10101 \\
\hline
01010
\end{array}
$$

and then add 1 to the last digit, as in decimal:

$$
\begin{array}{r}
01010 \\
+1 \\
\hline
01011
\end{array}
$$

To subtract in binary all you have to do is to take the number to
be subtracted, swap all its 1's for 0's and vice versa, and add 1 to
the last digit. The problem is now easy; take the sum 1101011 −
11010. The first thing we do is find the complement of −11010.

Since the number to be subtracted from has seven digits, we must consider that we are subtracting 0011010, and then turn all the digits round (+1100101). So:

$$1101011$$
$$+1100101$$
$$\overline{11010000}$$

Since the modulus is only seven digits, we knock off the 1 on the left because there will be no circuit for it, and all that remains is to add 1 to the last digit, giving us the correct answer of 1010001. Here is another, 1011111 − 101:

$$1011111$$
$$+1111010$$
$$\overline{(1)1011001}$$
$$+1$$
$$\overline{1011010}$$

Finally, 11010 − 11010:

$$11010$$
$$+00101$$
$$\overline{11111}$$
$$+1$$
$$\overline{(1)00000}$$

You can see that the basic adding circuitry in a computer can also subtract, provided there is the additional circuitry to control the sign (+ or −) and to produce the complement. The mechanism that controls the sign also crops up with another most useful application, and is based on something called a flip-flop. A flip-flop is a type of electronic switch which has two stable states, either off or on. The difference between it and an ordinary switch is that the latter will not necessarily stay in either the open or closed position in the absence of an external input; a flip-flop will stay in either position. In addition, a flip-flop at any instant will be in one of its two states; there is no intermediate state.

A circuit for comparing the signs in an arithmetical sum has only a fairly simple job to do, but it takes eight circuit components to make up. The job it has to do can be boiled down to deciding whether the signs of two inputs are like or unlike. There are four possible combinations:

Input A	Input B	Answer
+	+	like
+	−	unlike
−	−	like
−	+	unlike

The circuit which can produce the answer is shown in Figure 107. For each input there is a flip-flop, the state of which represents the

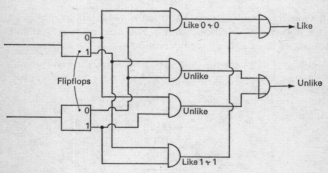

Figure 107

sign of the input. As in all other similar problems, the two possible states are represented by 0 and 1. Let us say that 1 stands for − and 0 for +. Now, if the flip-flop is in the 1 (conducting) state, current or a pulse will be transmitted to one of the two AND gates serving each possible answer. If the B flip-flop also shows 1, then current will pass to the same 'like-sign' AND gate as from the A flip-flop, but to the opposite 'unlike-sign' AND gate. The result is that the only place where further current flows is to the

Electricity

input of the like-sign OR gate, which then lets out a positive
answer, or a 1 signal. Had the B flip-flop been positive (0), then
current would have gone to the opposite 'like-sign' AND gate
from A, but to the same 'unlike-sign' gate, causing an output
from the unlike-sign OR gate.

In terms of computers, the sign of a number somehow has to be
represented in binary notation, and it is done conventionally by
placing a sign bit (a bit is computer jargon for a digit) in front of
a number, using a 'binary point' to separate them. This way
+1101 would be 0·1101, and −1101 would be 1·1101

$$1101 - 1101 = 0·1101 - 1·1101 = \begin{array}{r} 0·1101 \\ +0·0010 \\ +1 \\ \hline (1)0000 \end{array}$$

So much for addition and subtraction, what about multiplication and division? Multiplication should hold no great problems
because we have already seen how simple it is:

$$\begin{array}{r} 1101 \\ \times 1011 \\ \hline 1101 \\ 0000 \\ 1101 \\ 1101 \\ \hline 10001111 \end{array}$$

All that is needed is adding circuitry together with a means of
ordering the sequence and shifting the numbers to one side. The
computer just works through the multiplier from right to left
adding the multiplicand (1101) if the multiplier bit is 1 or adding
0 if it is 0. The resulting partial product is then shifted along one
position and the process repeated until the last bit of the multiplier is reached. The process of long division can be dealt with in
an equally straightforward manner.

Clearly, while all this is going on, the circuit has in some way got to store the multiplier and the multiplicand. The storage that is required is not for very long or of great capacity, so it would be impractical to put it onto magnetic tape, or anything like that. This is in fact where flip-flops come in handy again, because they can not only store binary numbers in the same way as a row of light bulbs but, unlike the bulbs, the information stored in them

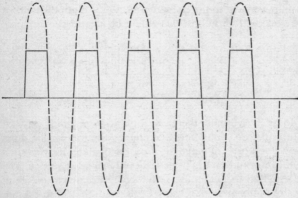

Figure 108

can be retrieved simply by attempting to pass current through them. Those that are set in their non-conducting stable state (0) will pass no current, those set for 1 will.

All the time we have been talking about these circuits, we have been thinking in terms of passing currents through gates and switches. However, very often it is better not to use steady currents, but pulses instead. Pulses have the advantage of being capable of transmitting binary information in a convenient way. To transmit the number 1101011 from one part of a computer to another using continuous currents would really require seven wires, five of them carrying current, two not. Using pulses, though, it can all be done in one wire, even if it does take a fraction longer. It is done like this: a train of pulses is generated at a certain frequency (Figure 108). Every pulse present represents 1, and if you want to represent 0 you simply suppress the pulse that would have occurred at that instant.

The generation of pulses is very simple. All you need to do in principle is to produce a sine wave from an ordinary oscillator, amplify it greatly, and then lop the peaks off it. Then if you want positive pulses only, you pass the whole thing through a rectifier.

There are obviously many requirements for a computer to store information of much greater complexity and for longer periods than we have so far encountered. While a good deal of it could be done with flip-flops, this would be a most cumbersome

Figure 109

way of doing it. We must therefore look at some other ways of storing information. Sometimes, of course, the job can be done perfectly well on reels of magnetic tape, particularly if, when it is wanted, the information has to be retrieved in a set sequence. The instructions given to a computer, what computations to perform, when to store information, retrieve it, print it out and so on, are often placed on magnetic tape. This is the program, and it can also be stored on punched tape or punched cards. However, tapes have beginnings and ends, and there is a limit to the speed at which they can be wound round. Consequently if you want to store tens of thousands of bits of information any of which may be wanted in a split second, you have got to find a storage system which is much more accessible.

If the storage is needed only for a short and precise length of time, such as in multiplying circuits, a time-delay device will do, and we met one of these in the chapter on PAL television receivers where the signal in one line had to be stored and re-displayed on the next. Another type of memory invokes the principles of magnetic tape, but does not use tape. Revolving drums or discs are used which are coated with the same sort of magnetic material as tape, but which do not have nearly the problems associated with beginnings and ends of tape being hundreds of metres apart. However, even these have their limitations because although it does not take long to find the place to start 'replaying' them, the information on them is still of a sequential nature, and they are still relatively slow.

The interesting type of storage in a computer is the magnetic core memory. The heart of this device is a large number of small ring-shaped or toroidal pieces of ferromagnetic ceramic material (Figure 110). They may also consist of a length of thin ferromagnetic metal tape either coiled or wound around a small bobbin. Each core is capable of storing only one bit of binary

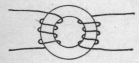

Figure 110

information, so a great many of them are needed; nevertheless, manufacturing considerations are the only things which limit their smallness.

Each core is wound with an input and a sensing coil, and if a pulse is passed through the input winding, magnetic flux will be produced which will align the magnetic particles of the core in a corresponding direction (remember the left-hand coil rule). Once the input ceases, the core remains magnetized; it has no north and south pole like an ordinary magnet, the poles are chasing their tails around the ring of the core. However, the magnetized core is still surrounded by a magnetic field, and the direction of the field determines whether a 0 or a 1 is stored. It is necessary in this case to use a positive pulse for 1 and a negative pulse for 0.

To retrieve information from a core, the second winding, the sense winding is used. To operate the sense winding, a further pulse is applied to the input of the kind which would magnetize the core in a direction representing 0. If the core already stores 0, the new input pulse will have very little effect on it, and very little will happen in the sensing coil. However, if the core stores 1, the application of a 0 pulse will switch its magnetic field right round, inducing a current in the sensing coil. The difficulty with this procedure is that every time information is retrieved from a core it is automatically reset to 0 and the information is lost. To over-come this, the output of the sensing coil may be used to set a flip-flop temporarily until the signal can be fed back again to the core input to re-code it.

This copes with a single core; what about the storage of a large number of bits? To sort this one out, we need to look a little more closely at the magnetizing properties of the cores. Figure 111 shows what is called a hysteresis loop. It is a way of showing the

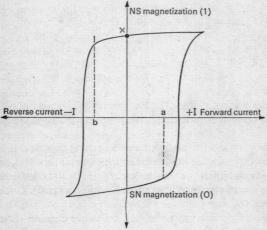

Figure 111

reluctance of the core to change from one state to another, and is analogous to the stiffness of door hinges. If you want to close a door on stiff hinges, you have to build up quite a bit of force on it before it will move much at all. There will come a point when it starts to budge, and then it will go relatively easily to the closed position. Then if you try to reverse it and open it again, you find it is once more difficult to budge. Again you have to build up a bit of force before it will start moving back.

Much the same happens with the magnetization of a magnetic-ally soft material. If you plot a graph of the amount of magnetizing current required to produce a given amount of flux density it will look like Figure 111. Let us start with the core magnetized in the 1 state, and look at point X on the graph. If a current of +I is applied to the input, nothing happens because the core is already magnetized that way. However as the current changes from +I to −I, let your eye travel right to left along the centre line of the graph. At the same time see how the magnetic flux density represented by X moves along only barely altering its value. Not until the current has reached point 'b' is the magnetizing force great enough to start dragging the flux density round. Then as the current nears its maximum the flux density rapidly changes and reaches its maximum in the opposite (0) direction.

So far, so good. Now let us turn the current back down towards +I. Does the flux density start changing again? Hardly at all; in fact not until the current gets to point 'a' does it start to turn round, and then finally as the current nears its greatest positive value the flux density moves quickly round. The change in flux is the equivalent of the stiff door moving. The moral of this story is that if you have a core magnetized in the 1 state, and you apply to its input a positive current only great enough to reach point 'b' and no more, then when the current is removed the core stays in the original 1 state. Exactly the same happens if it is in the 0 state and a negative current only sufficient to get down to point 'a' is applied at the input: when the current is removed the coil is still in the 0 state.

A similar state of affairs exists with the old-fashioned type of light switch where you have to move it way past the half-way point before the works inside click loudly into action. Then to turn it off again you have to move the switch well past the half-way mark once more. Consequently, if you move the switch only to the half way point and then let go, the switch stays exactly where it was.

What is all this leading to? It is going to give us a very clever way of selecting one out of hundreds of cores. Assume that we have an array of cores laid out in neat lines as shown in Figure 112. Let each core have two inputs as well as a sensing coil, and let all the cores be joined together along each horizontal line and each vertical line by one of their input coils. The wires joining the cores horizontally are kept insulated from those joining them vertically.

Now, suppose a pulse is sent along one of the horizontal wires, but that the strength of the pulse is not enough to pass the magic point 'b' on the hysteresis curve. When the pulse has gone, none of the cores will have been magnetized. However, suppose that at

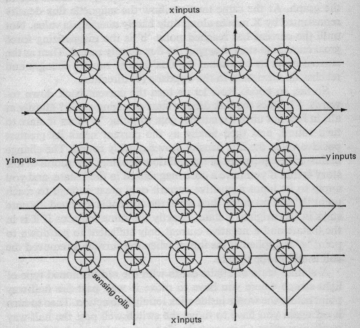

Figure 112

the same time, another pulse is sent down a vertical line, what will happen? The two lines will cross at one point only, and at that point there will be a core. Through both the inputs of that core a half-strength pulse will pass, and the effect will be that the total magnetizing force of both pulses together will be enough to pass the magic point and swing the magnetic flux of the core round.

What we have achieved is rather remarkable; we have found a

272

way of using countless numbers of cores, and yet have the ability to store a bit in any one we like to choose simply by sending pulses simultaneously down two intersecting lines.

Figure 112 shows a complete core memory in diagrammatic form. Any one of the 25 cores can have a bit written into it by picking the appropriate x and y selection wires and sending pulses down them. The same is done to read a core, but all the sensing coils are connected in series because there is no further

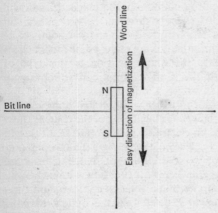

Figure 113

need to identify them. When a signal is present at the sense winding output, it is plain from which core it came, because we know which core was pulsed to extract the bit we require. It is still, of course, necessary to have a mechanism for replacing the information after a core has been read.

The latest type of memory uses tiny dots made from a thin film of magnetic material which can easily be magnetized in one direction, but only with difficulty at right angles to it (Figure 113). In the easy direction it is just as easy to magnetize it north–south or south–north. Across the dot run three conductors, a bit-line conductor, a sense-line conductor and word-line conductor. To write a bit on it, a pulse goes down the word-line conductor which has the effect of magnetizing the dot along the difficult axis. Simultaneously along the bit-line conductor, a pulse is transmitted which tends to magnetize the dot north–south in order to write 0, or south–north to write 1. The resultant effect of the two pulses combined is to magnetize the dot slightly north of the difficult axis for 1, or slightly south for 0. As soon as the pulses stop, the direction of magnetization will swing round to whichever easy direction it is nearest to. If 1 is to be written, the resultant effect of the two pulses will be to magnetize the dot 'east–north–east', and so when the pulses end, the magnetization will swing round to north. If 0 is to be written, the two pulses will together produce magnetization of the dot in an 'east–south–east' direction, and when the input pulses are removed, the magnetization will swing round to the south. Sensing of this type of memory is then basically the same as for a conventional core memory.

We cannot really go much further without answering the important question posed right at the beginning of the chapter: how does a transistor become an electronic switch? The first thing to realize is that the job of an electronic switch in a digital computer is to be able to give one of two possible outputs, 0 or 1, in response to a control signal from elsewhere in the circuit. Now when we talk of switches, we naturally think in terms of the on–off type, such as light switches. However, there are in fact quite a few pairs of states in an electronic device which can be used to represent 0 and 1. We have already come across the conducting and non-conducting states, which an on–off switch is capable of, but there are also positive and negative, pulse and no-pulse, zero voltage and positive voltage, zero voltage and negative.

The performance of a transistor as a switch depends not so much on its amplification properties, but on the behaviour of the two junctions between P-type and N-type materials within it. You remember that in a transistor you can either have two pieces of P-type semiconductor material with a wafer of N-type sandwiched between them, or vice versa. Either way, you end up with two junctions, each of which can in some respects be considered in isolation as a diode. If you apply a reverse bias to a diode, no current will flow through it, and it will behave like a high-value resistor; on the other hand, a forward bias causes it to let current through unimpeded.

Figure 114 shows a basic circuit using a transistor as a switch, together with the same circuit showing the transistor as two diodes. The diodes are connected in opposition to each other, and

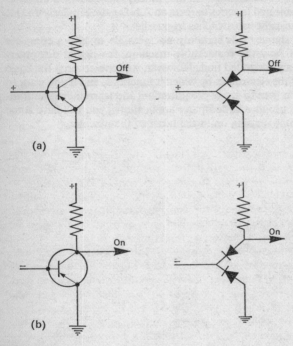

Figure 114

the point of connection is equivalent to the base of the transistor. The remaining connections to the diodes are the equivalents of the emitter and collector. In Figure 114a the switch is biased so that a negative voltage exists at both emitter and collector relative to a positive voltage at the base. This has the effect of reverse-biasing both diodes, and no voltage is developed across the output

275

resistor. In Figure 114b the polarity of the input is changed round so that both diodes are forward biased and a voltage is developed at the output. The transistor switch is in its 'on' position.

It is a fairly easy thing now to put two transistors together to form an AND gate. We have already seen that basically an AND gate is two switches in series, and indeed two transistor switches can be connected in series to form an AND gate. Similarly an OR gate is basically two switches in parallel.

In one chapter it is certainly not possible to give a complete picture of how the remarkable machine, the digital computer, works as an integrated unit. However, we have covered the basic aspects of the electronics by which it functions, and if you want to go on from here to study programming and learn more about inputs and outputs and computer applications, you will have some idea of what is going on in the heart of the machine.

Appendix

Summary of important facts.

Voltage is a pressure-like quantity, and is the *electromotive force* necessary to maintain a flow of electricity at a rate of 1 *ampere* (a quantity of 1 *coulomb* of electricity per second) through a conductor which opposes the current with a resistance of 1 *ohm*.

$$\text{current} = \frac{\text{voltage}}{\text{resistance}}.$$

voltage = current × resistance.

$$\text{resistance} = \frac{\text{voltage}}{\text{current}}.$$

For the same resistance, the higher the current, the higher must be the voltage.

For the same voltage, the higher the resistance, the lower the current.

Voltage is also a measure of potential, and can be used to express the *potential difference* between the two ends of a resistance; i.e. how positive one end is compared with the other. In this case, for the same current, the higher the resistance, the higher the potential difference across it.

Watts are units of power, and are the product of volume flow and the force behind it. The kilowatt-hour is a unit of energy and is equal to 3,600,000 watt seconds or *joules*.

watts = volts × amps.

One horsepower = 746 watts.

Conventional current flows from positive to negative, but in fact the electrons themselves flow from negative to positive. An electron carries a negative charge.

The *farad*, or more usually the microfarad (μF) is a unit of capacitance. A capacitance of 1 farad requires 1 coulomb of electricity to raise its potential by 1 volt. A microfarad is one millionth part of a farad.

The *henry* is a unit of inductance, such that a rate of change of current of 1 ampere per second produces an induced e.m.f. of 1 volt.

The *hertz* is a unit of frequency and is equal to one cycle per second. The kilohertz (kHz) and megahertz (MHz) are one thousand and one million hertz respectively.

The *joule* is a unit of energy and is equal to volts × coulombs.

277

Electricity

The *weber* is a unit of magnetic flux and is equal to 100,000,000 *lines*.

The right-hand wire rule

Clench your right fist and stick out the thumb, and if the conventional direction of current is the way your thumb is pointing, then the lines of force will follow the direction of your fingers.

The right-hand coil rule

If you wrap your fingers round a coil in the direction the current is conventionally flowing round the coils and stick out your thumb, then the thumb end of the coil will have a north-seeking type of attraction.

The right-hand current rule

If the thuMb (of the right hand) points in the direction of Motion, and the First finger in the direction of Flux, the seCond finger will point in the direction of Current flow.

The power factor

1. In a D.C. circuit you have only resistance to worry about; inductors behave like simple resistors, capacitors allow no current to pass at all and behave like insulators.
2. In an A.C. circuit, in addition to resistance you have also reactance, which is the effect of capacitance and inductance opposing current flow. With capacitance, the reactance falls as the frequency is increased; the opposite happens with inductance.
3. The overall impedance of a circuit takes into account resistance and reactance, which each have to be squared, added and the square root extracted from the total to give the impedance in ohms.
4. The ratio of resistance to impedance gives the power factor. Capacitance and inductance put current out of phase with the voltage, so that when the two are multiplied together to give power, there will be negative power as well as positive power, reducing the true power available. In a purely capacitive or inductive circuit, the negative power completely offsets the positive power, causing wattless current. The ratio of the true power to the apparent power (volts × amps) is again given by the power factor. In an A.C. circuit the power is therefore volts × amps × power factor, and for this reason machines are often described in terms of kVA (kilovolt amps) instead of kW (kilowatts).

The wiring of a domestic plug

The brown wire goes on the right-hand terminal of a plug, looked at from the back with the cover off (brown has an 'r' in it for *r*ight), and is the live wire. The live terminal of the plug is often marked 'L' and incorporates a fuse cartridge which should be of the correct value for the appliance. Blue is the neutral wire (and is a cold colour) and must be connected to the left hand 'N' terminal. Green and yellow is the earth wire: it *must* be connected, and goes on the top terminal of the large pin marked 'E'.

Glossary

For definition of electrical units, see Appendix.

ANODE: an *electrode* to which electrons are attracted and which is therefore positive.

ARMATURE: the rotating coils of an electric motor or generator.

ATOMIC NUMBER: the number of *electrons* in orbit round the nucleus of an atom or the number of protons in the nucleus.

BASE: the thin central region in a transistor, sandwiched between the *emitter* and the *collector*.

BIAS: a D.C. voltage applied to the grid of a *valve* or a *transistor* terminal to control the flow of electrons.

CAPACITOR: a device which can retain electricity in a pair of conductors, known as plates, separated by an insulating layer, the *dielectric*. The charge on the plates remains because of electrostatic attraction across the dielectric.

CARRIER: a high-frequency wave which is transmitted in order to convey a lower-frequency signal which is encoded on to it by *modulation*.

CATHODE: an *electrode* from which electrons are discharged and which is therefore negative.

CHOKE: an induction coil or *inductor*.

CHROMINANCE SIGNAL: the part of a television transmission which conveys information about the colour of the picture as distinct from the brightness.

COLLECTOR: the region of a *transistor*, and the terminal connected to it, towards which the holes in a P–N–P transistor or the electrons in a N–P–N transistor travel.

CONDENSER: synonym for *capacitor*.

CONDUCTOR: a material with a low electrical resistance.

DETECTOR: a device for extracting a signal from a modulated *carrier* wave – in its simplest form a *rectifier*.

DIELECTRIC: an insulator, such as separates the plates of a capacitor.

DIFFRACTION: the 'bending' of waves from a straight transmission path.

DIODE: a device, either a *valve* or *semiconductor*, which permits the flow of electricity at low resistance in one direction and offers a very high resistance in the other.

DOPING: the introduction of an impurity into a material such as silicon or germanium in order to make it a *semiconductor*.

ELECTRODE: a conductor by which an electric current enters or leaves an electrical device such as a *valve* or a voltaic cell.

ELECTRON: a basic particle of electricity, always having a negative charge.

EMITTER: the region of a *transistor*, and the terminal connected to it, from which the holes in a P–N–P transistor or the electrons in a N–P–N transistor are emitted.

FEEDBACK: the feeding of part of the output from an amplifier back to the input in inverted form, as negative feedback, in order to reduce distortion, or unchanged, as positive feedback, usually to maintain oscillation.

FIELD: any region in which some influence such as magnetism or electromagnetism exists.

FILTER: circuit which reduces the amplitude of certain bands of frequencies, allowing others to pass unaffected.

FLIP–FLOP: an electronic switch which will remain in either an 'On' or 'Off' state, and is therefore useful as a memory in a binary computer.

FLUX, MAGNETIC: the strength of magnetism in a region of interest, measured in webers.

FREQUENCY: the number of times per second an oscillating quantity completes an oscillation, such as from peak to peak.

GALVANOMETER: a meter for measuring small electric currents.

GATE: a component of a digital computer which is either open (non-conducting) or closed (conducting), and is thus a type of switch.

IMPEDANCE: the combined opposition to current flow offered by the *resistance* and *reactance* of a circuit.

INDUCTOR: an induction coil or coil of wire in which an opposing voltage is induced by a changing current either in the coil itself or in a conductor near it.

INSULATOR: a highly resistive material which will only allow electricity to flow through it with the aid of an extremely high *electromotive force*. The opposite of a conductor.

INVERSE DISTANCE LAW: the strength of an electromagnetic wave decreases in inverse proportion to the distance between the receiver and the transmitter.

INVERSE SQUARE LAW: the strength of the electrostatic attraction round an electron, as well as many other quantities, is inversely proportional to the square of the distance from the source to the measuring point.

Electricity

ION: an atom which does not have its normal complement of electrons and therefore has either a positive or a negative attraction.

LUMINANCE SIGNAL: the part of a television transmission which conveys information about the brightness of the picture as distinct from the colour.

MODULATION: the encoding of a signal into a *carrier* wave of much higher frequency, either by varying the amplitude of the carrier in proportion to the amplitude of the signal (Amplitude Modulation) or by varying the frequency or phase of the carrier (Frequency Modulation.

NEUTRON: a particle in the nucleus of an atom possessing no electric charge of any kind.

PAL: a system of colour television transmission in which phase distortion of the colour signal which would result in hue changes is counteracted by reversing the phase in alternate lines of the picture.

PIEZO-ELECTRIC EFFECT: the effect of pressure on certain types of crystal which produces an electrical voltage in proportion to the pressure.

POTENTIOMETER: a variable resistor.

POWER FACTOR: the effect of *reactance* which has to be taken into account in calculating the power of a machine from the voltage and current consumption.

PUSH–PULL CIRCUIT: an amplifier circuit in which separate halves of the circuit deal with the positive and negative halves of the signal.

REACTANCE: the resistance offered to alternating current, but not to direct current, by *capacitors* and *inductors*.

RECTIFIER: a *diode* employed to obtain D.C. from an A.C. current.

RING-MAIN: a simple method of wiring a house which avoids running individual wires to each lamp and power point. A separate loop of wire for each of the live, neutral and earth terminals runs round the house and connections can be made at any point across them, up to a given limit.

ROOT-MEAN-SQUARE: a means of expressing the value of an oscillating quantity by constantly squaring, averaging and taking the square root.

SEMICONDUCTOR: a material which in its pure state is an insulator, but which becomes a partial conductor when an impurity is introduced. Its importance springs from the fact that in an N–type semiconductor the current is conducted by means of electrons, which are negative, and in P-type material by means of 'holes' or electron deficiencies in atoms, which are effectively positive. When N-type and P-type materials are fused many useful phenomena result.

SHUNT: a component connected across a circuit or part of a circuit.

SIDEBAND: part of a radio signal of frequency above and below that of the carrier, the effect of *modulation*.

SUPERCONDUCTIVITY: the phenomenon of almost resistance-free conduction of electricity by certain conductors when cooled to near absolute zero temperature.

TRANSFORMER: a device which raises or lowers the voltage of an alternating current at the expense or gain of the current.

TRANSISTOR: a *semiconductor* device which performs functions similar to those of a valve.

VALVE: an evacuated glass tube containing a heated cathode, an anode, and sometimes a grid or grids such that electrons will only flow from cathode to the anode, and the strength of the flow is controllable by altering the voltage of the grid. The *cathode* emits electrons, the *anode* receives them.

Index